CONFLICT DYNAMICS

STUDIES IN SECURITY
AND INTERNATIONAL AFFAIRS

Conflict Dynamics

Civil Wars, Armed Actors, and Their Tactics

Alethia H. Cook

Marie Olson Lounsbery

The University of Georgia Press

Athens

Paperback edition, 2020

© 2017 by the University of Georgia Press

Athens, Georgia 30602

www.ugapress.org

Set in Minion Pro by Graphic Composition, Inc., Bogart, GA

Most University of Georgia Press titles are
available from popular e-book vendors.

Printed digitally

Library of Congress Cataloging-in-Publication Data

Names: Cook, Alethia H., author. | Olson Lounsbery, Marie, 1970– author.
Title: Conflict dynamics : civil wars, armed actors, and their tactics / Alethia H. Cook, Marie
    Olson Lounsbery.
Description: Athens, Georgia : The University of Georgia Press, 2017. | Series: Studies in security
    and international affairs | Includes bibliographical references and index.
Identifiers: LCCN 2016051438 | ISBN 9780820338330 (hardback : alk. paper) | ISBN 9780820351063
    (ebook)
Subjects: LCSH: Civil war—Case studies. | Insurgency—Case studies. | Tactics—Case studies. |
    Sierra Leone—History—Civil War, 1991–2002. | Congo (Brazzaville)—History—Civil War,
    1997. | Sri Lanka—History—Civil War, 1983–2009. | Insurgency—Burma—History—20th
    century. | Insurgency—Indonesia—History—20th century. | Insurgency—Peru—History—
    20th century.
Classification: LCC JC328.5 .C67 2017 | DDC 355.02/18—dc23 LC record available at https://lccn.loc
    .gov/2016051438

Paperback ISBN 978-0-8203-5883-3

To David J. Louscher, who taught me how to analyze and think critically, how to write professionally and function in the academic environment. Without him, none of this would be possible.
Alethia H. Cook

For my Dad, Luke's Pappy, and my biggest supporter
Marie Olson Lounsbery

CONTENTS

ILLUSTRATIONS

ACKNOWLEDGMENTS

Given the breadth of the topic and level of detail, this book has taken some time to complete. Through the process of collecting narrative information, assessing the cases, and writing chapters we have benefited greatly from the contributions, suggestions, and support of many people. Our collaborative exploration of civil war dynamics began with what we called the Rivalry Project. As we gathered the information needed to disaggregate cases effectively, we were supported first as junior faculty by East Carolina University, which provided research funds that allowed us to hire some very talented undergraduate students. The Harriot College of Arts and Sciences at East Carolina University contributed additional assistance in the form of a course release. We are grateful to the college and university for their support of our research efforts.

Our thanks to Stuart Turner, Kate O'Connor, Jason Robel, and Zachary Cooper for helping us in the initial phases of this project. Since that time, we have been fortunate to be able to draw continued assistance from a significant number of interested and highly competent undergraduate and graduate students, who were frequently supported by the university. These include Kyle Griffin, Amanda Sines, David Zeher, Ryan Cobey, Chris Munier, and Samuel Wagers. While researching and writing a book of this nature can be challenging, collaborating with witty and bright students made many of the more tedious tasks much more enjoyable.

We would also like to thank our friends and colleagues who provided support and feedback on the manuscript or on the Rivalry Project itself in its earlier years. These include Fred Pearson, Dursun Peksen, Scott Gates, Roy Licklider, Peter Francia, and Sharon Paynter. The quality of our work was increased through their expertise, words of encouragement, and friendship. In addition, we have appreciated the guidance and support, and definitely the patience, of our editors and the helpful staff at the University of Georgia Press, including Nancy Grayson, Walter Biggins, and Bethany Snead. Through their work and that of the anonymous reviewers they enlisted, the manuscript has been significantly improved from our initial draft to this final version, our theoretical framework is more fully developed, and its contribution to the literature has increased.

We also owe a great debt of gratitude to our families, who have supported us through this endeavor, allowing us the time needed to get the work done when necessary and providing welcomed distraction when it was needed.

ABBREVIATIONS

ABSDF	All Burma Student's Democratic Front
ACRM	Anti-Corruption Revolutionary Movement
AfDB	African Development Bank
AFPFL	Anti-Fascist People's Freedom League
AFRC	Armed Forces Revolutionary Council
AP	Popular Action
APC	All People's Congress
APFP	Arakan People's Freedom Party
APLP	Arakan People's Liberation Party
APRA	American Popular Revolutionary Alliance
ASDT	Timorese Social Democratic Association
ASEAN	Association of Southeast Asian Nations
BUP	Bloku Unidade Popular
CNRT	National Congress for Timorese Reconstruction Party
CPB	Communist Party of Burma
DEA	Drug Enforcement Administration
DI	Darul Islam
DKBA	Democratic Karen Buddhist Army
DOM	Daerah Operasi Militer
DRC	Democratic Republic of Congo
ECOMOG	Economic Community of West African States Monitoring Group
ECOWAS	Economic Community of West African States
ELN	National Liberation Army
EO	Executive Outcomes
EPRLF	Eelam People's Revolutionary Liberation Front
FLEC	Front for the Liberation of the Enclave of Cabinda
FRETILIN	Revolutionary Front for an Independent East Timor
FTO	foreign terrorist organization
GAM	Free Aceh Movement
HAM	Hak Asasi Manusia, "human rights"
IDP	internally displaced persons
IMF	International Monetary Fund
IPKF	Indian Peacekeeping Force
ISIL	Islamic State in Iraq and the Levant

ISIS	Islamic State of Iraq and Syria
JAT	Jemaah Ansharut Tauhid
JI	Jemaah Islamiya
JVP	Janatha Vimukthi Peramuna
KAF	Kawthoolei Armed Forces
KIA	Kachin Independence Army
KKY	Ka Kwe Ye, "home guards"
KLA	Kosovo Liberation Army
KMT	Chinese Kuomintang
KNDO	Karen National Defense Organization
KNLA	Karen National Liberation Army
KNU	Karen National Union
KNUP	Karen National United Party
KPLA	Karen People's Liberation Army
KRF	Kokang Revolutionary Front
LJ	Laskar Jihad
LTTE	Liberation Tigers of Tamil Elam
MCDDI	Mouvement congolais pour la démocratie et le développement intégral
MIR	Movement of the Revolutionary Left
MIR-EM	MIR—The Militant
MIR-IV	MIR-IV Etapa
MIR-VR	MIR—Rebellious Voice
MIT	Mujahidine Indonesia Timur
MNR	National Revolutionary Movement
MP-GAM	Majles Pemeritahan GAM
MRTA	Tupac Amaru Revolutionary Movement
MTA	Mong Tai Army
NAD	Nanggroë Aceh Darussalam
NCA	Nationwide Ceasefire Agreement
NDMC	National Diamond Mining Company
NGO	nongovernmental organization
NLD	National League for Democracy
NPFL	National Patriotic Front of Liberia
NPRC	National Provisional Ruling Council
NRC	National Reformation Council
OAU	Organization of African Unity
OPM	Organization for a Free Papua
PCT	Parti congolais du travail
PDF	People's Democratic Front
PDP	Papuan Presidium Council

PKI	Indonesian Communist Party
PKK	Kurdistan Workers' Party
PLP	Peoples Liberation Party
PMC	private military contractor
PRRI	Revolutionary Government of the Republic of Indonesia
PSI-MI	Revolutionary Socialist Party
PVO	People's Volunteer Organization
RPI	Indonesian Federal Republic
RSM	Republic of South Moluccas
RSO	Rohingya Solidarity Organization
RUF	Revolutionary United Front
SCOUHP	Supreme Council of the United Hill Peoples
SCSL	Special Court for Sierra Leone
SLA	Sierra Leone Army
SLA	Sri Lankan Army
SLMM	Sri Lanka Monitoring Mission
SLORC	State Law and Order Restoration Council
SLPP	Sierra Leone People's Party
SLST	Sierra Leone Selection Trust
SNUF	Shan National United Front
SSA	Shan State Army
SSIA	Shan State Independence Army
SSNA	Shan State National Army
SUA	Shan United Army
SURA	Shan United Revolutionary Army
TELO	Tamil Eelam Liberation Organization
TNT	Tamil New Tigers
TULF	Tamil United Liberation Front
UCDP	Uppsala Conflict Data Program
UNAMSIL	United Nations Mission in Sierra Leone
UNITA	National Union for the Total Independence of Angola
UNMOSIL	United Nations Observer Mission in Sierra Leone
UPADS	Pan-African Union for Social Democracy
UWSA	United Wa State Army

CONFLICT DYNAMICS

INTRODUCTION

In 2011, as the Arab Spring unfolded, a protest emerged in the city of Deraa, Syria, over the arrest of fifteen schoolchildren who had been accused of writing antigovernment graffiti (BBC 2015b). What began as a series of spontaneous protests was met harshly with state repression and has become a full-scale internationalized intrastate war with too many rebel groups to count, many of which transcend borders, spilling over into Iraq and Turkey. The conflict in Syria is truly dynamic. Initially, international efforts, led by the United States, sought to identify and support more moderate elements in their effort against the Assad regime, particularly in light of its use of chemical weapons. As the conflict has continued, however, one rebel faction has emerged and demonstrated great capacity to take territory and threaten both Assad and U.S. interests. The success of the Islamic State in Iraq and the Levant (ISIL, or ISIS, the Islamic State of Iraq and Syria) has led to a transition in U.S. policy. As a splinter faction of Al Qaeda that has expanded through terrorist tactics, ISIL has become a primary opponent in the U.S. War on Terror. In addition to employing air strikes, the United States has backed Syrian Kurdish rebels, who are fighting both ISIL and Assad. This has been much to the dismay of Turkey, a U.S. ally that has had its own decades-long battle with its Kurdish population and the Kurdistan Workers' Party (PKK), a rebel faction. The actors involved in and around Syria are indeed complex, as are the tactics employed by the various rebel factions involved and their supporters.

Clearly, civil instability continues to pose a serious challenge for the international community. Countries' seemingly internal struggles, such as those occurring in Syria, threaten to destabilize entire regions or, at the very least, spill into neighboring countries, prompting international response. Efforts to bring about resolution are challenged by resistant governments and emboldened rebels, both of which make tactical decisions repeatedly over time to achieve their goals. As a result of their decisions, and those of outside actors, civil disputes may endure at varying intensities over long periods of time and may become internationalized in the process.

Much of the early literature examining intrastate strife tended to focus on either the onset or the termination of violence using country- or conflict-level characteristics to examine both. Subsequent work continued to employ this approach in order to examine other aspects of this complex problem better. Yet scholars remained challenged by the curious nature of civil disputes. Countries like Myanmar and Indonesia, which are examined in this volume, have experienced many conflicts in different regions throughout their histories. These disputes involved varying numbers of armed factions of diverse capacities that evolved over time. Government efforts to subdue or eradicate factions also changed over time. Previous efforts to understand a set of conflicts like those in Myanmar or Indonesia tended to either collect all of those disputes into one country-level analysis or include all actors in one conflict-level examination. These approaches were suboptimal, as subsuming all of a conflict's complexity into a single unit ignored the importance and impact of key variations, potentially resulting in misunderstanding the situation.

Because of this, scholars have increasingly moved toward "disaggregating civil war" or "going beyond the state" as the unit of analysis. This involves the "intensive analysis of individual conflicts . . . more systematically" (Cederman and Gleditsch 2009, 489). By taking a more detailed, or microlevel, approach to intrastate disputes, the field has moved away from examining civil war as a single event. Instead, scholars now analyze the wide variety of groups and incidents that comprise civil conflicts and study their reciprocal relations to gain a more comprehensive understanding of what influenced the actors' capacities. Many in-depth case studies that have taken this approach have improved the understanding of specific conflicts (see, for example, Christia's analysis of Afghanistan [2012]). To move the field forward in this disaggregated approach, this book presents a theoretical framework through which the dynamic nature of relative group capacities and the resulting tactical decisions can be examined across a range of cases, in a systematic fashion, and over time as conflicts evolve. That framework is then applied to six case studies to illustrate its utility both for gaining better understanding of individual conflicts and for comparing across them.

What becomes clear is that civil conflicts do indeed ebb and flow over time, expanding and contracting through the relationships that emerge. Rebels may work together against a common enemy or may fight among themselves, as seen in Syria. Further, groups may find support from outside actors or end up facing them on the battlefield. Rebel group capacity to wage war is impacted dramatically by these relationship dynamics, which in turn influence, and are influenced by, the tactics they employ.

Analyzing intrastate conflict as a process is not a straightforward endeavor. Identifying groups operating within states is a challenge. Armed opposition groups are often shadowy figures prone to splintering. In addition, a country may experience multiple intrastate conflicts at any one time. At the very least, this complicates the approach of the government and of outside actors, but this may be particularly true when multiple intrastate rebel factions decide to act collectively by forming a coalition in opposition to the government. Conversely, intrastate rivals may begin to fight one another, making the government's work to suppress opposition easier. Unlike interstate conflict involving two recognized members of the nation-state system, intrastate conflicts involve a nation-state pitted against a difficult-to-define dynamic opponent. Further, once groups are identified, additional challenges emerge when attempting to analyze conflict processes systematically.

Conflict scholars have argued that during the course of civil war, opponents become demonized, constructive interaction disappears, and populations are socialized to the conflict, thus making resolution more difficult (Kriesberg 1998). The polarization of the parties sustains the conflict, extending its duration and increasing its intensity, even as changed circumstances may reduce or limit the relevance of the conflict's original causes. Examining civil wars or groups in isolation can provide a better understanding of what state- or group-level characteristics are associated with civil war onset or termination. However, it can overlook conflict, tactical, power, and organizational shifts that can move a conflict toward resolution or away from it. In essence, the factors that shape the warring actors and their decisions are missing. Thus, by focusing on the "guts" of a conflict, systematically, across a range of cases, analysis can progress beyond seemingly fixed characteristics to recognize the factors that change over time and the impact those have on tactical decisions.

Further, civil wars or conflicts do not happen in a vacuum. As was the case in the Middle East, events in Tunisia sparked similar events elsewhere. Civil wars spill over as refugees flee across borders (Weiner 1996), rebels seek safe havens in neighboring states, and external actors feel compelled to intervene. Decisions by external actors to engage diplomatically either through offers of mediation or pressure can influence group capacity, moving conflicts in different directions. The same applies to decisions by external actors to intervene militarily, as was seen in the cases of Libya and Syria. These attempts to exert influence by outside actors are themselves the product of a complex set of interactions. Ultimately, external actors aim to bring civil war to an end through various forms of intervention (Regan 2000a). That said, they certainly hope to do so in strategically important ways. In Syria, the United States would like to see ISIL defeated and would prefer Assad be removed. Conversely, Iran would like to see ISIL defeated but considers Assad an ally. Russian military intervention on behalf of Assad seemed to change the power balance entirely. All three interveners have sought to use their influence to bring about resolution in Syria, but under their own terms. For their part, various rebel factions have reacted to these efforts hoping to position themselves opportunistically amid this dynamic power structure. Civil conflicts and wars can be viewed in this regard as a series of actions followed by reactions that collectively determine the tactics rebels will employ to achieve their goals and the resulting impact those decisions will have on the conflict as it unfolds.

Civil wars have been identified as particularly perplexing events, more intense than their interstate counterparts (Miall 1992) with much higher rates of civilian casualties, and are seemingly more difficult to resolve (Licklider 1995). Yet, not all civil wars are intractable and deadly. Whereas some involve heavy civilian casualties and terrorist activity, others are more amenable to negotiation and mediation attempts. The ability to identify the types of factors that influence these tactical decisions among civil war actors would allow policy makers the opportunity to address such conflicts more quickly and effectively. If the answers to such questions lie in the details, that is, the conflict process, then the disaggregated conflict dynamic approach becomes not only informative but necessary. It can be assumed that particular actions and reactions by parties to intrastate conflict may be contentious based on a case or two, but the advantages to studying such moves over a larger set of cases in a more systematic fashion avoids the danger of assuming, particularly when the stakes appear to be very high.

To understand the tactical decisions made by civil war actors, a theoretical framework employing a systematic, disaggregated look at civil conflict has been developed. This was done by integrating previously disparate theoretical arguments that focused on specific aspects of intrastate strife into a cogent, interactive framework. The focus of this book is on the dynamic nature of civil wars, their actors, their capacity, and the conflict environment, all of which are thought to influence how rebels will attempt to achieve their goals. The goal of the book is to take a relatively comprehensive approach to examining the evolving nature of violence in intrastate conflicts and the actors involved by focusing on the conflict context, group and government capacity, and actor goals. To achieve this goal, the theoretical framework presented demonstrates how these variables influence tactical decisions, which subsequently impact the decisions of others. Two major undertakings were necessary to make this project possible.

First, theoretical arguments regarding the factors thought to influence how rebel factions and their government work to achieve their goals were examined and analyzed. Both static and dynamic characteristics of the conflicts are included in the study. Each conflict occurs in its own unique environment. The terrain of the country, its historical context, and the nature of the groups engaged are considered part of this environment. These factors are identified as static, meaning that they change only minimally over the duration of the belligerent relationship. Each can have an influence on the tactics selected by both government and its opposition and, therefore, on the trajectory any conflict may experience.

The nature of the conflict environment, although influential, is just one piece of the puzzle. Dynamic variables are also examined. These are aspects of the conflicts that could be expected to undergo significant changes in response to activities of the state and rebel groups. The most important dynamic variable is the relative capacity of the actors involved. Capacity consists of the size, cohesion, and leadership of each side, the degree to which it enjoys popular support, and the quality and quantity of weaponry available. Capacity is also influenced by the previous tactics in which each side engaged, particularly the success or failure of those actions. It is the *relative* capacity of the factions involved and their government that is important. The case studies presented confirm that the actions of warring actors are dramatically influenced by not only their relative capacity but also their perception of it. If one actor thought the other was about to gain or lose capacity, it could be enough to bring about calls for peace or the escalation of violence.

Tactical decisions and conflict trajectory are also thought to be influenced by one final dynamic variable, which is the overarching group goal. This may include desires for representation, policy/regime change, autonomy, or secession. Group demands can change over time, starting at any one of the goals and moving among them, depending on their situation and their experience over the course of the conflict. A government can have similar goals in that it may choose any of these as an acceptable or unacceptable solution to the problem with a group and will act accordingly. In other words, the government may prefer autonomy for a region rather than secession, which governments tend to do. Tactical decisions flow from these static and dynamic variables, as actors choose their actions for the future based on the success and failures of past and current decisions. Tactical options may include engaging in dialogue, appeals for international assistance, guerrilla warfare, or terrorism. These decisions or actions, along with the responses of other conflict actors, ultimately determine the direction or trajectory of a conflict.

International intervention, of course, is very important to the patterns of violence experienced by states in conflict. Intergovernmental organizations, nongovernment organizations, states, and individuals are examples of the types of actors that may choose or be invited to intervene. Among the relevant factors for this characteristic of conflicts are the motives of the intervener, whether the intervener seeks to change the behavior of the group or the state, the intervening power of the actor, and whether the intervention comes in the form of financial influence, diplomatic involvement, or military support. The addition of a third party into a conflict will impact group and government capacity, which varies depending on the type and direction of intervention. Capacity influences both tactical decisions and conflict trajectory.

The book proceeds with an intensive examination of six countries that have experienced intrastate conflict. The theoretical arguments proposed in chapter 1 are applied in order to gain an improved understanding of each case. In an effort to examine the complex nature of conflict as it changes over time and interacts across other actors, the project moves away from the typical approach of examining dyads (the state versus one rival) in conflict. Instead, the case studies examine a number of conflicts and conflict actors for the state during the period under investigation, which was from either 1945 or the date of independence until 2011.

Conflict has been distinguished from a war consistent with the work of civil conflict scholars. Conflict occurs between a recognized member of the nation-state system and an armed nonstate actor operating within its borders. Violent interactions between those actors must meet a minimum battle death threshold of twenty-five in a given year to be considered a civil conflict (Gleditsch et al. 2002). A civil conflict escalates to the level of civil war when the same actors reach a battle death threshold of one thousand in a given year (Small and Singer 1982; Gleditsch et al. 2002).[1] Some of the conflicts examined have evolved over time through their persistence into what DeRouen and Bercovitch (2008) have termed internal enduring rivalries, which can appear to be intractable in nature. As a result, intrastate conflicts that are episodic in nature, or those that are short bouts of violence that do not repeat, can be distinguished from those that endure involving multiple armed events over time. Further, in some cases, the repeated nature of the disputes involves political rivalries, or the same elites entangled in repeated interactions within the conflict itself. For clarity, political rivalry (i.e., conflicts involving elite-level actors) is distinguished from enduring rivalry (intrastate conflicts that have endured over time).

The complexity of the cases, as examined here in the number of rebel factions rivaling the state, ranges from one competitor in the case of Sierra Leone to as many as nine in the case of Myanmar. Governments' interactions with groups influence their responses to other groups and their future actions. When a government is facing multiple factions or conflicts at the same time, its ability to fight any one of them may be constrained. A government may also feel it has to repress one faction to demonstrate to other potential competitors that rebellion is costly. In other words, to understand conflict progression, and ultimately termination, the importance of decisions made in the midst of conflict, the history those decisions create, and group complexity that drives them must all be understood. This approach results in conclusions about how patterns of violence manifested in the six countries and the ability to make comparisons across the cases, which include Sierra Leone, Republic of the Congo (Brazzaville), Sri Lanka, Myanmar, Indonesia, and Peru. Each case was selected to illustrate important aspects of the theoretical expectations presented in chapter 1 across regions and conflicts.

The country of Sierra Leone, discussed in chapter 2, has been challenged by ineffective governance as it struggled to transition from a British colony to a functioning nation-state. Overcoming the legacy of this colonial history has proved difficult. The ethnically diverse nation has been ravaged by war as political elites vie for power and control over the country's resources, in particular its alluvial diamond fields. This case analysis brings into the discussion the role of external actors as facilitators of conflict (particularly Liberia's Charles Taylor) and as resolvers (including the British, the United Nations, and West Africa's ECOMOG). One interesting aspect of the case is the decision by the state to hire private military corporations in its efforts to boost its capacity versus the Revolutionary United Front (RUF) rebel faction. Unlike other cases, Sierra Leone has only one conflict and it was relatively short-lived, but the country experienced a significant amount of governmental change in the form of coups d'état. The shifting nature of the government pitted against the externally backed RUF is explored in detail, helping to illustrate the impact of such changes on the course of conflict and its resolution.

The Republic of the Congo also had a rather short conflict history. Although the country has experienced multiple intrastate conflicts, they have been episodic in nature involving political rivals, flaring up briefly only to end in a negotiated outcome. Examining this case in light of the theoretical model proposed in chapter 1 provides a better understanding of the influence that goals have on tactical decisions made by rival actors. Each of the episodes of violence occurring in the Congo was a manifestation of elite political divisions defined almost entirely by the players that led them. Of course, the histories of these rivalries became intertwined as well with rivals merging as loyalties shifted. The analysis presented in chapter 3 makes it clear that group goals are indeed a force driving conflict trajectories.

The long-term civil war in Sri Lanka has spawned one of the most unique and innovative rebel organizations of modern history, the Liberation Tigers of Tamil Elam (LTTE), which is discussed in chapter 4. The LTTE developed a primitive air force and navy, as well as spearheaded the use of suicide bombings as a tactic. The group had one of the most sophisticated and developed organizational structures of the rebellions examined. Despite these advantages, the government's victory in 2009 may indicate that the group has been defeated. However, while the conflict with the LTTE was the dominant conflict in the country, it was not the only one. The government had to face other Tamil and Sinhala nationalist groups as well, which challenged its capacity to respond. In some cases the LTTE fought both other Tamil nationalist groups and the government at the same time. This chapter examines the factors that influenced the group's strategic decisions through time as well as the impact of international interventions and negotiations on the group and the Sri Lankan government. One of the most important points this case illustrates is the potential importance a charismatic leader, in this case Velupillai Prabhakaran, can have on conflict dynamics.

Myanmar, formerly Burma, represents the most complex of all the cases examined in this book and is presented in chapter 5. This case provides an excellent illustration of the fact that intrastate conflicts do not occur in isolation. The country has experienced over nine different conflicts of varying types. Their histories are frequently intertwined as groups coalesce at times, effectively increasing their capacity relative to the government even in the presence of competing goals. At other times, factions of one conflict have also taken up arms alongside the government, pitted against another of the government's opponents, diminishing the capacity of one while bolstering the other. The Myanmar government has been forced to wage war in several parts of the country through much of its history, facing multiple opponents and a frequently hostile set of external actors. Examining the enduring nature of these conflicts and how they have unfolded over time as tactics have shifted provides a unique insight into how multiple conflict trajectories are formed in the same political space.

Indonesia, the subject of chapter 6, is a truly fascinating case for the study of intrastate conflict. In the immediate post-independence period, the country experienced civil unrest from a variety of different groups that sought changes ranging from more representation and differing policies to secession. Each of these conflicts was resolved in a different way by the government, and each had unique factors that impacted strategy selection, evolution of the conflict, and interventions. Some of the conflicts were resolved relatively quickly, while others have persisted. The diverse conflicts evolved along unique paths and demonstrate the theoretical arguments of this book in different ways. The Indonesian case provides an analysis of a Southeast Asian country with a large number of groups in conflict with each other and the government. It is also a case where the success of international intervention varied based on the characteristics of the specific conflict and its actors. Indonesia has had one ideological and four identity-based conflicts since independence. The country's archipelagic nature increased the importance that the geography of the country had for the conflict dynamics.

Peru has experienced four distinct intrastate conflicts in the post–World War II time period and is discussed in chapter 7. Each of these conflicts shared the same ideological goal of seeking to move the country toward the left politically. The conflicts diverge, however, in the rebel groups' ability to survive, in the tactical decisions they made, and, not surprisingly, in their capacities relative to the government. Two Peruvian disputes are episodic, whereas two others are more enduring. The case of Peru demonstrates that when actors make tactical decisions that best match their capabilities, they can flourish. In even the enduring rivalries, however, tactical decisions that resulted in diminished group capacity are evident. The case demonstrates that conflict trajectories are indeed formed through a set of actions and reactions over time.

The final chapter reflects on the importance of both static and dynamic

TABLE I.1 Rivalries and Groups Examined in This Book

Country	Intrastate rivalry	Rivalry dyads	Episodes of armed conflict
Myanmar (Burma)	Government	Communist Party of Burma; Communist Party of Burma—Red Flags; People's Volunteer Organization	1948–1988
	Arakan	Arakan People's Freedom Party; Arakan People's Liberation Army; Arakan Rohingya Islamic Front; Harkate Jihadul Islam; Mujahid Party; Rohingya Patriotic Front; Rohingya Liberation Organization	1948–1961 1964–1978 1991–1992 1994
	Kachin	Kachin Independence Army	1949–1950 1961–1992 2011
	Karen	Democratic Karen Buddhist Army; Karen National Union; Karen National Defense Organization; Karen National Liberation Army; Karen National United Front; Karen National United Party; Karen People's Liberation Army; Kawthoolei Armed Forces	1949–1992 1995 1997–1998 2000–2003 2005–2011
	Mon	Mon National Defense Organization	1949–1963 1990 1996
	Shan	Noom Suik Harn; Shan State Independence Army; Shan National United Front; Shan State Army; Kokang Revolutionary Front; Shan United Revolutionary Army	1959–1970 1972–1973 1976–1988 1993–2002 2005–2011
	Wa	United Wa State Army	1997
Congo (Brazzaville)	Government	Cocoyes; Ninjas; Cobras; Ninjas-Ntoumi	1993 1997–1999 2002
Indonesia	Government	Darul Islam Movement; Revolutionary Government of the Republic of Indonesia (PRRI—1958–1961); Permesta Movement (1958–1961)	1953–1961
	Aceh	Free Aceh Movement (GAM)	1989–2005
	Papua	Free Papua Movement (OPM)	1965–1984
	South Moluccas	Republic of South Moluccas	1950
	East Timor	Revolutionary Front for an Independent East Timor (FRETILIN)	1975–1998
Peru	Government	National Liberation Army (ELN)	1965
	Government	Movement of the Revolutionary Left (MIR)	1965
	Government	Sendero Luminoso	1982–1999 2007–2010
	Government	Tupac Amaru Revolutionary Army (MRTA)	1989–1993
Sierra Leone	Government	Revolutionary United Front (RUF)	1991–2002
Sri Lanka	Tamil	Liberation Tigers of Tamil Eelam (LTTE); Eelam People's Revolutionary Liberation Front (1985); Tamil Eelam Liberation Organization (TELO—1984–1985)	1983–2009
	Government	Janatha Vimkuthi Peramuna (JVP)	1971; 1989–1990

Source: UCDP/PRIO (2014).

factors in influencing conflict trajectory. Each of the six countries and many conflicts examined provide insight into tactical decisions that actors make in the midst of conflict, how those decisions are reciprocated, and how these interactions influence future activities. The lessons learned through these in-depth case analyses are presented as concluding thoughts on the conflict process. Implications of these findings for the direction of future research on the topic of civil conflict, war, and rivalry are also provided.

CHAPTER 1

Conflict Dynamics
A Comparative Framework

Civil conflicts are incredibly complex. While there may be similar factors that influence relationships, tactics, strategies, and patterns of violence, each situation is also unique because of the way in which those factors interact. Two conflicts may seem very similar at first glance but end up with entirely different outcomes. As they evolve, unique aspects of the participants, geography, group goals, resources, and relative capacities can result in dramatic changes. These realities make examining patterns of violence problematic. Frequently, the nuances of each case are what matters.

Some intrastate conflicts are enduring in nature. They tend to ebb and flow, involving periods of armed struggle intermixed with times of little to no violence. Efforts to address underlying grievances and bring about conflict termination may occur, but in such cases resolution attempts are frequently unsuccessful, leading some to label them as "intractable" or as enduring rivalries (Kriesberg 1998).[1] Other conflicts, however, may be episodic, or short-term affairs involving a brief period of armed struggle that terminates and never reemerges. Intrastate conflicts can vary in intensity as well. Some, although lasting for decades, may involve low-level violence and displacement, whereas others may experience extremely high levels of violence and occur at various times throughout the conflict history or over a short period of time. The intensity of episodic conflicts can vary in similar ways. Further, intrastate conflicts can vary dramatically in terms of the tactics employed by the actors involved. In some cases, innocent bystanders are targeted, sometimes on a massive scale, while in others, guerrilla warfare dominates or negotiations are prevalent. What accounts for these divergent experiences? By taking a closer look at the actions and reactions occurring within intrastate conflicts over time, one can get a better sense of how and under what conditions conflicts unfold and how more enduring rivalries evolve as compared to their more episodic counterparts. This book examines both specific rivalries that have evolved between actors over time and the more general context of the conflicts.

Examining the dynamic interactions of actors engaged in intrastate conflicts is challenging. Nonstate actors tend to be secretive. This may be necessary in order to survive against their typically more powerful opponent. Rebels may exaggerate their numbers or their support in order to achieve legitimacy. Although such actors may have access to weaponry, it is often unclear what the acquisition channels are or the types of weapons they possess until they are used on the battlefield. Governments in the midst of armed conflict also may not be forthcoming with information about their actions. Repressive approaches to dealing with such opposition may be frowned upon by international actors. As a result, it is not always immediately clear what a government has done when it engages with its nonstate opponent. Of course, over time, its actions, along with those of its opponents, typically become a part of the historical record, which is examined in the form of a series of conflict case studies. Although it may not always be clear what exactly transpired, which actors and how many were involved and under what conditions, through the use of historical and archival accounts a general sense of how intrastate conflict actors interacted and the tactics they employed can be developed. Patterns of violence can also be recognized and analyzed to determine what contributed to changes.

Among the most important aspects of civil conflicts are the decision-making processes that occur on both sides about whether to attempt to resolve their differences through peaceful negotiations or to resort to violence, and if one or both sides choose to employ violence, do they also include campaigns of terror? According to Coker (2002), one of the consequences of globalization has been a shift from instrumental violence (between states or communities) to expressive violence (carried out as a form of communication or ritual, or for a symbolic purpose). Factors that contribute to this decision-making process include politics, economics, military considerations, ideologies, and cultures. Another important influence is the role elites and leaders play as compared to that of rank and file members of groups (Cronin 2002/2003).

What follows is a framework that seeks to explain patterns of violence and group dynamics in intrastate conflicts by examining rebel group actions, their tactic selection processes, and the addition or subtraction of additional players. Each of these factors influences and is influenced by the others; the various combinations of factors determine to a large extent the direction any particular conflict will take. This focus is a particularly neglected aspect of conflict dynamics that involves factors related to the rebel group and its conflict with the government. This is not to say that government capabilities, actions, and other characteristics are not important. In fact, they are. But they are presented here as an intertwined relationship of the group, its characteristics, and its capabilities.

FACTORS INFLUENCING SELECTION OF TACTIC

Actors engaged in civil conflict make tactical choices in order to achieve their political goals. Their choice in tactic will influence subsequent decisions by conflict opponents as each set of actors makes revised assessments of their position in the conflict relative to their opponent. These actions and reactions are the factors that influence the direction that a conflict will take and how long it will ultimately endure (Olson Lounsbery and Pearson 2009). Tactical decisions and the impact subsequent actions have on the patterns of violence in a conflict are important in understanding their progression. There are a large number of factors that have been identified in the literature that have the potential to influence the tactics of nonstate actors.[2] However, these characteristics alone do not provide a sufficient understanding of conflict dynamics. What is necessary is that researchers gain insight into the interaction of the variables as the conflict evolves.

Group and government decisions to employ one set of tactics over another at any point is likely influenced by two sets of factors. The first is thought to be static in nature involving the context of the conflict, while the second set of factors is more dynamic in nature and evolves over time.

Conflict actors are impacted by the environment in which they operate. The characteristics of the conflict environment are primarily static or slow to change. A country's terrain, for instance, is unlikely to experience significant alteration due to ongoing strife but would likely influence tactical decisions made by rebels and government actors as each pursues their goals. Available mountainous or jungle terrain may allow insurgents to evade governmental pursuit more effectively than those operating in urban settings, for example (Fearon and Laitin 2003). Conflict occurring with such terrain advantages would be expected to endure longer than others.

Conflicts and rivalries unfold in the context of the nation's political, social, and cultural history as well. Factors such as colonial legacies (Henderson and Singer 2002) and group identity hierarchies (Gurr 1993) lay the foundation for the types of conflicts that may emerge, but they also are likely to influence tactical choices, and therefore conflict progression. A conflict that emerges out of a history of unfair treatment during a country's colonial history, which itself becomes embedded in the nation's culture, may make the targeting of civilians, particularly of opposing identities, more acceptable than those emerging under a different historical and cultural context, for example.

A third static factor of the conflict environment thought to influence tactical decisions has to do with the nature of the group itself. Groups that tend to be defined by their ethnic, religious, or cultural identity have a tendency toward more secessionist goals (see Gurr 1993), whereas ideological groups are typically more focused on regime change or political revolution (see Licklider 1995 and Regan 2000a for further discussion of this conflict dichotomy). Groups, and therefore rivals, that define themselves in ethnic, religious, or cultural terms that they view are different than the identity of their government may also find terrorist tactics more acceptable than ideological groups that wish to change the nature of the political regime but do not necessarily see themselves as a distinct identity relative to the rest of the population. As a result, the nature of the group engaged in the conflict will likely influence what sorts of tactics will be acceptable in order to achieve conflict goals.

Although conflict progression may be influenced by these static factors, the action-reaction sequences that unfold over time are dynamic in nature. Understanding the changing environment that influences tactical decisions is the next topic for discussion.

In contrast to the static variables, those that are dynamic are more likely to shift over the course of the conflicts in reaction to other factors. Each set of actors engaged in a conflict may be affected by the actions of the others or by societal reactions. These variables influence the future decisions and actions of both nonstate actors and their government. They are expected to behave similarly regardless of which takes action.

The tactics that each actor employs will likely have an impact on the selection of tactics by others involved. Today's actions can be expected to influence tomorrow's decision making and subsequent actions taken. Government repression, for instance, may result in increased support for a nonstate group, or it could cause an opponent to engage in more violent actions. In fact, some groups may engage in violence in the hopes of driving their government to become increasingly repressive (Bueno de Mesquita and Dickson 2007; Bueno de Mesquita 2005).[3] This could increase the support for nonstate actors both domestically and internationally, as these communities unite in rejection of the government's use of violence. This demonstrates that groups and governments understand that their actions will provoke reactions from the other and emphasizes the importance of studying the dynamic interactions of the combatants. Tactical decisions, and therefore conflict progression, are thought to be influenced by the relative nature of group and government capacity, as well as group goals.

Group size, its leadership, and its cohesion are determinants of capacity. When one actor in a conflict has a significant numerical disadvantage, it may feel compelled to resort to nontraditional tactics (terrorism or guerilla warfare) in order to cope with the asymmetry (Olson Lounsbery and Pearson 2009). An increasing disadvantage with respect to size may also drive a group toward increasing levels of violence. As the size of a group or number of government troops devoted to a conflict increases, one would expect the engagements to move away from terrorism and toward other tactics. One of government's advantages in intrastate conflict is that it not only usually enjoys a numerical advantage in the number of troops but also often has the ability to determine the proportion of its troops that it will commit at any given time. Governments may therefore have a surge capacity that is not enjoyed by the nonstate combatants. Confidence emerging from the size of one's group relative to its opponent

FIGURE 1.1 Characteristics of Tactical Choice

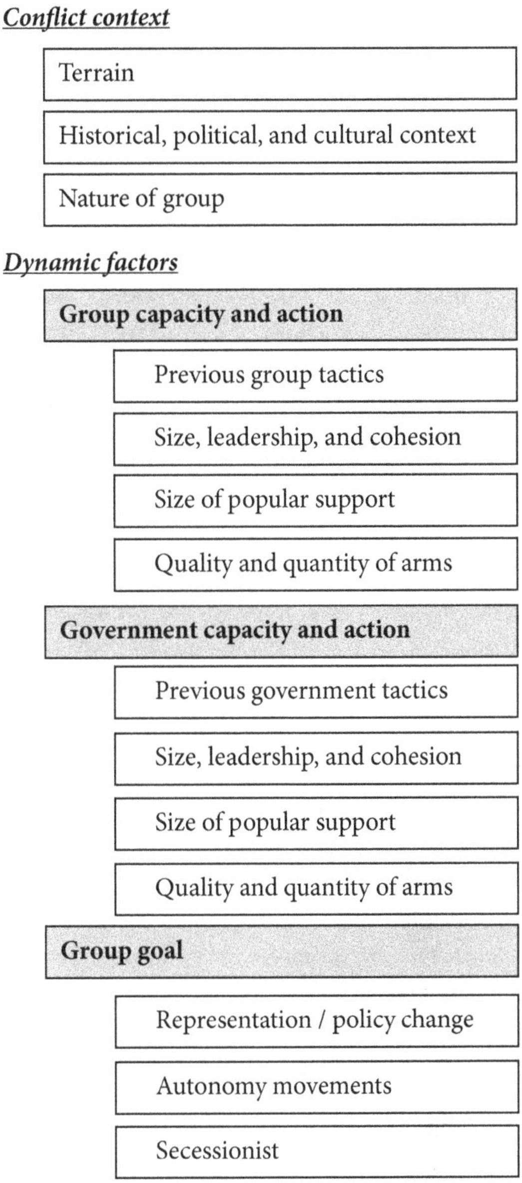

Conflict context

Terrain

Historical, political, and cultural context

Nature of group

Dynamic factors

Group capacity and action

Previous group tactics

Size, leadership, and cohesion

Size of popular support

Quality and quantity of arms

Government capacity and action

Previous government tactics

Size, leadership, and cohesion

Size of popular support

Quality and quantity of arms

Group goal

Representation / policy change

Autonomy movements

Secessionist

is likely to deter that group from engaging in good faith negotiations, choosing instead to pursue uncompromising military victory. Leadership and cohesion are also important factors and are discussed in greater detail below.

As indicated, civil war and rivalry research tends to view rebel groups, as well as their opposing governments, as both static and singular. Simplifying conflict to a set of bilateral interactions helps with systematic analysis but does little to capture the realities of the relationships. As conflicts evolve, participants may be altered in a number of different ways. One of the more common intragroup changes in the midst of civil war involves group cohesiveness. What may have originally started as a bilateral set of interactions between the government and one rebel group may become multilateral, involving several groups. Governments may experience internal divisions as well. For the most part, governments are more likely to present a united front toward rebellion, but members within the government may disagree over the approach or on issues unrelated to the rebellion. Segments of the government's military could potentially revolt and join the rebellion. Internal divisions tend to weaken all parties, and divided governments are no different.

There are many different issues that could lead to a division among rebels. Cunningham (2006) argues that there are three reasons for splinters to form: differing policy preferences, leadership disputes, or disagreements within the group over the strategy to pursue. It is suggested here that policy preferences may involve differences over group goals. Leadership disputes may emerge simply because of clashing egos or serious differences of opinion over how best to pursue group goals, or what those goals ought to be. Leadership differences may also emerge over group strategy.

One might also expect that success, or lack thereof, on the battlefield might bring to light differences within groups. If a group is doing well in its military campaign, there is probably less of a chance that disagreements over policy or strategy will occur. Potential leadership rivals are also likely to be held at bay. When, however, battlefield losses accumulate or earlier successes cannot be repeated, members may begin to reevaluate leadership, strategy, or policy (i.e., group goals), thus creating conditions conducive to splintering. Battlefield losses and a general lack of success in a military campaign tend to force groups and governments to reassess a military approach (i.e., policy preferences or choice of strategy). In such situations, negotiations are possible, which can have significant implications for intragroup cohesiveness.

It seems counterintuitive that attempts to negotiate a peace could contribute to escalation of violence and the splintering of groups. The fact is, however, that negotiated settlements rarely result in lasting peace. As Licklider's (1995) study demonstrated, while military victory tends to be a relatively stable outcome for civil conflict (regardless of the desirability of such an outcome), less than 13 per-

FIGURE 1.2   Negotiation Processes Cause Factions within a Group to Splinter

Source: Olson Lounsbery and Cook (2010), 76.

cent of negotiated settlements were able to sustain peace after five years. Part of the reason for this may be that one side or the other enters into the negotiations in bad faith. They may be bowing to international pressure to engage in the negotiations or trying to gain some strategic advantage through participation. However, they may have no intention of following through on whatever agreement is struck. One might expect such a scenario when one group appears to be losing the military struggle and another winning.

A contributing factor could also be that groups and governments are not unitary actors, as has been indicated. Both sides tend to involve a range of members, from those who can be considered more moderate to those who are more extreme, each of which will have its own motivations to negotiate or not. When they splinter, a more moderate faction is likely to emerge along with a more extreme faction. Multiple splinters will similarly result in a range of factions from moderate to extreme (Bueno de Mesquita and Dickson 2007). Even if the leaders on each side engage in negotiations in good faith and have every intention of honoring the agreement, their followers or other elites could disagree with the settlement or the negotiation process. "Despite the successful negotiated outcomes that can result between major parties, a common effect of political processes is the splintering of groups into factions that support the negotiations (or their outcome) and those that do not" (Cronin 2006, 25). This dynamic is captured in Figures 1.2 and 1.3. If the leadership of either side lacks the capacity to enforce the agreement among their own members, violence can re-emerge.

Of course, splintering may occur before negotiations emerge. Such splintering is still going to produce more and less extreme factions. This can work to the government's advantage. If the government seeks to come to terms with the moderate faction(s) (i.e., negotiate), it can potentially isolate the more extreme members by co-opting selected group members. In diminished numbers, extremist factions could potentially be defeated more easily. By negotiating with one faction, that relationship de-escalates, while at the same time the government is likely to escalate its campaign against the more extreme group or groups (Driscoll 2012). Splintering, in turn, can lead to increased violence in one conflict dyad as the extremists who objected to the negotiations vow to continue the fight, and a de-escalation in another if an agreement is reached with more

FIGURE 1.3   Government Uses Negotiations with the Intention of
Splintering a Group

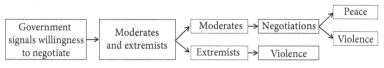

Source: Olson Lounsbery and Cook (2010), 76.

moderate factions. This divide-and-rule dynamic is depicted in Figure 1.3. The
increased intensity on the negotiation-resistant dyad could potentially be short
lived, however. The capacity of the splinter faction will be significantly diminished. In order to survive, a shift in tactics may be necessary.

When a civil war government indicates its willingness to engage in negotiations to end a conflict, the possibility of groups emerging that wish to "spoil"
negotiations becomes problematic. "Peace creates spoilers because it is rare in
civil wars for all leaders and factions to see peace as beneficial. Even if all parties
come to value peace, they rarely do so simultaneously, and they often strongly
disagree over the terms of an acceptable peace" (Stedman 1997, 7). A spoiler can
be either a party to the conflict or external to the process. A spoiler will always
be an actor who does not find peace to be in his or her interest. In some cases,
the existence of a portion of the group could be threatened by the conflict's termination (Bueno de Mesquita 2005). If individuals have based their identities on
group membership, settlement may be an unbearable threat. As a result, splinter factions tend to prolong civil wars (Cunningham, Gleditsch, and Salehyan
2009; Driscoll 2012).

In addition to the presence of a spoiler, there are other factors that may
have an impact on group splintering. Previous research has demonstrated that
there are specific conflict characteristics that statistical analysis shows predis-
pose groups to splintering (Olson Lounsbery and Cook 2010). Group splintering may be more likely early or late in the conflict as compared to the times in
between. Early on the group has yet to establish strong leadership and group
cohesion. Later in the conflict fatigue and disagreements may be more likely,
and groups tend to be more likely to engage in negotiations (Cronin 2010). The
intensity of the violence, as measured in casualties, also tends to increase the
likelihood of splintering. The size of a group may also influence splintering. As
the size of the group increases, the likelihood of splintering decreases. It is also
more likely that splintering will occur when the conflict is over territory rather
than over ethnicity.

Clearly, group divisions complicate the conflict process and have significant implications for patterns of violence. Divisions within the government may escalate conflict, but when rebels splinter, the implications for government action are more complex. If the government is doing well in its military campaign (or perceives it is doing well), it is unlikely to change its course of action. If there is doubt, however, as to the ability to succeed fully, the government may choose to de-escalate with a more moderate group while escalating with another.

It should be clear at this point that when rebel groups decide to part ways, for whatever reason, their ability to wage war against a typically stronger government is diminished. Their resources are fragmented, and the government may use those divisions against one another. This recognition may result in coalition forming among rebel groups. What is known about rebel group coalitions is somewhat limited and can be considered a neglected area of research.[4] One can, however, speculate that coalitions emerge because larger groups are more likely to achieve success on the battlefield. If members can overcome their differences and present a united front, they stand a better chance of winning. The decision to unite or reunite is a rational decision, as a result, because groups want to maximize their utility (Bottom et al. 2000). Creation of a rebel group coalition requires, however, that more moderate and more extreme members compromise on group goals, strategy, or leadership, or perhaps on all three. Players will in essence be forced to give up their preferences that may have led to the splintering in the first place. Riker (1962), in his work on political coalitions, has referred to this as "shaving the quota." Because coalition forming requires shaving the quota, coalitions are likely to emerge when groups are failing on the battlefield. They may also be viewed as tenuous peace agreements.

Rebel group and governmental leadership are central to this discussion as well. Charismatic leaders who have the ability to persuade and woo followers can dramatically increase a group or government's capacity. Boulding (1989) has described this type of power as integrative. It costs less than leaders who have to employ threats or inducements to gain membership or following. Rivalries and the groups involved that include charismatic leadership can sometimes become heavily dependent on that integrative power and the personality involved. When that leader is arrested, killed, or otherwise deposed (sometimes referred to as decapitation of the group), those movements or governments may collapse. Further, where leadership personality plays a central role in defining a rival, efforts to collaborate across conflict actors may be challenged by the egos involved.

As indicated earlier, civil wars are particularly complex because states may actually be engaged against multiple rebellions at once. All of these rebellions will share a common enemy (i.e., the government). As a result, it is possible that coalitions may be formed not just within any one conflict among rebels with a shared identity, but coalitions may also be formed across conflicts. By uniting two or more rebel factions across conflicts, rebels enjoy larger numbers, shared resources, and potentially a greater chance of success. These types of coalitions are significantly challenged if there are divergent goals, leadership, and strategy. But they do, nonetheless, occur. Regardless of whether rebel coalitions form across conflicts or within one (i.e., between factions), rebels who emerge as a united front, creating one entity with increased capacity, will typically do so with the hopes of escalating the conflict in pursuit of a rebel victory. It should be noted, however, that even without coalition building the presence of multiple rebellions in a state dilutes a government's capacity to respond to any one conflict, as it must divide its resources against multiple rivals.

Popular support is another important resource for civil war actors. Both the government and groups benefit from increasing levels of public support for their side. Supported groups can see their capacity increase as recruiting and fundraising are facilitated and safe houses and other assistance are provided. More important, a group that experiences high levels of public support would have less impetus to resort to terrorism, as attacks on civilians would likely be counterproductive, unless the civilians are seen as complicit with the government's actions. Further, rebels with significant support may be able to use that support as leverage at the negotiating table, making nonviolent approaches more likely. If public support for the group was never experienced or decreased significantly, it could increase the group's willingness to resort to terrorism. The same arguments apply to governments engaged in conflict. During periods of high support they will find more public compliance with taxation, laws, and calls for the draft, for instance. Attacks on the public under these conditions would likely undermine a government's goals.

Quality and quantity of arms will also have an impact on tactical decision making. Access to superior firepower has an obvious impact on the capacity of combatants. As such access decreases, more aggressive tactics may be employed in attempts to offset perceived or real military inferiority. This is related to popular support in that groups with high levels of support may have additional funds to purchase more or better weaponry. Increasing parity in weapons between combatants would favor traditional military maneuvers or guerilla warfare rather than terrorism (Sislin and Pearson 2001). In some cases in identity-based conflicts, groups can augment their support by fundraising within their diaspora community (i.e., people of the same kinship group who have fled, often because of fighting, and now live abroad). Of course, armaments are expensive and are easily depleted in battle. As a result, the ability of a group or its government to fund its campaign is important. The government has a clear advantage in this regard as it can typically tax its population and utilize wealth produced by the state to buy weaponry through legal channels (barring any weapons embargo that may be put in place). Rebels rarely have this resource building capacity and tend to fund their endeavors in several ways. They may look to outside assistance (discussed in depth later in this chapter), they may acquire their weapons through theft or success on the battlefield (Pearson et al. 1998), or they may capture resources such as diamond mines or oil fields.

Finally, group goals are treated as dynamic in this study. Although group goals can be multiple in nature and complex, three primary goals have been identified. The first goal is representation, policy, or regime change. Groups may engage against the government in attempts to have their interests included more fully in the policy process or to change the nature of the system itself. Groups with such goals are unlikely to engage in terrorism. Their goals are to get more participation in the existing regime, not to eliminate it. Violence in such a case would likely be counterproductive. The second and third goals are often referred to as self-determination movements. These are the most common forms of violent political conflict within states (Marshall and Gurr 2003). Autonomy movements may seek greater self-rule but are attempting to achieve this within the existing governing system. Secessionist campaigns have the greatest chance to result in violence against civilians, as their goal is to remove themselves from the existing system entirely. Seceding groups are no longer bound by societal norms or the desire to remain within the state system. Goals can change during the course of conflict. It may be that frustration leads a group to progress from demands for policy change to seeking secession as their calls for change are unheeded by government. However, it could also be the case that a group's goals begin with autonomy or secession.

Collier and Hoeffler (1998) have suggested that rebels are frequently motivated more by greed than by grievance issues. Rebels may be more interested in capturing state resources than any true reform. In such campaigns, greed goals are rarely stated as such. Instead actors tend to couch their movements in the more altruistic goals identified above. If greed is an underlying motive of leadership, however, it should be expected that tactical decisions will be influenced by that reality. Terrorism may be more likely, but so too may negotiated outcomes. Resources are more easily negotiated than goals that are more closely tied to group identity (Rothman and Olson 2001). Rebel leaders may be willing to come to terms with revenue sharing of a diamond mine, for example.

As was previously stated, no one variable discussed above provides an adequate explanation for strategic and tactical decisions during conflicts. Only by understanding the dynamic interaction among these variables can one hope to gain insight into why groups and governments behave as they do. It is only recently that scholars have started to study the dynamic aspects of civil wars (see the work of Olson Lounsbery 2005; DeRouen, Bercovitch, and Wei 2009; Olson Lounsbery and Pearson 2009). Figure 1.4 presents an interaction framework that illustrates the process that leads to ebbs and flows in political violence.

FIGURE 1.4   Tactical Choice Interaction Framework

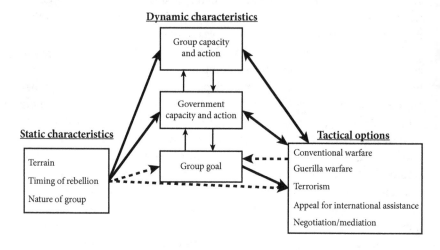

TACTICAL OPTIONS

In addition to the static and dynamic variables, the figure also lists potential tactical options that are available to the combatants. In the text above, factors that may cause rebels to turn toward or away from terrorism were discussed. Those are examples of this kind of shift in tactics in response to dynamic inter-actions. In this section, the focus is on tactical options and what might influence their selection.

Rebels engaged in an intrastate conflict with government have already made the decision to take up arms and engage in armed conflict. Once that armed conflict ensues, groups reconsider their approach in light of both performance on the battlefield and the behavior of their opponent. Armed insurrection can take three different forms: conventional warfare, guerrilla warfare, or terrorism. These tactical decisions are not mutually exclusive. Conventional warfare is distinguished from guerrilla warfare by the way in which nonstate actors engage with the government. Guerrilla warfare by definition involves hit-and-run tactics allowing rebels to engage briefly with the government followed by a retreat to a safer place. Conventional approaches to armed conflict involve more sustained combat.

One of the challenges in studying this phenomenon is making the distinction between terrorism and other forms of political violence. It is particularly difficult to differentiate between guerrilla warfare and terrorism, as both are asymmetric warfare strategies employed by the disadvantaged combatant.[5] There are a huge number of potential definitions of terrorism from which one could draw. Even before 9/11 brought the issue into the mainstream, Bruce Hoffman identified 109 separate definitions for terrorism in the scholarly literature (Hoffman 1998, 35–40). A common distinguishing characteristic among the definitions is the targeting of civilians or so-called innocents (see, for example, Feldmann and Perala 2004, 104). This raises the question of what combatant characteristics and conflict dynamics may push a group to identify citizens as legitimate targets for violence.

Given the Global War on Terrorism and its prominence as an issue in international relations, this is something that must be better understood. Attacks against civilians may be conceptualized as the most extreme manifestation of political violence. Both groups and governments may target civilians during the course of conflict. On occasion, civilians are targeted because of their perceived support for one side in the conflict. At other times, violence may become completely indiscriminant. Rebel groups and governments in the conflict may decide to engage in violence against civilians.

At the onset of strife it can be assumed that the government will enjoy many strategic advantages over the rebel group. A potential disadvantage for the government, however, may be an inability to distinguish civilians from combatants, who by definition will be unlikely to wear a uniform or insignia. This can lead to confusion about what a government's intentions were when attacks killed civilians. The ability of a group to choose one tactic over the other is a function of its capacity vis-à-vis the government, terrain, and group goals. All are thought to escalate a conflict and contribute to more enduring violence should such tactics prove successful.

As the conflict progresses, armed or violent tactical options may be replaced by a desire or a need to negotiate a resolution, particularly if other approaches are failing. Negotiations involve unassisted efforts by rebels to engage in a dialogue with the government over issues of the conflict aimed at resolution, or at least conflict de-escalation. Due to the typically asymmetric nature of intrastate conflict, unassisted negotiations do not occur as frequently as third-party assisted, or mediated, attempts. This is not to say that negotiations do not occur in intrastate rivalries, but when they do occur, they rarely address underlying grievance issues of the rivalries (Olson Lounsbery and Cook 2010). In order to get parties to come to the negotiating table in good faith and address core conflict issues, third-party influence is frequently necessary.

Intrastate rivalries, despite the fact that they tend to be "internal" struggles, tend to draw attention from the outside world. Further, civil wars and rivalries are generally contagious (Forsberg 2009). Violence, whether on purpose or unintended, draws attention from other states and the international community. In fact, intervention into civil wars is a frequent occurrence (Regan 2000a). External actors, whether nation-states or intergovernmental organizations, become involved in civil wars by offering financial aid or threatening sanctions (economic intervention), troops or military aid (military intervention), or third-party assisted mediation (diplomatic intervention). According to Pearson and Baumann (1993), interventions vary depending on the direction of intervention. External actors may be motivated to support an ally government, but they might also choose to intervene in support of the rebellion. Not all interventions are as specifically targeted, however. Some may be designed to be neutral in nature, with the goal of stopping the fighting. Civil wars may also involve intervention in the form of cross-border raids as neighboring countries find themselves impacted by fleeing refugees or rebels. The impact of the internationalization of civil wars is well explored, but its relationship to tactical decisions and conflict patterns is complicated by several factors. Some of these factors relate to interactions already discussed, while others emerge as new complicating processes. In order to understand the intervention-conflict progression relationship better, one must recognize that all interventions are not alike. What motivates intervention will impact its type (diplomatic, economic, military) and direction (at whom the intervention is targeted), which will then determine, along with other factors, how it influences patterns of violence.

Figures 1.2 and 1.3 demonstrate what the impact of diplomatic intervention may be on the subnational actor engaged in conflict. Figure 1.4 suggests the factors that would motivate a civil war actor to seek outside assistance. Figure 1.5 depicts the decision-making dynamics of the international intervener, which is another significant piece of the puzzle. The motivation for such assistance may or may not be a request made by a civil war actor. The appeal for international assistance in the group tactic options box in Figure 1.4 captures this type of request. This is not to say that an international actor would not decide to intervene without receiving a request from the government or rebels, but the focus here is on understanding why groups or relevant governments would choose to make such a request as a tactical decision.

By definition, civil wars occur within the borders of a recognized nation-state with one of the warring parties being the government of that state (Small and Singer 1982; Gleditsch et al. 2002). As a result, international legal norms that value state sovereignty would suggest that civil war states would naturally be hesitant to request or allow an intrusion into their own affairs. As mentioned previously, for the most part at the onset of a conflict, civil war governments enjoy a preponderance of power (Bapat 2005). Under these conditions, a government is unlikely to request external assistance in any form because such action may convey weakness and potentially challenge the validity of that government's sovereignty. At the onset, a government facing internal armed challengers would typically attempt to use this initial advantage to deal with the opposition swiftly. It is fairly unlikely at this stage that a civil war government will view external intervention, in any form, as either necessary or beneficial.

FIGURE 1.5   International Intervention Dynamics

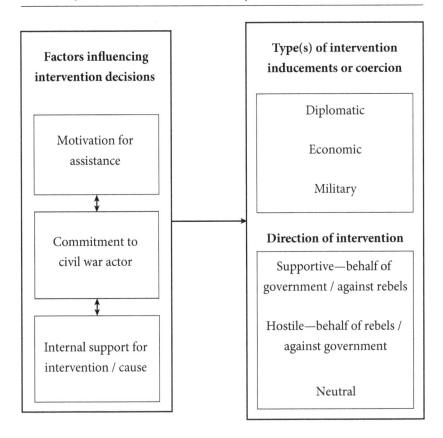

Should the armed conflict continue despite initial attempts by the government to alleviate the threat, however, requests for external assistance become more likely. Bapat (2005) has suggested that civil war governments are most likely to request assistance once it becomes clear that their military efforts alone are not bringing about a swift enough end to the insurrection. If requests for military intervention on behalf of a civil war government are granted, this will likely signal an escalation of the conflict as the government ratchets up its efforts to defeat the rebels. Governments are unlikely to request diplomatic assistance (which could potentially lead to a mediated settlement) at this time, as it would be inconsistent with the goal of defeating their opponents militarily. Economic interventions allow civil war governments to address potential grievances, thereby undermining support for armed factions that may have used such grievances as a rallying cry. Under these conditions, one would expect that economic intervention would also signal an initial escalation of conflict followed by de-escalation if the rebel support base becomes undermined. If, however, military or economic intervention assistance does not achieve the desired military victory for the government, requests by the civil war government for diplomatic intervention in the form of third-party-assisted negotiations become more likely. This phase, when it involves the failure to produce a military victory, can be characterized in many situations as a mutually hurting stalemate that is ripe for resolution (Zartman 1989; Zartman and Touval 1985). The fear of further loss and the fatigue of fighting can lead actors to reevaluate and reconsider their commitment to violence (Zartman 1993; Fison and Werner 2002; Powell 2004; Slantchev 2003). Fighting is expensive, and costs accumulate over time. Actors tend to look for alternatives to fighting when victory remains elusive and costs continue to be incurred (Greig 2001; Zartman 2000). Diplomatic intervention then becomes an alternative worthy of consideration.

It is not the case that all such calls for mediation involve a mutually hurting stalemate, however. If a civil war government makes requests for military or economic assistance, but those fall on deaf ears, are not reciprocated to the extent necessary to win the war, or simply do not produce the desired result, a situation can arise where the rebel group faction(s) move closer to achieving military victory. A civil war government, facing defeat, may seek external diplomatic assistance for the purpose of negotiating an exit to the conflict or a safe departure from the country. Whether negotiations are being sought to end a stalemated war or to complete a victory, the expectation is that, if successful, de-escalation becomes very likely. If requests fall on deaf ears, however, a failed negotiation may result in the escalation of violence. If intervention is too limited to assure victory, de-escalation is likely regardless of the outcome of the talks. Military victory will bring about resolution regardless of whether the former leaders find their own safe haven or are able to negotiate a role in the postwar government.

Relative to their governments, rebels are more inclined to seek external assistance early in the conflict, albeit for similar reasons. Although the international legal norm valuing sovereignty would suggest that most interventions will occur on behalf of the civil war government and with its consent, in practice this is not always the case. When such interventions do occur on behalf of rebels, their situation tends to be improved regardless of intervention type. Given the asymmetric power relationship, and the already perceived legitimacy of the civil war government, rebels are at a distinct disadvantage early in the conflict. When external actors decide to intervene on their behalf, the nonstate actor's cause can gain legitimacy.

For rebels, diplomatic intervention may occur in some important ways. First and foremost, as conflict unfolds and violence ensues, external actors may call for talks. While those calls may be unheeded by warring governments for reasons mentioned above, the suggestion of such discussions serves as recognition that assistance is needed. Should talks emerge where the mediator advocates on the nonstate actor's behalf, rebels are more likely to elicit peace agreements, and the provisions of such agreements are likely to be more meaningful, such as power sharing (Olson Lounsbery and DeRouen 2015; Svensson 2009). As conflict continues, however, if rebels have had negative experiences in negotiations, their preference for diplomatic assistance may wane. Further, if they are able to receive material forms of intervention, which actually work to bolster their capabilities, a diplomatic solution may no longer seem to serve their needs.

Economic intervention on behalf of rebels can also improve their chances. Engaging in armed struggles requires weaponry, which rebels typically lack as compared to their governmental opponent, especially early in the conflict. Even over time, however, rebels will need to replace spent weapons or to arm additional recruits. As a result, absent some other form of revenues, rebels frequently look to outsiders for assistance (whether it be economic aid, training, or actual foreign military intervention on their behalf). An influx of such resources can allow groups to continue the fight or escalate a conflict in significant ways.

The most expensive form of intervention from the perspective of the intervener is foreign military intervention. When it is forthcoming, however, the power hierarchy of the conflict can be changed dramatically, increasing the chances for rebel victory (Balch-Lindsay, Enterline, and Joyce 2008). Given the asymmetric nature of most civil wars, it is not uncommon for rebels to seek such assistance. Of course, doing so means that rebels will lose some of their autonomy and decision-making ability. This was the case with the Kosovo Liberation Army (KLA) when NATO engaged with Serbia on their behalf. The KLA was forced to accept what they perceived as unacceptable terms or face complete withdrawal of support (PBS 1999). The desire to maintain their autonomy may deter rebels from seeking foreign military intervention, though they are more likely to accept such assistance than the opposing government.

Actors engaged in intrastate conflict make tactical decisions repeatedly over time. Many issues factor into each decision, including their capacity vis-à-vis their opponent, prior successes and failures, and goals. At various times in a conflict or rivalry rebels and governments may choose to employ violent approaches (i.e., conventional warfare, guerrilla tactics, or terrorism), seek outside assistance, or make appeals for dialogue. These tactics could be cycled through sequentially or could be entered into at any point. In fact, groups and governments are likely employing more than one tactic at a time.

Static factors may have an influence on each aspect of the dynamic conflict but will not be altered by them. Static factors may also have some impact on group goals and the choice of tactic, by bracketing the range of possible responses. It would be unlikely that any of the static characteristics would be a determining factor for a group's goals. Tactic selection is clearly a very dynamic process. The tactic being pursued by each side is heavily impacted by the conflict dynamics identified in this chapter as well as by the other side's previous actions, providing a feedback decision-making loop. Groups and government may pursue the same tactics over a long period of time, or their behaviors could change in reaction to some event. Tactical decisions influence escalation and de-escalation and determine the strategies that are adopted by not only combatants on both sides but by international actors as well.

To evaluate the theoretical framework presented here, conflict chronologies were created using the *New York Times, Keesing's World News Archive,*[6] and published interviews with key actors, scholarly research, and reports on each of the six countries and the conflicts occurring within them. Chronologies were comprehensive in nature capturing events, such as battles/attacks, negotiations, interventions, and group dynamics, but also discussions of group and government capacity, such as troop levels or territory captured. Through the use of chronologies, not only could group and government tactics be identified, but the conflict environment and the context under which tactical decisions were made, such as engaging in negotiations or shifts toward targeting civilians, could be better examined. What follows is the application of the theoretical framework presented on each of the countries examined here. The variables identified in the frameworks are drawn from the case chronologies.

CHAPTER 2

Resources and Conflict
Sierra Leone

Examination of civil conflict in Sierra Leone provides insights into factors that influence patterns of conflict and group interactions. The country experienced underlying tensions and relatively bloodless coups. The former British colony even managed to transition to independence without significant bloodshed. In the 1990s, however, the situation escalated into a civil war that was exceptionally brutal. Of particular interest is the fact that both rebels and government troops intentionally targeted civilians. The extent to which a scarce natural resource, in this case diamonds, is responsible for the atrocities committed in Sierra Leone is a point of debate. In addition to the problems caused by the country's gem wealth, violence has been tied to the dire economic conditions, official corruption, regional disparities, ethnicity, and political competition. While each of these aids in the understanding of tactical decisions at specific points in time, it should be recognized that each was experienced as it related to diamonds. Corruption, for instance, was often tied to smuggling and the maldistribution of wealth.

The purpose of this chapter is to examine patterns of violence and the interrelationships among groups in Sierra Leone. It focuses on conflict dynamics during the two most important periods of violence experienced in Sierra Leone, the mid-1960s, when there was conflict over the type of government and control, and the civil war period from 1991 to 2000.

COUNTRY GEOGRAPHY AND HISTORY

Sierra Leone is a small state located on the coast of western Africa, situated on the North Atlantic between Guinea and Liberia. Its capital, Freetown, is on the western coast and distant from the diamond mines in the south and east as well as the border with Liberia (two factors whose significance is discussed later in the chapter). Its terrain varies from the coastal mangrove swamps in the west to the mountainous areas of the east. It peacefully transitioned to independence from the United Kingdom on April 27, 1961. Essentially, the area that became the country was designated by the British for the relocation of freed slaves. This factor, combined with the previously existing presence of tribes in the various

FIGURE 2.1   Sierra Leone

Diamond Extraction Area

regions of the country, gave it its ethnic diversity. The country is home to about fourteen different ethnic groups (Hirsch 2001) with the Mende (35 percent) and Temne (31 percent) being the largest and most influential (U.S. CIA 2012). As political parties developed in the country, the Mendes, who lived mostly in the south, took control of the Sierra Leone People's Party (SLPP). The Temnes, from the north, came to control the All People's Congress (APC). The country is also somewhat divided geographically, with the north tending to be more prosperous than the south. The country is consistently among the poorest in the world. Education and literacy are very limited, and life expectancies are low.

The presence of diamonds, a finite natural resource, in the country had an important impact on the civil war that occurred. This is unique compared to other cases included in this book as it is the only one where a scarce resource has influenced conflict. The most important characteristic of the diamonds in Sierra Leone is that they are alluvial. In contrast to kimberlite diamonds that are mined from concentrated deposits or veins underground, alluvial diamonds have been weathered out of their original deposits and rest in riverbeds. So-called point resources, like kimberlite diamonds, can be controlled and defended from predation more easily than dispersed assets such as alluvial diamonds, which are more lootable (Snyder and Bhavnani 2005; Le Billon 2005; Homer-Dixon 1999). This has been the case in Sierra Leone.

Diamonds were discovered in Sierra Leone in 1930. In 1934, the Sierra Leone Selection Trust (SLST) was granted a ninety-nine-year monopoly on the country's diamonds. Almost immediately efforts were underway by tribal chiefs and others to undermine the monopoly. By independence in 1961, the country drew 60 percent of its export earnings from diamonds (Gberie 2005, 23). During the late 1960s, the SLST was operated under the auspices of Siaka Stevens (president of Sierra Leone, 1968–1985) and his friend, Mohammad Jamil, a Lebanese diamond merchant (Ndumbe and Cole 2005; Keen 2005). Beginning in the 1970s, Stevens maintained a relatively high level of control over the country's diamonds. He effectively nationalized the SLST in 1971 by creating the National Diamond Mining Company (NDMC) in which the government held a 51 percent share (of which Stevens personally held 12 percent) and SLST 49 percent (Gberie 2005, 32). This personalization of control and cronyism continued until the late 1970s (Smillie, Gberie, and Hazleton 2000).

Through this control, the country was able to reap some tax benefits from the sale of diamonds. Stevens used government forces to protect the diamond mines and resources. However, throughout the 1970s, the Lebanese diamond merchants became more and more powerful, allowing them to decrease their reliance on government forces, build their own private armies, and increase smuggling operations. Jamil was the most prominent of the Lebanese merchants,

gaining power and governmental presence. He "had vital stakes in the fish-
eries, tourism and manufacturing sectors, paid the salaries of senior military
and police officers, and even attended cabinet meetings. He was also allowed to
maintain a well-armed 500-strong personal security force" (Gberie 2005, 35).

The combination of cronyism and personalization of the diamond industry
increased the tendency for diamond smuggling to occur. Furthermore, Stevens,
fearing a military coup, worked to undermine the strength of the military by
cutting spending and capping the size of the army at two thousand troops. Instead, he relied on small, paramilitary troops loyal to him for his protection
(Snyder and Bhavnani 2005, 582). This situation was exacerbated by the rampant
corruption in the country. Stevens used his power to diminish the efficacy of
official government agencies in order to assure his personal wealth (Reno 1998,
115–118). William Reno described Stevens's actions as the creation of a "shadow
state." While official channels were being weakened and impoverished, Stevens
surrounded himself with cronies who controlled both the government and the
diamonds (Reno 1998; Reno 1996). John Hirsch went a bit further and declared
that Stevens "destroyed and corrupted every institution of the state" (Hirsch
2001, 29). Between the economic problems of the country and Stevens's undermining of the government, educational institutions almost completely collapsed,
diminishing the well-being and futures of Sierra Leonean youths.

Stevens handed over power to his personally selected successor, Major
General Joseph Saidu Momoh, in 1985. Stevens did so not in spite of his lack of
power and popularity, but because of it (Reno 1996). He wanted to assure that
his successor lacked the capacity to interfere in his profits. Shortly thereafter,
governmental control of the diamonds collapsed. Momoh was less popular than
Stevens, faced an increasingly dire economic situation, and had neither an effective mechanism for managing the trade nor the capacity to stop the smuggling.
His time in office was characterized by the exceptionally poor performance of
the economy. This was due, in part, to Momoh's attempts to implement the
conditions that the International Monetary Fund (IMF) placed on the country, which exacerbated the already miserable economic situation. In addition
to these challenges, Momoh also faced increasing demands for transition to a
multiparty system (Zack-Williams and Riley 1993).

Momoh's regime was also characterized by decreasing governmental control of the country's diamonds. This decline is captured in the country's export
numbers. In 1970, the country exported an estimated two million carats of diamonds. By 1980, licit exports had dropped to 595,000 carats, and then down to
48,000 carats in 1988 (Ndumbe and Cole 2005; Keen 2005; Smillie, Gberie, and
Hazleton 2000). It is difficult to capture how much of this loss was due to smuggling versus diminished production. Several sources point out, however, that
Sierra Leone's neighbors have been exporting far more diamonds than mineral

surveys indicate are to be found within their borders (Gberie 2003; Hirsch 2001; Smillie, Gberie, and Hazleton 2000), suggesting that smugglers were exporting Sierra Leonean diamonds through neighboring countries. According to one author, by the mid-1980s, 70 percent of the diamonds leaving the country were through illicit channels, depriving Sierra Leone of a much-needed source of income (Snyder and Bhavnani 2005, 582). These trends continued into the 1990s.

Since independence, the country has been plagued with underlying tensions. Rather than being the exception, the targeting of civilians (terrorism) by rebels has been the norm, while the government has focused its attacks almost entirely on the rebels, except in 1997, when a coup brought rebels into government (which is described in greater detail later in the chapter). This has contributed to the international campaign against so-called blood diamonds. The acts committed against civilians have been particularly brutal, including rapes, murders, burning down of homes with people trapped inside, and mutilation of citizens' hands or arms to keep them from working in the diamond industry or voting. Those committing the atrocities have often been youths who were captured by rebels or government members and compelled into service through brutality. Rampant drug and alcohol use among the Revolutionary United Front (RUF) rebels and military members also served to fuel the violence.

It was not until 1990, however, that the number of battle deaths suffered exceeded the twenty-five per year threshold to be identified as warfare. Once the civil war started, however, it became particularly brutal. During the civil war, by some estimates over seventy-five thousand were killed, about five hundred thousand fled the country, and in excess of two million people were internally displaced (Smillie, Gberie, and Hazleton 2000).

SIERRA LEONEAN CONFLICT

In the case of Sierra Leone, there is only one armed conflict identified by the Armed Conflict Dataset (UCDP/PRIO 2014), which is that between the government's Sierra Leone Army (SLA) and the Revolutionary United Front (RUF). The Armed Forces Revolutionary Council (AFRC) seized governing power in 1997 and joined forces with the RUF. The Kamajors (a group of tribal hunters and protectors) consistently fought against the RUF. They therefore aligned themselves with the government, with the exception of the period of the AFRC/RUF junta's rule, at which time they fought against the government. As mentioned previously, Siaka Stevens governed Sierra Leone from 1968 to 1985, first as its elected prime minister and later as its authoritarian president. While his election came out of the country's desire for democracy, its aftermath shifted the country in quite the opposite direction. The post-election conflict had a profound impact on the country. In March 1967 the country held elections that were indecisive but

TABLE 2.1   Timeline of Key Events in Sierra Leone's Conflict, 1930–2000

Date	Event
1930	Diamonds discovered in Sierra Leone
1934	Sierra Leone Selection Trust was given a 99-year monopoly on the country's diamonds
April 27, 1961	Independence. Sir Milton Margai, head of the Sierra Leone People's Party (SLPP), elected prime minister.
1964	Sir Milton Margai died; his brother Sir Albert Margai succeeded him as prime minister and then attempted to amend the constitution to make the country a one-party system but failed
March 21, 1967	Brigadier David Lansana led a coup that prevented the transition of power, in spite of the fact that election results seemed to favor Siaka Stevens and the All People's Congress (APC)
March 23, 1967	National Reformation Council (NRC) arrested Lansana and suspended the constitution, bringing a military junta into power
April 18, 1968	Coup by noncommissioned officers (Anti-Corruption Revolutionary Movement—ACRM) brought Siaka Stevens to the presidency (May 26, 1968), a post he held until October 1, 1985
1972	Stevens effectively privatized the country's diamond assets
1978	APC and extractive industries joined forces to bring about a one-party system, with Stevens at the head
October 1, 1985	Major General Joseph Saidu Momoh was elected and served as president until April 29, 1992. It is largely recognized that Stevens arranged the elections to assure Momoh succeeded him.
August 1990	Civil war in Liberia caused the mobilization of the Economic Community of West African States (ECOWAS) forces, which included Sierra Leonean troops. Their participation angered Liberia's Charles Taylor. Momoh complained that hosting Liberian refugees was stretching national resources thin. Momoh oversaw the redrafting of the constitution, to return a multiparty system to the country.
March 23, 1991	The Revolutionary United Front (RUF), led by Corporal Foday Sankoh, invaded Sierra Leone. The small force (about 100 rebels) included Liberian fighters loyal to Charles Taylor.
April 12, 1991	By this time Sierra Leone had asked the United States and the UK for assistance in dealing with the rebels
May 1991	RUF began a campaign against the civilian population to demonstrate the government's inability to protect its citizens
April 29, 1992	Coup ousted Momoh. Captain Valentine Strasser headed up the new National Provisional Ruling Council (NPRC).
November 1992	NPRC offensive against RUF began
December 29, 1992	NPRC foiled a coup attempt
March 1993	Intensified rebel violence. Troops from Taylor's Liberia sent to assist Strasser.
January 1994	Recruitment drive for the NPRC brought in the uneducated and children, resulting in an army that was without discipline or command. *Sobel* (soldier by day, rebel by night) phenomenon began.

TABLE 2.1 Continued

Date	Event
December 1994	Strasser requested the UN use its good offices to mediate the conflict
Mid-1990s	Practice of mass amputations began
January 1995	RUF overran Sierra Rutile and Sieromco Mines, a major blow to the government
February 1995	Private security Ghurkhas contracted by the government to fight the RUF, which was moving toward the capital, Freetown
March 1995	Executive Outcomes (EO) contracted by Strasser to repel the rebels from Freetown and mining regions
January 16, 1996	Coup replaced Strasser with Brigadier Julius Maada Bio, who served as chairman of the Supreme Council of State until March 29, 1996
February 26–27, 1996	Elections held
March 17, 1996	Ahmad Tejan Kabbah (SLPP) won the presidency in a runoff election
March 1996	Kamajors experienced increasing power
March 25–26, 1996	Bio and Sankoh met and negotiated a temporary ceasefire and provision of aid to areas controlled by RUF
March 29, 1996	Bio handed power over to the elected government. Ahmad Tejan Kabbah (SLPP) became president of the Republic of Sierra Leone.
April 22, 1996	Sankoh and Kabbah engaged in peace talks, resulting in the signing of an indefinite ceasefire agreement on April 23, the Abidjan Peace Agreement, which was never implemented
May 29, 1996	Peace negotiations stalled on the issue of EO withdrawal
July 1996	Plans to reduce the size of the military and cut rice rations resulted in unrest
August 1996	International Alert (a mediation firm from London) sought to renew peace negotiations
September 8–9, 1996	Abortive coup attempt against Kabbah's government
November 30, 1996	Kabbah and Sankoh signed the Abidjan Peace Agreement
January 31, 1997	EO departed
March 6, 1997	Sankoh flew to Nigeria to purchase weapons and was arrested for carrying firearms when attempting to board a plane to return to Sierra Leone on March 12
March 15, 1997	Sankoh, in his absence, was ousted from the RUF and replaced by Sam Bockarie
May 26, 1997	Coup released Major Johnny Paul Koroma and many other rebels from prison. He became chairman of the Armed Forces Revolutionary Council (AFRC) and served in that capacity until February 12, 1998. Looting and mass violence ensued; much of it targeted civilians.
May 27, 1997	AFRC suspended the constitution and banned political parties
May 28, 1997	RUF rebels ordered to support the AFRC
June 1, 1997	Nigerian attempt to oust the junta failed. RUF was invited by Koroma to join the junta. Army and RUF merged to form the People's Army.

(continued)

TABLE 2.1 Continued

Date	Event
July 18–19, 1997	ECOWAS met with People's Army representatives in an attempt to restore peace and constitutional rule
October 8, 1997	UN embargoed military equipment and petroleum products
October 24, 1997	Conakry Peace Agreement, brokered by ECOWAS, signed
December 1997	Sandline International, a private military company, met with Kabbah to discuss supporting military activities
March 10, 1998	Ahmad Tejan Kabbah (SLPP) became president of the Republic of Sierra Leone and served in that capacity until September 17, 2007
December 1998	Increased violence from the RUF, in response to Sankoh being sentenced to death and battle deaths at the hands of Economic Community of West African States Monitoring Group (ECOMOG)
Early January 1999	RUF rebels invaded Freetown, killing at least 5,000
July 7, 1999	Lomé Peace Agreement signed
October 1999	UN authorized the creation of the larger UN Mission in Sierra Leone (UNAMSIL) peacekeeping force
April 30, 2000	The Lomé Peace Agreement collapsed when RUF fighters abducted 500 peacekeepers and returned to full-scale violence

Source: Compiled by the authors from *Keesing's World News Archive*, Hirsch (2001), 113–133, and other materials listed in the references. Shading indicates shifts in executive power.

seemed to favor Stevens and the All People's Congress (APC). The results were never officially announced, as a coup was carried out on March 21 by Brigadier David Lansana, who placed Stevens under house arrest and declared martial law. On March 23, however, the National Reformation Council (NRC), composed largely of young military officers and members of the police, staged another coup. This three-day period was accompanied by relatively low-level violence— rioting and looting, with four dead (*Keesing's World*, March 1967, 21949). The officers formed a junta that governed for the following year. Reportedly, Stevens spent that time training guerillas in Guinea in anticipation of overthrowing the NRC. The Anti-Corruption Revolutionary Movement (ACRM), a group of non-commissioned officers, removed the government on April 18, 1968, in a relatively bloodless coup. Stevens was sworn in as prime minister on April 26 (*Keesing's World*, May 1968, 22698). This period of episodic unrest is important in that it provided the "justification" for Stevens's declaration of a state of emergency, centralization of power, and distrust of the military. "Following the declaration of the state of emergency in 1968, the Army and the police carried out a combined operation which resulted in the massive arrest of the (opposition) SLPP stalwarts and their supporters including Paramount Chiefs in the Southern and Eastern Provinces. Apart from physically attacking the people or looting and damaging

TABLE 2.2   Conflicts in Sierra Leone, 1991–1999

Conflict	Groups participating	Primary geographic location(s)	Duration of conflict	Periods of outbreak of violence	Incompatibility
Revolutionary United Front (RUF)	RUF	Widespread	1991–1999	1991–1997	Government
RUF	RUF; Armed Forces Revolutionary Council (AFRC); Kamajors	Widespread	1991–1999	1998	Government
RUF	RUF; AFRC	Widespread	1991–1999	1999	Government

their properties, the forces actually shot and killed people" (Zack-Williams 1999, 144, quoting Lavalie 1985). By 1971, Stevens had moved the country from a coalition form of governance to one-party rule (Zack-Williams 1999).

As mentioned above, Stevens used his position to enrich himself and the top members of his party. He "consolidated his hold on power by nationalizing and clientelizing Sierra Leone's diamond sector" (Le Billon and Levin 2009, 701). He chose to step down in 1985 and transitioned power to his hand-picked successor, Major General Joseph Saidu Momoh. Diamond fields were deindustrialized under Momoh, and the government lost control of the country's most significant source of wealth. More critically, the RUF was largely financed by diamond smuggling beginning in the mid-1990s and throughout the country's civil war (Le Billon and Levin 2009, 702). On April 29, 1992, Momoh's ineffective regime was overthrown by the National Provisional Ruling Council (NPRC), which brought Captain Valentine Strasser to power.

Stevens's efforts to assure that the military was too weak to control his actions or depose him resulted in an army at the beginning of the war (1991) consisting of a mere three thousand troops who were poorly armed, trained, and fed. Their weapons were reportedly World War II–era guns, many of which could not even fire (Gberie 2011; Francis 1999; Zack-Williams 1999). While military leaders profited from the system, rank-and-file personnel were impoverished. Corruption and the economic shambles of the country demoralized both government and military personnel. This was reflected in both entities' reluctance or inability to secure the country's diamond revenues in government hands. In fact, in some instances the army is reported to have worked to protect diamond smugglers' operations rather than the country and its citizens (Keen 2005).

The rebels were led by Foday Sankoh, a former colonel in the Sierra Leone Army who had trained in rebel tactics in both Liberia and Libya in the late 1980s. He was, at one point, imprisoned by the APC government, which contributed to his anger at the government (UCDP).[1] While Sankoh was training in

Libya, he met Charles Taylor of Liberia, and the two agreed to support one another's rebellions (SCSL 2004; Abdullah 1998). Taylor came to power in Liberia in 1998 after a successful rebellion in which Sankoh participated (D. Brown 2000).

The RUF began as a small group of rebels. Sankoh returned to Sierra Leone with two men with whom he had trained in Libya and Liberia, Abu Kanu and Rashid Mansaray. Throughout its existence, the RUF was supported extensively by Taylor and his military forces as well as receiving training, equipment, and other support from them (Gberie 2003, 3; Gberie 2005).[2] They also worked with private firms to increase both sets of actors' capacity to earn money by enslaving captured citizens in the diamond fields (Badcock 2015). At its peak, the group reportedly had as many as fifteen thousand men (UCDP). This increase in numbers was made possible through both voluntary enlistment of poor young people in Sierra Leone and the forced conscription of others.

Early on, the RUF stated that its goals included the removal of corrupt leaders, liberation of the peasants, and creation of a military-led democratic government. According to the Uppsala Conflict Data Program (UCDP), it is unlikely that these stated goals accurately reflect the RUF's agenda, especially as the conflict grew. The UCDP report suggests that the RUF had no previously stated ideological foundation. It also pointed out that the RUF's practice of targeting civilians with indiscriminant violence contradicts their stated desire to free the peasantry (UCDP). In reality, the group was largely devoid of ideological motivation for their actions. Its members were primarily unemployed or underemployed young men who were often active in underground activities. According to Abdullah, "they [were] prone to criminal behavior, petty theft, drugs, drunkenness, and gross indiscipline" (1998, 208). Recruiting and conscripting among this class of people led to serious leadership challenges within the RUF's ranks. In fact, decisions about increasing an individual's leadership responsibilities in the organization were sometimes determined based on the candidate's relative capacity to control the troops (SCSL 2009). Kanu and Mansaray objected to the violent tactics that Sankoh was employing, and they were subsequently imprisoned and then executed (BBC News 2003; D. Brown 2000; Abdullah 1998).

There is a fairly common perception that the civil war in Sierra Leone was fought over diamonds (see, for example, Gberie 2003). However, as in most cases, the true cause of the war was far more complex. Clearly, the wealth associated with the diamonds was a factor, especially given the abject poverty suffered by most in Sierra Leone. Furthermore, the funds from the diamonds financed both corrupt governments and rebel organizations (Le Billon and Levin 2009). If nothing else, the diamonds served to prolong the conflict by increasing the capacity of whichever side controlled them, at least for a period of time. However, there are good arguments that there were broader socioeconomic underpinnings to the war. According to Archibald and Richards, a "combination of poverty and injustice, especially affecting youth," was the reason for the civil war (2002, 345). According to some, ethnicity was not a factor in the war (Gberie 2005, 2011; Francis 1999; Zack-Williams 1999). However, Ndumbe argued that it played a role as the Mende and Temne ethnic groups struggled against one another for control of the diamonds (Ndumbe and Cole 2005). From a somewhat different perspective, Zack-Williams (1999) argued that the war came about because of the illegitimacy of the state and the inability of the ruling class to bend the lower classes to their will.

CONFLICT PROGRESSION AND DYNAMICS

The initiation of the civil war in Sierra Leone had its origins in the civil war that was taking place in neighboring Liberia in 1990. Liberian refugees were flowing into Sierra Leone in large numbers, causing Momoh to complain that they were stretching his country's resources. The Economic Community of West African States (ECOWAS) mobilized peacekeeping troops into Liberia to help quell the violence. This force included Sierra Leonean troops, which irritated Charles Taylor, who felt personally betrayed by Momoh's participation (CQ Press 2011b).

Sankoh and the RUF, with Taylor's support, began deadly incursions into Sierra Leone in early 1991 and had penetrated to about 150 kilometers into the country by mid-May (Brecher and Wilkenfeld 1997). The support that Taylor provided clearly increased the RUF's capacity versus the government in these important early phases of the conflict, as well as throughout its progression. Taylor was not merely motivated by his anger at Momoh's participation in ECOWAS and his permitting the organization to use the country's airport at Lungi as a repair depot (Hirsch 2001, 32; Zack-Williams 1999); Taylor was also reportedly profiting from the Sierra Leonean diamonds that were being smuggled through his state (UCDP; Gberie 2003, 2005). Furthermore, Taylor's support of the RUF actions was also motivated by a desire to distract the ECOMOG force that was actively fighting his National Patriotic Front of Liberia (NPFL) rebels in Liberia (Rashid 2016). The NPFL was Taylor's Liberian rebel group, which even loaned troops to the RUF for the invasion (UCDP).

Beginning in 1992, the government was providing training to the Kamajors within the country. These were typically Mende groups of men who were hunters within their communities. They became conceptualized as protectors within their villages and provided self-defense primarily in the south and east of the country. In this case, it is clear that the government was attempting to increase their capacity versus the RUF forces by incorporating the Kamajors into the government's defensive forces (UCDP).

The disempowerment of the military of Sierra Leone that was carried out by

FIGURE 2.2   Patterns of Violence in Sierra Leone, 1991–2000

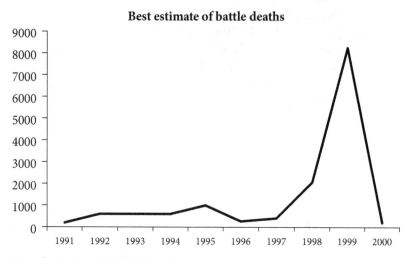

Drawn from Lacina and Gleditsch (2005).

Stevens created an environment in which the three hundred or so trained rebels enjoyed the advantage at the initial stages of the conflict. By the end of 1991, Momoh was seeking assistance from all quarters to fight the rebels. Guinea and Liberia sent troops starting as early as May, and Momoh expanded the Sierra Leone army to about six thousand, though the new recruits were largely unfit for duty (Gberie 2005). In spite of the increase in government power, the war rapidly took a serious toll on the economy and civilians. By early 1992, about three hundred thousand Sierra Leoneans had fled to refugee camps in Guinea, and four hundred thousand were internally displaced (Zack-Williams 1999).

Another coup occurred on April 29, 1992. Momoh was replaced by Captain Valentine Strasser, who was one of the young, white coup participants who were reportedly so surprised at their success that they had not even selected some-one to lead them if they won (Fritz 1994). The coup was relatively bloodless. Strasser began his regime by releasing resources that were being hoarded by APC cronies, which gave him instant popularity (Gberie 2005). Strasser funded supplies for the army through alluvial diamonds. However, the rebellion im-pacted the diamond industry, diminishing the impact of his actions. "The offi-cial diamond mining company [was] closed due to rebel attacks, and much of the country's productive base [had] been in rebel hands during 1992" (Zack-Williams and Riley 1993). The 1992 taking of the Kono (diamond-rich) region was planned and supported by Taylor. After the RUF had taken the region, San-koh provided Taylor with diamonds in exchange for even more ammunition

(SCSL 2004). Furthermore, Charles Taylor's assistance to the RUF helped keep the country destabilized, which allowed him to continue to exploit Sierra Leone's diamonds. While by this time the majority of Taylor's NPFL troops had left Sierra Leone, some remained to fight alongside the RUF, and Taylor continued to participate with the coordination of RUF actions through regular contact with Sankoh (SCSL 2004).

In the mid-1990s, the RUF tactics escalated in their brutality, shifting from occasional amputations to a massive campaign of severing the limbs of civilians. This shift in tactics occurred for a number of reasons. Amputations were carried out before elections to deter people from voting, either through the actual process or fear that the same would happen to them. After the elections, the rebels also punished those who voted for Ahmed Tejan Kabbah, the SLPP candidate, who would have had permanent ink on their fingers from voting. The tactic may also have been developed in order to intimidate the citizenry by displaying their willingness to engage in brutality. Still other explanations for the use of amputations by the RUF indicate that it was done to keep the people from harvesting rice that would feed government troops (*Economist* 2003) or to render the people unable to work in the diamond fields. There are no reports of the citizenry turning against the RUF, aside from the actions of the Kamajors. However, unlike typical peasant movements, the RUF was relatively unsuccessful in recruiting members, as indicated by the need for it to resort to conscription (Abdullah 1998). Had citizens turned against the RUF, this would have diminished the group's capacity. It may be that the fear of the group, the distrust of government, and poverty experienced in the country limited the amount of backlash to the group's tactics. It may also be that rather than opposing the group, the citizens fled. By February 1995, estimates indicated that an additional 185,000 people had fled the violence to Guinea, 90,000 to Liberia, and another 600,000 were living in refugee camps within the country (*Keesing's World*, February 1995, 40395).

Gberie (2005) argues that the RUF increased the use of amputations as a tactic when the Kamajors became a more serious opponent in the mid-1990s (14). The RUF also engaged in looting, rapes, murders, and the burning of entire villages. Similar acts of violence were carried out as a means of controlling the country's diamond wealth and smuggling operations (UCDP). The fighting was mostly restricted to the diamond-rich eastern and southern regions of the state.

By early 1994, Strasser had lost most of his public support, diminishing his capacity versus the RUF. "Members of the regime were accused of diamond smuggling; Sierra Leoneans were getting tired of the youthful antics of the young officers and their inability to end the war; and many saw the transition to civilian rule as a prerequisite for ending the war" (Zack-Williams 1999, 150). The RUF was on the offensive throughout the year, eventually expanding the geographic scope of the conflict from the previous focus on the east and south of the country, and pushed into the north. In December 1994, Strasser asked the UN to use its good offices to ensure the peace due to the desperate situation his NPRC now faced. Subsequently, in January 1995 the RUF captured a major bauxite mine, which was one of the last economic assets over which the government had control (UNDP; Gberie 2005). The United Nations began some small-scale attempts to engage the rebels in dialogue but these were rejected by Sankoh, as he was negotiating from a position of power versus the government.

One of the unique aspects of the Sierra Leone civil war as a case study is the fact that the government chose, at several different points, to increase its capacity versus the RUF by hiring private military contractors. In February 1995, Strasser hired the Gurkha Security Group to bolster his military forces. However, the Gurkhas were compelled to withdraw alongside the military when rebel forces beat them back and killed their leader, Robert Mackenzie (Gberie 2005). In May 1995, Strasser hired Executive Outcomes (EO), a private security force from South Africa. Details about the arrangement differ from source to source. Hirsch states that Sierra Leone paid the company an estimated $1.5 million a month, and diamond concessions were given to the company's subsidiary, Branch Energy (Hirsch 2001). EO has denied that it is affiliated with Branch Energy. Regardless, it should not come as a surprise that EO's primary focus was on retaking and protecting the country's diamond fields (Francis 1999). Even without the concessions, it would have been in EO's interest to secure the diamond assets so that the country would be able to pay their fees. While the organization mobilized equipment and technology, there were a relatively few personnel devoted to the battles (P. Richards 2005). After EO's arrival, rebel forces were driven back from Freetown and suffered significant losses. There is disagreement, however, about the extent to which EO contributed to the government's success (Smillie, Gberie, and Hazleton 2000; Hirsch 2001; Francis 1999). It is possible that the timing was coincidental.

The government's side, at this point, was essentially a coalition of the SLA, the Kamajors, and the EO contingent. The Kamajors numbered about thirty thousand, which were augmented by about four hundred EO troops, both of which mobilized in support of government capacity (Francis 1999, 330). In addition, EO helped to train other tribal groups, including the Donsos, Gbethis, and Tamboros, who joined the coalition (SCSL 2004). The EO troops also contributed to the government's strength by recruiting and training the Kamajors. By the end of 1995, the government had achieved a greater level of success against the rebels and had partial control over their actions (UCDP).

On January 16, 1996, mere weeks before scheduled elections, a divide within the NPRC resulted in Strasser being replaced by his deputy, Brigadier Julius Maada Bio, in a bloodless palace coup. Bio announced that he had initiated the coup because Strasser was attempting to remain in power rather than hold the elections (Synge 2002). Elections were then held in February 1996, which brought Kabbah of the SLPP to power. This kind of split in the government could be expected to lead to diminished government capacity versus the rebels. However, shortly after Bio came to power he made it clear that he intended to hold elections quickly (SCSL 2004). During the period leading up to the elections, Sankoh and his leaders in RUF ordered "Operation Stop Election," which was a campaign of violence against citizens to deter voting.

Furthermore, in mid-1996 the RUF suffered significant casualties, reducing their capacity versus the government and motivating them to request peace talks (Ndumbe and Cole 2005, 95). The RUF placed preconditions on the negotiations, which included a call for power sharing, budget provisions for education, housing and other benefits for citizens, and withdrawal of all foreign troops including ECOMOG and EO (Zack-Williams 1999, 151). The November 30, 1996, peace talks ended with the signing of the Abidjan accord. The terms of the peace agreement would allow the RUF to become a political party, would give amnesty to the rebels, and would institute policies toward a more equitable distribution of the country's wealth (UCDP). The peace was short lived, as it created a split in the RUF between those who supported the agreement and those dedicated to the continuation of violence. Abdullah (1998) argues that for many battle commanders and the lumpen (uneducated peasants) elements of the RUF, termination of the conflict threatened their survival. In addition, Sankoh was arrested in a coup among his top leaders, who objected to his failure to respect the Abidjan negotiations (SCSL 2004). The SCSL found that Taylor influenced this disagreement in the RUF in order to maintain his influence over the organization (SCSL 2003). However, while the leadership cadre in the RUF agreed that Sankoh should be removed, a move stimulated at least in part by his reluctance to move forward with the peace accord, the lower-level leaders and rank-and-file rebels remained strongly in support of Sankoh (Abdullah 1998). Subsequently, rebels seized the opportunity to act once the EO force was withdrawn from the country in accordance with the treaty (Gberie 2005).

The May 26, 1997, coup, whose aftermath marked a peak of violence in the country, grew out of the Abidjan accord. Members of the military, led by Major Johnny Paul Koroma, overthrew the government, at least in part because of fears of the demobilization it required. While the members of the military did not prosper within the system, demobilization threatened what little they did get, including housing, clothing, and subsidized rice. The coup participants were demoralized military personnel, the so-called sobels, soldiers by day and rebels by night (Kandeh 2003; Francis 1999). The coup appears to have been launched by Koroma for personal gain (UCDP). Koroma invited the RUF to join his movement, and they were folded into the AFRC to become the People's Army (UCDP;

Gberie 2003, 2005). The coup was followed by twelve hours of shelling of Free-town by the People's Army and a full week of rampant violence. Reportedly, this violence occurred because the RUF quickly took over control of the People's Army from the government troops (IRIN News 2000). This provides a powerful illustration of how tactical decisions can have an impact on group or govern-ment cohesion. Throughout the period of the junta's rule, Taylor continued to provide support in exchange for large quantities of diamonds (SCSL 2004).

The Sierra Leone government was therefore in the hands of the AFRC, with the support of the RUF. The result of this was the creation of a governing junta that engaged in rampant violence against civilians. It is the only time the UCDP identifies government one-sided violence against civilians in Sierra Leone. The RUF rebels were now part of the governing structures of Sierra Leone. As the two forces joined, the Sierra Leone Army adopted the RUF practice of using ampu-tations to control the population (UCDP; Gberie 2005).

In response to this dramatic shift in government and its practices, the Kam-ajors broke with the government and joined with other irregular forces in the country to form the Civil Defense Forces, which aligned against the AFRC/RUF government (Hoffman 2002). In other words, the same conflict continued, but the rebels now had governing power while those previously aligned with the government rebelled against the AFRC/RUF government. The AFRC/RUF junta subsequently declared the Kamajors illegal, at which point the Kamajors vowed to return Kabbah to power. The RUF hated the Kamajors because they were hav-ing success in their campaigns against the RUF forces. The SLA, now under con-trol of the AFRC, disliked the Kamajors because they felt the Kamajors were tak-ing a position in society that rightfully belonged to the SLA (Abdullah 1998).

This marked the point where the United Nations first imposed sanctions on the AFRC/RUF government of Sierra Leone. The sanctions included an arms em-bargo, oil embargo, and travel ban against AFRC members and their associates.

The Kamajors, Nigerian troops, and ECOMOG peacekeepers (who entered the conflict in July 1997) coalesced (increasing Kamajor capacity) and mobilized against the AFRC/RUF. Their successes brought about negotiations. On Octo-ber 24, 1997, the Conakry Peace Plan was signed. It was mediated by ECOWAS and signed by major states and international organizations. It included provi-sions to end hostilities, bring Kabbah back into power, demobilize troops (by ECOMOG), return refugees, release Sankoh from captivity, grant immunity to AFRC rebels, and facilitate humanitarian assistance (Gberie 2005, 114). The plan failed to produce any lasting results, in part because of the government's lack of capacity to do so, but also because of Koroma's decision to stay in power for two to four years longer than he had agreed to in the negotiations (Woods and Reese 2008). ECOWAS subsequently levied sanctions against the AFRC and

Koroma and mobilized thousands of Nigerian troops to pressure the junta to step down (UCDP).

In spite of the fact that they had lost power in early 1998, the AFRC/RUF alliance continued to fight against the government (i.e., they reverted back to their original role as rebels) and other forces aligned against them. In March 1998, Sankoh was captured, flown to Nigeria for a trial, convicted, and sentenced to death on October 23. In response, the RUF, now under the command of Sam Bockarie, went on the rampage for the remainder of 1998. Koroma, another RUF leader, at this point lacked the funds to pay his troops. To solve this problem, he ordered a new operation called "Operation Pay Yourself," in which troops under his command were encouraged to loot extensively as a form of compensation (SCSL 2004).

In January 1999, in what the UCDP referred to as the "peak of atrocities committed against civilians during the conflict," the AFRC went on a campaign, codenamed "Operation No Living Thing," of indiscriminant violence against the Sierra Leone capital of Freetown that lasted over two weeks. The RUF joined in the attacks only after the AFRC had initiated the violence (SCSL 2004). The period was described by Gberie as "a regime of horror lasting nearly two weeks and so intense and bizarre that it almost defies description" (2005, 126–127). Human Rights Watch said of the action:

> Civilians were gunned down within their homes, rounded up and massacred in the streets, thrown from the upper floors of buildings, used as human shields, and burnt alive in cars and houses. They had their limbs hacked off with machetes, eyes gouged out with knives, hands smashed with hammers, and bodies burned with boiling water. Women and girls were systematically sexually abused, and children and young people abducted by the hundreds. The rebels made little distinction between civilian and military targets. They repeatedly stated that they believed civilians should be punished for what they perceived to be their support for the existing government. (Human Rights Watch 1999a)

ECOMOG joined with the Kamajors, thereby increasing their capacity, to defend against the rebels. They enjoyed some initial success but were beaten back by ferocious attacks by the rebels. At one point, when the rebels claimed to have taken most of Freetown, Bockarie declared that his forces would not let up until Sankoh, who had been arrested and sentenced to death, was released. Kabbah agreed to release Sankoh if the rebels agreed to abide by the 1996 peace agreement, but Bockarie rejected these terms. Subsequently, in 1999, Bockarie and Sankoh had a falling out over diamonds (Jones 2003). Reportedly, Sankoh felt that Bockarie had strengthened himself during Sankoh's imprisonment by selling diamonds to reorganize and rearm the RUF (IRIN News 2003). Bockarie fled to Liberia with several hundred of his followers, diminishing RUF capacity. ECOMOG forces were joined by Nigerian reinforcements and what remained of the Sierra Leone civil defense forces. At this point, the coalition against the RUF included the SLA, the Kamajors, ECOMOG, and Nigerian forces. They managed to drive the rebels out of the capital, but the rebels left a path of maimed and killed civilians along their retreat (*Keesing's World*, January 1999, 42708). Estimates of the dead from this campaign alone are between three and five thousand people (SCSL 2004).

From January to July 1999, peace negotiations were overseen by a mediation committee composed of ECOWAS states, the UN, and other regional and international government representatives, including Taylor. The parties signed what came to be known as the Lomé Peace Agreement, which called for the transition of the RUF into a political party and provided a position in the government for Sankoh (SCSL 2004). It also included cessation of hostilities, demobilization provisions, and the establishment of the United Nations Observer Mission in Sierra Leone (UNMOSIL) to serve as a peacekeeping force. This force was expanded to six thousand troops and renamed the UN Mission in Sierra Leone (UNAMSIL) (Hirsch 2001, 86). The AFRC had been routed in the January 1999 conflict over Freetown and was therefore not party to the negotiations or the resulting settlement agreement. As expected, the agreement contained provisions to accommodate demands of the RUF, which was tasked with developing an initial plan. One of the key provisions in the agreement was that Sankoh would lead a commission to manage the country's mineral wealth (Gberie 2005; O'Flaherty 2004). Many were shocked that the Lomé Agreement also pardoned all combatants and collaborators for anything they might have done during the conflict (Gberie 2005).

The Lomé Agreement was unsatisfying to many in the RUF, including Sankoh, who soon began to challenge the authority of Kabbah and the UNAMSIL troops (UCDP). On April 30, 2000, the peace collapsed as the RUF captured five hundred UN peacekeepers and then resumed full-scale rebellion. The RUF later argued that it captured the peacekeepers in response to their attempts to forcibly disarm RUF members (*Keesing's World*, May 2000, 43552). The UN expanded UNAMSIL's mandate (to include fighting alongside government and militia forces) and increased its size to address this resurgence of violence (UCDP).

The rebels were eventually repelled by British forces, which had joined the UNAMSIL and battered government forces in October 2000, thereby forming a coalition to increase the government's capacity versus the RUF and saving Kabbah's presidency (Kandeh 2003). The British were brought into UNAMSIL to replace Indian forces that were departing, which would have diminished the government's capacity. In November 2000, after UN and ECOWAS mediation, the RUF rebels finally agreed to the ceasefire and to abide by both the Abuja and

Lomé agreements. This included provisions for disarmament and demobilization. "With hindsight it can be seen as the seminal moment at which a process of definitive consolidation of peace got underway" (O'Flaherty 2004, 37). On July 5, 2000, the United Nations issued a declaration banning the trade in uncut diamonds from Sierra Leone until its government created and implemented a certification plan that would guarantee the diamonds had not come from RUF-controlled areas (*Keesing's World*, July 2000, 43661). This ban was a clear threat to one of the RUF's funding sources and subsequent capacity, though it is unclear how the ban would have impacted the large proportion of diamonds that were smuggled out of Sierra Leone and exported from other countries.

In spite of the agreements, fighting continued into 2001. In March the UN passed a resolution to maintain the presence of UNAMSIL for another six months and increase its size by seven thousand troops. The resolution condemned rebel use of child soldiers and the rebels' human rights abuses, and it demanded that terms of the peace agreement be honored by the groups. Finally, in May 2001, under the combined weight of the UNAMSIL, the Kamajors, and troops from Guinea, the rebels were driven out of the diamond fields in the east of the country. The RUF agreed to cease all hostilities on May 16, 2001, and an official announcement of the end of hostilities was issued by Kabbah on January 18, 2002.

Since the end of the civil war, the RUF has reinvented itself as a political party. The Revolutionary United Front Party has developed some legitimacy and power in Sierra Leone. However, in spite of the fact that the country's political system has ten political parties, only the APC and SLPP hold any significant power and the ability to influence policy making in the country. Evidence of this is found in the U.S. CIA's identification of only those two parties by name in its country profile for Sierra Leone, along with a note that there are "numerous other parties" (U.S. CIA 2016).

There have been international and domestic calls for the apprehension and punishment of those who sought to profit from the conflict. The most important achievement in this regard was the 2012 conviction of Charles Taylor for aiding and abetting war crimes and crimes against humanity that were committed by the RUF fighters. A UN Special Court sentenced Taylor to fifty years in a British prison, where he would be housed in a maximum-security facility (Blair 2012).

The 2015 arrest of Michael Desaedeleer was another step toward accountability. The businessman is the first to stand accused of enslavement and pillaging of blood diamonds during the civil war. According to the EU National Court complaint against Desaedeleer, his actions contributed to the enslavement of civilians in diamond pits and the RUF's delivery of the proceeds to Charles Taylor (Badcock 2015).

According to a 2015 report from the African Development Bank (AfDB), the country's postconflict recovery is a notable success. It argues that the country has "embarked on a peace-building and state-building agenda, re-establish[ed] democratic government and institutions, conduct[ed] three successful elections, and manag[ed] peaceful political transitions" (Litse 2015, 1). The country has also maintained economic growth averaging 8 percent over the five years preceding the report (Litse 2015). While these achievements are laudable, it should also be recognized that the country's own development goals, which focused on decreasing poverty, increasing equality, and improving citizens' health, have not been met (Sandy 2016). These problems were exacerbated by the terrible toll the Ebola virus took on the country in 2015 and the subsequent accusations that the government mislaid millions in relief funds and attempted to cover up the extent of the Ebola problem to protect its international image (Agence France-Presse 2015c; Freeman 2015).

CONCLUSIONS

As compared to the other case studies in this book, the civil war in Sierra Leone has some unique characteristics. It was, in comparison, a relatively short-lived conflict. The conflict dyad in the case was also fairly consistent, with the RUF battling with government forces and the Kamajors, aside from the brief period of time during which the AFRC joined with the RUF to govern.

The RUF had some distinctive characteristics. Rather than being a peasant rebellion, the organization recruited and conscripted young, unemployed, drug-addicted riffraff to fill its ranks. Those who did not volunteer were forced into the organization by violent coercion. Essentially, the rank-and-file members of the organization had nothing to live for and no ties to the community. This may help explain the extraordinary violence against civilians that was committed by the group. While many rebel organizations are fighting for their cultures, religions, families, and society, the RUF rebels fought because they had little else to do and no support system beyond the members of the group.

The case of Sierra Leone is also compelling in that while the intensity fluctuated, the tactics employed by both sides remained relatively constant over time. The Sierra Leone government tended to concentrate its efforts on the rebel group, with the exception of 1997, when the rebel group was a major player in the junta government. Throughout, the RUF (and AFRC in 1997) engaged in atrocities against civilian targets. What varied was the extent to which the violence was widespread, the number of people maimed or killed, and the frequency of attacks. In times when its capacity decreased versus that of the government, the RUF chose either increased ferocity in its attacks or calls for mediation. That decision seems to have been strongly influenced, in each case, by the group's perception of its relative strength versus that of the government.

The UN hostage taking in May 2000 was a tactic the rebels had not previously employed. Within the theoretical framework of this book, the act can be interpreted as a response to the decreased capacity of the rebels. While the RUF was permitted to establish a political party, thereby offering some representation of the interests of the rebels, the rebels faced the complete loss of identity that would accompany the dissolution of the RUF as a rebel organization. Disarming the rebels was a clear threat to their conceptualization of their capacity relative to that of the government, resulting in employment of this unprecedented tactic.

Another important aspect of the conflict is the role that the relationship between Sankoh and Taylor had on influencing its progression. Both men upheld their agreement to help the other's rebellion. Taylor continued to influence the conflict throughout its duration. He provided guidance, strategy, weapons, and training, in addition to serving as a source of instability aimed at continuing the conflict. He prospered extensively from the smuggling of diamonds through his country and from the payments in diamonds he received for weapon transfers to the rebels. This single man served as a major catalyst for the initiation of the invasion and for its continuation. Even when Sankoh was imprisoned, he was able to maintain contact with Taylor (SCSL 2004).

In spite of the debate over the role of diamonds in the country's conflicts, it is clear that they had influence over the violence that was experienced. Both greed and grievance played a role in the events that took place. As is often the case, the wealth of the country was concentrated regionally and within specific ethnic groups. The extent to which individuals' motivations for controlling the diamonds were idealistic versus being profit driven is impossible to determine. Most likely, the issues of region, ethnicity, and greed intertwined so extensively in this case that their division would be artificial.

However, the diamonds had significant impact in that they were vital to maintaining each side's capacity. Absent the diamonds, it is unlikely that Taylor would have shown such sustained interest in the conflict. In addition, without the diamond revenues, the government would not have been able to generate the funds necessary to hire the private military contractors (PMC). While the PMCs may not have had a major impact on the conduct of the war, they did increase the government's capacity and may have served to extend the duration of the conflict by providing the country's tribal factions military training. They also assisted in strategizing for the government. None of this would have been forthcoming if the government had not had the funds to pay, which would not have been likely absent the diamonds. The diamond fields also became important factors in determining each side's strategy in the conflict, in that both sides maneuvered to try and control the wealth that they represented.

Capacity in this case was largely determined through the formation of coalitions and the control of diamonds. The Kamajors were a consistent force against the RUF and formed coalitions with whatever actors were opposing it. The government collaborated with ECOWAS, ECOMAG, Liberian forces, British troops, Sandline International, EO, and the Gurkhas. In addition, EO helped train the Kamajors and other tribal groups so that they could join with the government as an effective force. In the interim, the RUF joined forces with Taylor and his troops, as well as working with the AFRC when it was in power. All of these coalitions increased each side's capacity and served to extend the duration of fighting and increase the number of casualties.

The group dynamics in the RUF and in the Sierra Leone government were characterized by fragmentation, contention, and shifting alliances. Coalitions formed when they were deemed desirable to boost the capacity of one side against the other. However, these tended to be temporary arrangements that dissolved once their preeminence was challenged. Interpersonal disputes, whether in government or the RUF, led to shifts in leadership that sometimes resulted in changing tactics based on the preferences of leadership.

CHAPTER 3

Elite-Led Episodic Rivalry

Republic of the Congo

The Republic of the Congo has received little attention in the media or among scholars studying intrastate conflict. This is due in large part to its relatively peaceful history, particularly when compared with its similarly named neighbor, the Democratic Republic of the Congo (DRC, formerly Zaire). Despite the absence of attention paid to Congo-Brazzaville,[1] this smaller country has also known war. In fact, the Republic of the Congo's history includes multiple armed rivalries of the episodic nature in a conflict over government control. As a result, this case provides a good comparison case to the more enduring conflicts examined in other chapters.

The Republic of the Congo has experienced three primary conflicts, as well as a splinter faction within one group that has maintained its struggle, surpassing the primary conflict from which it emerged. Although these conflicts began as political rivals as early as 1964, when the Congo effectively became a one-party state (Amnesty International 1999), armed struggle among rivals did not occur until the democratization process unfolded beginning in 1991. To this point, armed conflict in Congo-Brazzaville has claimed nearly 12,000 lives, with the bulk of those civilian. Approximately 860,000 people have been displaced, while "hundreds, if not thousands, of women" have been raped (Norwegian Refugee Council/Global IDP Project 2005). Despite the serious impact these armed struggles have had on the population of Congo-Brazzaville, the conflict itself is almost entirely elite-led, which is not surprising given the management of its oil resources, involving regionally based ethnic rivalries among the political class (UCDP). As a result, as these elites (along with their supporters) vied for power in a changing political environment, they employed a variety of tactics and waffled between dialogue and armed struggle.

GEOGRAPHY AND HISTORICAL CONTEXT

The Republic of the Congo is situated in West Africa bordering Gabon, the Central African Republic, the Democratic Republic of the Congo, and Angola. Notably, the population of the Congo is heavily concentrated in the southeastern portion of the state. In addition, the people of Congo-Brazzaville are a rather educated and urban society, with 70 percent of its citizens living in Brazzaville (the political capital), Pointe-Noire (its economic capital), or somewhere along the railway that connects the two cities (U.S. Department of State 2009b). The Congo includes dense jungle terrain in the north, but with the bulk of the population located in the southern portion of the country, traditional guerrilla warfare did not become the tactic of choice in the conflicts. At times, groups and their leaders have been made to flee Brazzaville, for example, and tend to return to their regional strongholds. However, most of the fighting in the first two waves of violence occurred in and around Brazzaville or along the railway. The exception is the third wave, which occurred almost entirely in the Pool region in the southern portion of the country with similar tactics. The map of Congo-Brazzaville is presented in Figure 3.1.

This concentration of the Congo's population also means that armed struggle is inevitably going to have a significant and destructive impact on civilians, which was certainly the case in the conflict examined here. Geographic factors in relation to the nation's population seem to translate to urban-centered conflict involving massive refugee flows, arbitrary arrests, rape, and torture. These tactics, not surprisingly, tend to alienate a potential mass base of support for any of the groups despite the ethnic or regional identities involved.

The location of the Congo within its region also has implications for tactics employed. With neighboring states so close in proximity sharing somewhat intertwined histories, it is not surprising that appeals for intervention were made and conflict spillover was evident. Some neighboring states, as a result, served as mediators, while others came to the aid of one rival over another. Decisions made by external actors to intervene are partly a function of the political and cultural histories involved.

The Republic of the Congo became independent from France in 1960. The treatment of the various ethnic and regional groups in Congo-Brazzaville by the French created a backdrop for the more recent conflict. The southern groups tended to receive social advantages, while northern groups were identified more readily for military service (Magnusson and Clark 2005). Regional differences roughly coincide with ethnic differences. The largest ethnic group in the Congo is the Bakongo (or Kongo), with 48 percent of the total population (Minorities at Risk 2009). The Bakongo have, for the most part, lacked the cohesion of some of the smaller ethnic groups and have suffered politically as a result (Magnusson and Clark 2005). By contrast, the Mbochi are approximately 12 percent of the population (Minorities at Risk 2009) but were disproportionately represented in military service (Magnusson and Clark 2005). In addition, the Mbochi have benefited from the three Mbochi presidents who served during periods of high oil revenues, which could be passed on to presidents' supporters. This has created resentment among the non-Mbochi ethnic groups (Clark 1997).

FIGURE 3.1   Republic of the Congo

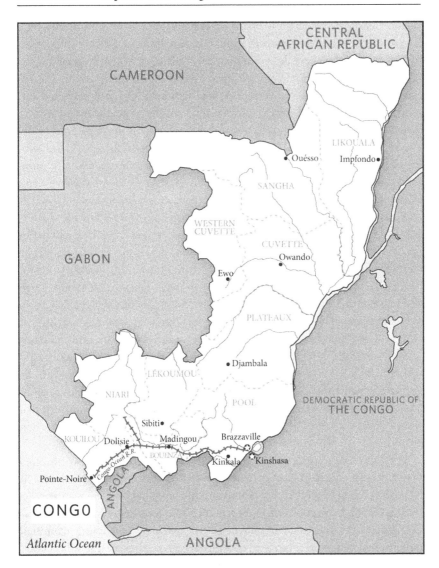

In addition, Congo-Brazzaville includes members of the Nibolek identity, which is composed of three southern regions (Niari, Bouenza, and Lékoumou) (Eaton 2006). The Pool region, on the other hand, tends to be dominated by the Lari people (deBeer and Cornwell 1999). These regional and ethnic differences feed into the political conflicts and political rivalries examined in detail below.

The Congo's colonial history solidified preexisting ethnic divisions. The decision to have the Mbochi overrepresented in the military, however, had significant implications for group and government capacity postdemocratization. When Pascal Lissouba, a southerner, was elected in 1992, his concern over the loyalty of the military appears to have been justified, leading to the creation of his Cocoyes militia, as well as appeals by Lissouba for international assistance. Ethnic divisions exacerbated during colonialism fed into the political rivalries and resulting conflicts discussed in detail later in this chapter.

Pleas for international assistance were themselves informed by the region's colonial history. Clark (1998, 34) suggests that a regional cleavage existed in post-independence French colonies.[2] On the one side were regional leaders he identified as Francophilic, or those aligning with France. This included Congo-Brazzaville's President Sassou N'Guesso (1979–1991), along with Gabon's Bongo and remnants of the former Rwandan army and of Mobutu's guard. Clark also identifies regional leaders he considers Francophobic, or those aligning against France. These included Uganda's Museveni, Rwanda's Kagame, and the DRC's Kabila. As Clark describes it, President Lissouba's (1992–1997) relationship with France was complicated, but he tended to find more in common with the Francophobic than the Francophilic. This regional cleavage provides another layer of complexity in the Congo rivalries and helps explain why some external actors became involved in the way they did (see the discussion of intervention below).

The nature of the groups involved in the Republic of the Congo also informed the tactics employed. The conflicts were both regional and ethnic in nature. It is not surprising that ethnic cleansing and the targeting of civilians became a tactical choice. When political elites and their followers engaged in the process of carving out their spheres of influence by using regional and ethnic identities, nongroup members were likely to become targets or refugees. The splinter faction that emerged from one conflict, the Ntsiloulous faction of the Ninjas, took an even stronger identity-based tone. Pasteur Ntoumi has claimed that he was sent by God to save the people of the Pool region, creating a distinct "us versus them" division evident in many intense conflicts. Conditions in the Pool region have been referred to as "a humanitarian disaster" (*Economist* 2007). It is not surprising that he too employed terrorist tactics particularly focused on non-Lari speakers and those "not abiding by their religious rules and for not giving

TABLE 3.1 Timeline of Key Events in the Republic of the Congo's Conflicts, 1960–1997

Date	Event
August 15, 1960	Republic of the Congo gained independence with the country's first president, Fulbert Youlou
1963	Youlou resigned in the face of strikes and labor demonstrations. Succeeded by Alphonse Massamba-Debat.
1964	National Revolutionary Movement (MNR) formed as Congo's only legal party
1968	A new Marxist-Leninist party called the Congolese Labor Party (PCT) was established through a military coup led by Marien Ngouabi
March 18, 1977	Ngouabi assassinated. Power transferred by the PCT to Jacques-Joachim Yhombi-Opango.
February 5, 1979	PCT leader Denis Sassou-N'Guesso took power following Yhombi-Opango's resignation
October 1990	Sassou announced the introduction of a multiparty system to begin in 1991
1991	Multiparty democracy emerged
1992	Pascal Lissouba was inaugurated, bringing his political party, the Pan-African Union for Social Democracy (UPADS), into power
November 17, 1992	Lissouba dissolved the National Assembly after Sassou abandoned a coalition with UPADS
November 1993	Armed rebellion led by opposition leader Kolelas and his Ninjas began
1994	A truce emerged between Lissouba and Kolelas, ending the first wave of violence
August 1995	President Lissouba announced that the military would be restructured to include ethnic groups more friendly to him
December 24, 1995	Peace pact signed providing for disarmament and integration of former combatants
February 14, 1996	Violent mutiny occurred in Mpila
June 5, 1997	Army surrounded Sassou's compound, beginning the second wave of armed struggle
1997	Sassou and his Cobras successfully took control of Brazzaville

Source: CQ Press (2011a).

support to the war effort" (UCDP). The elite-led nature of the groups has clearly fed into this problem as well.

REPUBLIC OF THE CONGO CONFLICTS

The four primary conflicts in this evolving conflict over government control are presented in Table 3.2. Political rivalry in Brazzaville took root immediately following independence. The first two presidents of the Republic of the Congo, Fulbert Youlou and Alphose Massamba-Debat, were ethnic Kongo from the southern part of the country. More important, both also embraced political patronage, choosing to appoint ethnic Kongo disproportionately to positions in government and civil service. A shift in leadership from Massamba-Debat to Marien Ngouabi, an ethnic Mbochi from the north, meant a swing in political and administrative positions from ethnic Kongo to Mbochi (Franck and Rainer 2012), thus effectively tying political leadership and civil service to group identity. These identity-based benefits trickled down into other aspects of society, as well (see Franck and Rainer 2012 for a detailed discussion of the impact of political patronage in the Republic of the Congo). Subsequent leaders would continue this approach to leadership.

The first, and most successful, rival to emerge in the conflict examined here was Denis Sassou N'Guesso, an ethnic Mbochi hailing from the north. He emerged as the leader of the Parti Congolais du Travail, or Congolese Labor Party (PCT) and therefore of the Republic of the Congo in 1979 during the country's one-party, Marxist-Leninist existence. The PCT had been the only legal political party since 1969, having succeeded the 1963 National Revolutionary Movement (MNR). During this time, the government's approach to political rivals was to arrest them (Amnesty International 1999). As a result, although rivalries existed, they did not reach the point of armed struggle. This changed, however, in the 1990s.

Multiparty democracy emerged in 1991 followed by the 1992 inauguration of Pascal Lissouba (U.S. Department of State 2009b) and his Union Panafricaine pour la Démocratie sociale, or Pan-African Union for Social Democracy (UPADS) party. At this point Sassou was considered political opposition to Lissouba's UPADS, as was Bernard Kolelas and his political party, Mouvement Congolais pour la Démocratie et le Développement Intégral (MCDDI).

The democratic experience in the Congo was short lived, however. Lissouba won the second round of elections in 1992 by partnering with Sassou in order to form a government. Unhappy with the PCT cabinet posts received, Sassou dissolved the coalition and formed a new one with Kolelas, allowing them to gain the majority in Parliament (Clark 2002a). Lissouba dissolved Parliament and called for new elections, which sparked political protests and ultimately

TABLE 3.2   Conflicts in the Republic of the Congo, 1993–2002

Rivalry	Groups	Location	Episodes of violence	Incompatibility
Sassou-N'Guesso Rivalry	Cobras	Brazzaville	1997	Government
Kolelas Rivalry	Ninjas	Brazzaville	1993–1994; 1998–1999	Government
Lissouba Rivalry	Cocoyes	Brazzaville; southern Congo	1997–1999	Government
Ntsiloulous Rivalry	Ninjas	Pool region; Brazzaville	1998–1999; 2002	Government

Source: UCDP.

armed struggle. This was the first of three waves of violence in postdemocratized Congo.

In this first phase, the bulk of the fighting occurred within the neighborhoods of Brazzaville. In order to bolster support, Sassou, Lissouba, and Kolelas had employed instrumentalist tactics playing to ethnic affinities (Clark 1998).[3] As a result, the three major parties tended to draw from their respective segment of Congo society. Sassou identified with the Mbochi, while Lissouba, who was a Nzabi, most closely identified with the Nibolek identity. Kolelas, on the other hand, found his base of support in the Pool region among the Lari (de-Beer and Cornwell 1999) as did Ntoumi (UCDP). In the wake of the 1992 elections and the resulting follow-up parliamentary elections, frustrated groups engaged in disorganized violence as Brazzaville, a city of already distinct ethnic districts, succumbed to ethnic cleansing, with districts becoming even more homogeneous (UCDP/PRIO 2014; Amnesty International 1999). By most definitions, these efforts would be considered terrorist tactics. With the introduction of more organized rivals and their militias, these tactics continued. Civilians were targeted even more destructively when then-president Lissouba ordered the shelling of the predominantly Lari-speaking Bakongo and Makelekele districts loyal to Kolelas (Clark 2002a).

Kolelas and his militia, the Ninjas, joined the rebellion in the Bakongo district against the Lissouba government in November 1993 (UCDP/PRIO 2014). Sassou and his Cobras, for the most part, played a minor role in this bout of violence (Clark 2002a) and participated to a lesser extent in the Mpila district (UCDP/PRIO 2014). Lissouba, unsure of the loyalty of the Congo military, which traditionally was composed more of northern Congolese than his own southern groups, felt compelled to create his own militia of loyal supporters and did so with the Cocoyes, who began to purge their own neighborhoods of Diata and Mfilou (Clark 2002a). By early 1994, the first wave of violence, which had resulted in one to two thousand deaths, ended with a truce between Kolelas and Lissouba's government. The tactical shift toward a negotiated peace was the result of a series of negotiations, with and without external mediation. The militias, however, remained with zones of influence carved within Brazzaville and mirrored the regional/ethnic divisions that exist within the country at large.

The second wave of violence began in 1997, this time between the Lissouba government and Sassou. This wave was by far the most deadly, resulting in six to fourteen thousand deaths. As political campaigning began, Sassou announced that he planned to campaign in the northern Cuvette. Both Sassou and former president Yhombi-Opango (who had joined the Lissouba government) hailed from the region. As Sassou campaigned in Yhombi-Opango's hometown of Owando, Yhombi-Opango's supporters took exception. Several died as a result of the preelection violence (Clark 2002a). This episode escalated dramatically, however, as Lissouba, amid rumors of a military coup, in June ordered the arrest of some of Sassou's men thought responsible for the Owando violence. The attempted arrest took place at his well-guarded compound in Brazzaville where Sassou ordered his supporters and militia to resist (U.S. Department of State 2009b). Lissouba had also given the order to disarm Sassou's militia (Clark 2002a). What followed were four intensive months of armed struggle between Lissouba, the Congolese army (at least those who remained loyal to Lissouba), and Cocoyes versus Sassou and his Cobras (Clark 2008). Despite continued efforts at negotiating a solution, with the help of an Angolan intervention (see below), Sassou was able to capture Brazzaville and declare himself president by October 1997 (Amnesty International 1999; Clark 2002a). The rivalry and armed struggle, however, continued until 1999. During that time, Kolelas and his Ninjas joined the struggle in collaboration with Lissouba. Both Lissouba and Kolelas were forced to flee the Congo. A splinter faction of the Ninjas emerged in the Pool region in late 1998 as a result. This new faction, Ntsiloulous, was led by the charismatic Frederic Bitsangou, or Pasteur Ntoumi, who was able to capitalize on divisions emerging in Kolelas's absence. Through his religious preachings, Ntoumi with his Ntsiloulous was able to emerge as a challenger to the leaderless Ninjas (UCDP/PRIO 2014).

The second wave of violence was not restricted to Brazzaville. As Sassou took the capital, rivals operated in the southern Congo (deBeer and Cornwell 1999), particularly along the Congo-Ocean Railway (U.S. Department of State 2009b) and in the Bouenza region (Havermans 1999). This bout of violence ended with another negotiated outcome. This time, however, Kolelas and Lissouba were in exile and did not take part in the negotiations. As a result, neither was involved in the third wave of violence, which emerged in 2002.

Unlike the previous two armed struggle episodes, the violence that plagued the Congo in 2002 emerged out of the Pool region and was led by Ntoumi and his splinter faction. The violence began with an alleged attack on a train by Ninjas. Armed incursions into the Pool region by the Congolese army, followed by

FIGURE 3.2   Patterns of Violence in the Congo, 1991–2003

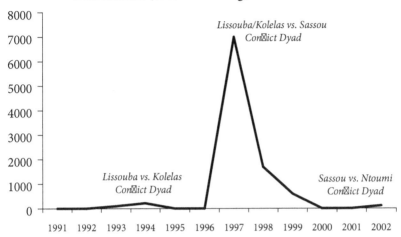

Best estimate (or low if missing) of battle deaths

Drawn from Lacina and Gleditsch (2005).

the brief spread of violence to the city of Brazzaville, resulted in eighty to one hundred deaths (Muggah, Maughan, and Bugnion 2003). Once again, the violence ended with a negotiated agreement in early 2003, although the rivalry continued with sporadic violence reported as late as 2007. A graphic depiction of the ebbs and flows of violence is presented in Figure 3.2.

While armed struggle has not renewed since 2002, political protest emerged in 2015 when Sassou announced a referendum on the constitution that would allow him to stand for a third term of office. Oppositional clashes resulted in four people killed (Agence France-Presse 2015a). In fact, election protests and low-level violence continued following Sassou's successful capture of power with Angola's help.

CONFLICT PROGRESSION AND DYNAMICS

Understanding tactical decisions of these rivalries in the Congo involves examining the dynamic factors presented in chapter 1's theoretical model. While exact sizes of the militias involved in the Republic of the Congo are difficult to obtain, it seems clear that the core number of supporters was relatively small. Nonstate actor data collected by Cunningham, Gleditsch, and Salehyan (2009) suggest that the pro-Sassou faction included approximately 2,250 rebels when conflict emerged in 1997. It is not surprising that Sassou's faction was probably the largest. Although his ethnic and regional identity was not demographically the largest in the Congo, the Mbochi were, as indicated earlier, well represented in the Congolese military. Cunningham, Gleditsch, and Salehyan (2009) also provide estimates of rebel group size for the Cocoyes and Ninjas, with both groups numbering near 1,000, or fewer than half of Sassou's Cobras. The Ntsiloulous Ninja splinter group had approximately 1,750 rebels in 2002. These estimates, however, may not tell the whole story. After the first two episodes of violence, the negotiated outcomes involved disarming and integrating rebels into the government's army. Reports of this integration include much larger numbers of rebels. Marshall (2000, 12), for example, estimated the number of ex-militiamen in a range between 10,000 to 15,000 in the aftermath of the 1999 Ceasefire and Cessation of Hostilities Accord.

Although rebel group size tends to be a rather dynamic variable, for the case of the Congo, the actual armed insurrection portion of each conflict was fairly short in nature. In addition, after successful negotiations, some disarmament and military integration did occur. According to Amnesty International (1999), as many as four thousand former militia were integrated. The first episode of violence involved the Kolelas militia versus the Lissouba government and militia. With the conflict ending in negotiations, it can be deduced that the numbers of Kolelas's militia declined following 1994. The Ninjas continued to exist, however, as did Sassou's Cobras. In fact, Sassou remained heavily armed. The questionable loyalty of the military remained as well, despite Lissouba's attempt to restructure the armed forces, providing for more regional and ethnic balance (Amnesty International 1999). It is not surprising then that it was Sassou's rivalry with Lissouba that sparked violence in 1997.

Regardless, the size of these groups indicates that traditional and guerrilla warfare was unlikely. Both tactics require larger numbers to achieve success. These more traditional tactics also require sympathizers or nonarmed supporters who are willing to provide safe houses, supplies, food, and so on. Although the identity of the armed factions operating in the Congo involved regional and ethnic affinity, the goals of the groups, or at least the goals of the leadership, did not necessarily encourage large-scale support. In fact, the large-scale human rights abuses and ethnic cleansing tactics employed did more to alienate potential supporters than encourage them. The lack of mass support helps explain the short duration of the episodes of armed events within the conflict.

While Congolese rivals lacked a certain amount of internal support, the same cannot be said for external support. In fact, regional actors contributed greatly to tactical decisions by actors in the conflict. Key regional actors, such as Gabon's President Omar Bongo and Special Representative Mohamed Sahnoun from the Organization of African Unity (OAU), as well as the French and U.S. embassies, worked extensively to bring rivals to a negotiated political solution. Their efforts led to the decision by Kolelas to come to terms with President Lissouba in 1994. Discussions continued when violence reemerged in 1997. In fact, Bongo and Sahnoun appeared to have an agreement carved out that would have brought the armed struggle to an end with the assistance of external peacekeepers. The agreement crumbled, however, when the UN Security Council balked and delayed action on the issue (Zartman and Vogeli 2000). Both Lissouba and Sassou turned to allies to help break the stalemated situations in which they found themselves.

External intervention and the impact such support had on tactical decisions was not always peaceful. During his presidency, Lissouba was able to divert weapons purchased for the Congolese Armed Forces, mainly from Russia and South Africa, to his Cocoyes (Amnesty International 1999). He was also able to acquire training for his militia from Lordon-Levdan, an Israeli company (Amnesty International 1999). Lissouba, however, was unable to secure support from Rwanda or Uganda (Galloy and Gruénais 1997), although former members of the Zairian Armed Forces who had fled to Brazzaville joined Lissouba and his efforts against Sassou (Amnesty International 1999). Lissouba's campaign also received support from neighboring rebel group UNITA (National Union for the Total Independence of Angola), which at the time was engaged in its own intrastate struggle in Angola. Lissouba had supported UNITA in its struggles (as well as backing FLEC, Front for the Liberation of the Enclave of Cabinda). As a result, when Sassou appeared to be at a distinct disadvantage facing a unified coalition of Lissouba and Kolelas, Angola came to his aid with 2,500 troops (at its peak) (UCDP) in August 1997. Sassou also received help from Chad, Gabon, France, and Elf-Congo (a French oil company) (Galloy and Gruénais 1997) as well as South African and Serbian mercenaries, the former Rwandan government forces, Rwandan Interahamwe militia, and elements of Mobutu's Zairian army (Eaton 2006). With this support, the tide shifted clearly and rather decisively toward Sassou. By October of the same year, Sassou had captured Pointe-Noire and Brazzaville. Not surprisingly, the regional division noted by Clark (1998) and discussed earlier appears relevant here with Sassou gathering significant Francophile support.

Another dynamic aspect of Congo rivalries has to do with group cohesion. The three main rivals formed coalitions at times when it was in their interest to do so. Although Kolelas and his Ninjas were instigators of the first outbreak of violence in 1993, as parties involved were "dissatisfied with an electoral measure of their strength" (Zartman and Vogeli 2000, 272), Lissouba and Kolelas signed a truce in 1994, which included Sassou, and agreed to disarm their militias (UCDP/PRIO 2014) as indicated above. That did not happen entirely, but the rivalry between pro-Lissouba and pro-Kolelas factions appears to have terminated at that time. Sporadic fighting occurred into 1995 (deBeer and Cornwell 1999). However, in early 1995 Kolelas's MDCCI gained cabinet posts, including the Interior Ministry. These moves appeased the Ninja rivals at the time. When violence emerged in 1997 between Cobras and the Lissouba government (along with his Cocoyes militia), Kolelas actually served as a mediator rather than resume his rivalry with Lissouba—that is, until Kolelas formally joined the Lissouba government as prime minister of what Lissouba suggested was a new government of national unity (UCDP/PRIO 2014; Amnesty International 1999). Not surprisingly, within a year of Kolelas's decision to join Lissouba, the Ntsiloulous movement took shape. Sassou, for his part, declined the ministerial posts offered to him and his party (Amnesty International 1999). Sassou's refusal to join the Lissouba government meant he would now be also facing a new rivalry with Kolelas and his Ninjas.

As indicated above, the government changed hands in 1997 when Sassou, assisted by outside forces, took control over Brazzaville and Pointe-Noire. Violence and armed struggle continued until December 1999 when four days of intense negotiations produced the Cessation of Hostilities Agreement (Marshall 2000). Interestingly, neither Lissouba nor Kolelas was party to the negotiations. The agreement was made between the Armed Forces of the Congo, led by General Moukoki, and by five leaders of the armed opposition militias representing the Cocoyes and Ninjas, including Ntsiloulous (UCDP/PRIO 2014). Not only were Lissouba and Kolelas not a part of the discussions, but both denounced the agreement (Marshall 2000). Following the accords, both Lissouba and Kolelas were exiled, tried in absentia, and convicted (U.S. Department of State 2009b). This seems to be the equivalent of cutting the head off of a snake as these rivalries were largely defined by their leadership. Both the Sassou-Lissouba and the Sassou-Kolelas rivalries appear terminated as a result. This seems more evident when Sassou granted Kolelas amnesty in December 2005 and pardoned Lissouba in 2007 (U.S. Department of State 2009b). This is not the case for the Ntsiloulous rivalry, however, which continued its campaign, reemerging again in 2002.

It appears that group capacity may help to explain, in part, why terrorist tactics were employed in the way they were. Once civilians were targeted, it was unlikely that other forms of insurrection would follow, which would have required large mass support. Mass support was not necessarily forthcoming, but clearly external actors were willing to fill that role. Certainly arms were plentiful. Lissouba's stint as president allowed him to train and arm his militia. Sassou's external supporters provided him with weaponry and later with troops. In fact, during the first wave of violence involving the Lissouba-Kolelas rivalry, Kolelas was able to obtain weapons and other military assistance from Sassou (Amnesty International 1999). Sassou's access to external military aid had serious implications for his rivalry with Lissouba. Without such support, it is likely that Lissouba would have been able to secure his presidency, particularly once he came to terms with Kolelas. External intervention in this way appears to have brought about the end of the Sassou-Lissouba and the Sassou-Kolelas rivalries, although certainly not right away. The second bout of violence lasted more than a year following the Angolan intervention.

Armaments were not the only resources that impacted conflict trajectory in the Republic of the Congo. Approximately 87 percent of the Congolese economy is dependent on the primary commodity of oil (U.S. Energy Information Administration 2014). The revenues generated by the oil industry add an interesting element to the conflict discussion, as does the influence of external actors on those revenues. Mbochi presidents benefited from the wealth generated by the industry until 1985 when oil prices collapsed (Eaton 2006). Control over oil revenues has certainly been identified as a significant motivating factor in these elite-led rivalries (Norwegian Refugee Council 2005). In addition to lining pockets, revenues from the industry had been particularly useful for paying civil servants, particularly in a country of urbanized and educated citizens. "Presidents Ngouabi and Sassou-Nguesso clearly used oil revenues to patronize major segments of the population. Most important, new university graduates were guaranteed jobs in the civil service through the end of the Sassou-Nguesso regime, greatly reducing the potential for protest movements rooted in the middle class" (Clark 1997, 67). In fact, in the Republic of the Congo wealth generated by the state disproportionately benefited the identity group of its leadership. For example, Franck and Rainer (2012) found that ethnic favoritism in education is particularly acute in the Congo. The collapse of prices meant that the Congo became even more dependent on French support. In addition, Sassou borrowed on the promise of future oil revenues to pay employees, even raising pay in the late 1980s, while the country experienced structural adjustment imposed by the International Monetary Fund (IMF).

The implications of such actions became evident when Lissouba became president. The Congo was, by 1990, *the* most heavily indebted country per capita in the world (Eaton 2006). In order to continue to pay state salaries and keep the economy from collapsing (not to mention maintain domestic political support), Lissouba attempted to solicit French support and aid, but he did not have the success that Sassou had had with them. The French, by all accounts, benefited heavily from Congolese oil and their close relationship with Sassou. Lissouba, however, struggled to maintain those ties. In 1993, when Lissouba's request from Elf-Congo for a loan of three hundred million dollars against future production was denied, he reached out to the American firm Occidental Petroleum (referred to as the "Oxy affair") (Clark 1998). Occidental, eager to gain access to Congolese oil, agreed, allowing Lissouba to pay civil servant wages and therefore prevail in the 1994 elections. In response, the French devalued the African Financial Community Franc (Clark 1998; Clark 2002a). When the Sassou-Lissouba rivalry became violent in 1997, the French remained neutral rather than backing the democratically elected Lissouba (Clark 2002a), tacitly paving the way for the string of other external actors (identified earlier) that ultimately supported Sassou's efforts.

The Congo is among the top five oil-producing states in sub-Saharan Africa (U.S. Energy Information Administration 2014). Clearly, access to oil resources influenced Congolese rivalries in several important ways. Internally, the government (regardless of which rival was in control) benefited by using those resources to pay civil servants, who were then more likely to continue their support. Externally, because the Congolese economy was so dependent on oil revenues, when oil prices collapsed, the ability to offset the economic blow was dependent on external support. That such support was forthcoming for one rival but not for another seems to have influenced the outcome of the Sassou-Lissouba rivalry, as well as the democratic experience in the Congo (Clark 2002a).

Tactics employed by rivals were also influenced by group goals. The Congolese groups are clearly political rivals. During elections, there was evidence of instrumentalist tactics used to bring in the vote, but ultimately the leadership was more interested in controlling the political system rather than changing it. Typically, identity-based conflicts tend to involve struggles for autonomy, representation, or secession. Throughout the brief conflicts and political rivalries examined here, neither Sassou, nor Kolelas, nor Lissouba worked to achieve more political rights for their groups in the form of autonomy and certainly not for secession. Their primary interest appears to have been either control of the presidency or, at the very least, a larger portion or position in the government for themselves and members of their political party, as well as the benefits from the oil revenues that those political positions would reap. As a result, it is not surprising that mediation and negotiation are evident throughout the conflict histories discussed here, as compromise is often possible when financial benefits can be divided. In fact, the Lissouba-Kolelas rivalry ended in such a way through the efforts of third-party mediators discussed above.

It is possible that the Sassou-Lissouba/Kolelas rivalry could have ended in a similar way had it not been for the Angolan intervention in 1997, which by all accounts changed the power dynamics to favor Sassou. Up until the Angolan intervention, mediation appeared to be making progress. Negotiations seemed to be providing for a national unity government monitored by an African force (deBeer and Cornwell 1999). Five ministerial posts were offered to Sassou in September, but by then it was too late. A lack of action on the part of the United Nations and military action by Angola had changed the game, making military victory for Sassou evident.

Rivals in the Congo engaged in violence in an effort to achieve their ultimate goal, which was to control the governing structure of the Congo (as well as to benefit economically), but such political goals are also amenable to negotiations. Following the December 1999 negotiations involving military leadership, the nature of the conflict led one participant to conclude: "We are soldiers who have been trained for war, but never knew war with all its atrocities. Only the belligerents know war. Never again! Never again should the politicians be permitted to use the army and the youth to fight their wars" (Marshall 2000, 8), suggesting that the political rivalries examined here were negotiable. The resulting violence could have been avoided. Of course, that may be true of the Lissouba-, Kolelas-, and Sassou-led rivalries, but Ntsiloulous continued. However, even Ntoumi was willing to negotiate with the government for political power and did so to end the 2002 conflict.

The success and failures each rival experienced over the course of the conflicts examined here have influenced subsequent behaviors, as the chapter 1 model would predict. Intrastate rivalry in the Republic of the Congo emerged early after independence. During the Marxist-Leninist, one-party rule, dealing with political opposition was fairly straightforward and effective. Opposition was suppressed or arrested. This was effective and not surprisingly was employed multiple times in the Congo-Brazzaville rivalries. The 1991 transition to democratic rule meant changing this tactic, however. Political opposition could no longer be oppressed and ignored. Government response to opposition had to change. The lessons of the past, however, were not immediately learned. When Lissouba lost his winning coalition in 1992, parliamentary rules called for him to dissolve Parliament and call for new elections. When Kolelas and Sassou were unable to win at the polls, they formed militias. Their efforts were successful in ultimately gaining the political power they had hoped to achieve. Kolelas was able to do so through negotiations. Lissouba attempted to employ the same tactic with Sassou, having successfully embraced one rival in Kolelas. However, Sassou, who once may have been amenable to negotiating more political power, was no longer interested as his pleas for external assistance proved successful.

Sassou's success on the battlefield seems to have informed his treatment of Ntsiloulous as well. With Ntoumi and his rebels making headway in the Pool region, Sassou chose to increase the number of armed incursions into the region while reducing access of humanitarian agencies (Muggah, Maughan, and Bugnion 2003). Sassou did extend an olive branch to Ntoumi in 2003 when he agreed to amnesty and army integration in exchange for Ntsiloulous disarming. Ntoumi's demands for a national unity government were not met. Further, when Ntoumi showed up to take his seat as the general delegate in charge of the promotion of peace and postconflict reconstruction, the government blocked his way, and clashes ensued (UCDP). Sassou's military approaches worked in the past and seem to have informed his subsequent actions with Ntoumi.

CONCLUSIONS

Conflict in the Republic of the Congo can be described as a political struggle among elites as they vied for power. The implications of the conflict, particularly given the patronage governing approach and oil wealth generated by the state, reverberate throughout Congolese society. While the conflict itself seems to have come to an end, the rivalries that existed within the conflict and the identity-based divisions that drove the episodes of violence remain.

If the goal is to understand tactical decisions in the midst of conflict, the case of the Congo appears to illustrate the factors that bring about conflicts that are relatively shorter in duration. It seems evident that when civilians bear the brunt of the violence, particularly when conflict goals are elite driven and political in nature, the ability to generate mass support is unlikely even if the implications of the dispute translate into economic benefits based on identity. Such goals, however, do tend to make negotiated outcomes more likely and rivalry termination a possibility, particularly with persistent mediation efforts.

Outside actors played an important role in shifting rivals toward and away from violence. Gabon's Bongo and the OAU's Sahnoun, among others, assisted in negotiations throughout, finding success at times, most notably in 1993 and 1994. To his credit, President Lissouba embraced a negotiated outcome, making such a resolution possible.

External support also provided the means for a return to violence as well. External actors provided the weapons necessary for each of the rivals examined to maintain their own militia in this volatile and untrusting environment. Sassou's connections outside of the Congo were a function of his political alliances in a regional context. Drawing on that support, he effectively achieved a military victory over Lissouba and Kolelas, even while negotiating with portions of their militias. Armaments provided by these external players made the outbreak of violence in both 1992 and 1997 possible in the first place. Had arms flows into the Congo not been so plentiful, it is possible that political rivalries would have stayed in the political realm.

CHAPTER 4

Ethnic Conflict over Time

Sri Lanka

Sri Lanka's civil conflict has been characterized by continued waves of violence. The country's Sinhala and Tamil populations have vied for governing power since independence. By 1983, the situation erupted into civil war, with the Tamils fighting for an independent homeland in the northern and eastern regions of the country. The violence escalated and de-escalated through more than twenty-five years of conflict, with lulls in violence resulting in the civil war's classification into four distinct periods, Eelam Wars I–IV. Fighting peaked in 2008–2009 with over eight thousand casualties per year, as the sides fought to the military defeat of the dominant Tamil rebel group, the Tamil Tigers (UCDP). This case is unique, as compared to the others in this book, because it is a single protracted rivalry and because the Tamil Tigers were an innovative terrorist organization.

GEOGRAPHY AND HISTORICAL CONTEXT

Sri Lanka is an island in the Indian Ocean off the southern tip of India. The geography of the country consists of largely low, flat rolling plains, with some mountainous terrain in the south and central regions. The fact that it is an island, sharing no borders with neighboring countries, likely limited the amount of intervention in the country's civil wars, aside from that of India, whose own Tamil population incentivized intervention. Tactics on both sides tended to focus on trapping the other side with their backs to the sea. The rebel groups engaged largely in guerrilla tactics, as well as terrorism, as they did strike civilian targets.

The conflict in Sri Lanka is rooted in British colonial rule. The British, using their common divide-and-rule practices, favored the minority Tamils versus the Sinhala majority, resulting in their disproportionate representation in universities and in employment in government and business at the time of independence. Some Sinhalese also perceived the Tamils as being collaborators with the imperialist British rule (Bhattacharji 2009). Singer (1992) cited arguments that the north and east of the country, where the Tamils have traditionally been concentrated, had so little agriculture or industry that the Tamils had to become better educated and enter these types of employment as there were no other options. It is likely that neither the British colonial powers nor those who ruled

FIGURE 4.1   Sri Lanka

Sri Lanka upon its independence understood the extent or complexity of the societal fragmentation of the country (Little 1994). The Sinhala, having achieved majority rule upon independence, reacted to this perceived disproportionate representation of the Tamils aggressively. Tamils were denied citizenship and the right to vote. The Official Language Act of 1956 declared Sinhalese to be the official language of the country. In 1963, university admissions policies were changed to give significant preference to Sinhalese applicants (Raman 2009). This was followed in 1971 by a revision of the university system that drove Tamils out of university teaching and research positions (Nieto 2008, 576–577). In addition, "from 1956 to 1970 the proportion of Tamils employed by the state fell from 60% to 10% in civilian employment and from 40% to 1% in the armed forces" (577). The new constitution of 1972 went so far as to eliminate minority protections that were included in the 1947 constitution (Hopgood 2005). These actions served to demoralize and disenfranchise the Tamil population of the country, as well as leaving them geographically isolated and concentrated. The situation was so egregious as to have caused Hopgood (2005) to comment that "for nearly six decades, since the former British colony of Ceylon secured its independence in 1948, the Tamils have experienced systematic and unrelenting discrimination from the majority Sinhalese population in Sri Lanka" (43). According to DeVotta (2000), in addition to these problems, the Tamils perceived that government resources were unfairly allocated. This included Sinhala resettlement policies (discussed later in the chapter) and the unfair allocation of international aid given to stimulate development or even funds designated to foster recovery from the 2004 Asian tsunami.

In addition to these factors, the Sri Lankan Tamils objected to a resettlement campaign that was undertaken by the government, which resulted in the movement of largely Sinhala citizens from the south and west into the traditional Tamil areas of the country. The Tamils saw this as a form of colonization of their homeland. The Tamils felt that the programs were put into place with the purpose of diluting their concentration in historically Tamil-occupied regions. This would have the effect of diminishing Tamil impact on elections and undermining their persistent claim that their territorial concentration was justification for autonomy or independence (DeVotta 2000).

SRI LANKAN CONFLICTS

The Sri Lankan situation is dominated by one major rivalry, that of the Sinhala versus the Tamils. There were actually a number of different Tamil groups who claimed to represent the interests of the Tamil minority population. However, none approached the persistent power versus government that the Tamil Tigers

TABLE 4.1 Timeline of Key Events in Sri Lanka's Conflicts, 1956–2012

Date	Event
1956*	Sinhalese designated official language of Sri Lanka
1972*	New constitution seen by Tamils as giving Sinhalese permanent social and political dominance
1976*	Liberation Tigers of Tamil Elam (LTTE) got its name and began low-level campaign
July 23, 1983*	Killing of 13 SLA soldiers by an LTTE landmine led to a backlash of anti-Tamil violence and beginning of the Sri Lankan civil war
August 1984*	LTTE declared full-scale revolution
May 1985*	By this time LTTE controlled Jaffna City and much of the peninsula, formed a temporary alliance with other pro-independence Tamil groups
May 1986*	Sri Lankan Army (SLA) offensive
September 1987*	Indian Peacekeeping Force (IPKF) arrived, was quickly drawn into conflict with the LTTE, and suffered significant losses
September 1989*	IPKF declared ceasefire with LTTE
March 1990*	IPKF withdrawn from Sri Lanka
June 19, 1990	LTTE reportedly used a chemical agent against Sri Lankan Armed Forces installation, the first known chemical attack by a guerrilla or terrorist organization (Hoffman 2009)
March 1991*	LTTE assassination of Defense Minister Ranjan Wijerante
May 1991†	Assassination of Indian president Rajiv Gandhi by the LTTE
May 1993†	Assassination of Sri Lankan president Ranasinghe Premadasa; LTTE denied responsibility
November 1994*	Chandrika Kumaratunga elected president of Sri Lanka. Promised talks with LTTE, loosened economic restrictions on LTTE-held areas, and arranged a ceasefire.
April 1995*	After many breaches, a truce and talks broke down
January 31, 1996*	LTTE suicide bombing killed 80 in Colombo
July 1999†	Assassination of Sri Lankan member of Parliament Neelan Thiruchelvam, a Tamil who was working on a peace initiative with the government
1999*	Fighting escalated, with the advantage shifting between the LTTE and government troops throughout the year
December 1999†	Two suicide bombings in Colombo by the LTTE, one of which injured President Chandrika Kumaratunga; 21 died in the attacks
2000*	Norway engaged in mediation
April 2000*	Months of fighting resulted in LTTE capture of the Elephant Pass, the largest defeat of the SLA in the war. LTTE operated as a conventional army rather than using guerrilla attacks.
June 2000†	LTTE assassination of Industry Minister C. V. Goonaratne
April 2001*	LTTE ended ceasefire, and SLA mounted a failed offensive in Jaffna
2002*	Indefinite ceasefire signed by both sides; Sri Lankan Monitoring Mission (SLMM) created to maintain the peace

TABLE 4.1 Continued

Date	Event
2003*	LTTE pulled out of peace talks after six rounds, but ceasefire held
2004*	"Karuna faction" defected from LTTE, was initially defeated by LTTE, but then joined forces secretly with the SLA
December 26, 2004*	Asian tsunami devastated the eastern and northern regions dominated by the LTTE, which resulted in a lull in hostilities. Death toll for Sri Lanka was set at 30,000.
2005*	Tensions increased as the LTTE accused the government of refusing to distribute tsunami aid to Tamil areas in an attempt to force a settlement on the LTTE
August 2005[†]	LTTE assassination of Foreign Minister Lakshman Kadirgamar
2006*	The ceasefire eroded
April 2006*	Peace talks were canceled as violence escalated in the east
July 2006*	Eelam War IV began at the end of July
2007*	Fighting continued, with government mounting offensives on all fronts
January 2, 2008*	The government officially abrogated the ceasefire of 2002 followed by the SLMM departure on January 16. Government forces continued on the offensive against the LTTE, which fiercely resisted but was becoming increasingly isolated.
January 2008[†]	LTTE assassination of member of Parliament from the United National Party, T. Maheswaran
January 2008[†]	LTTE assassination of Nation-Building Minister D. M. Dassanayake
February 2008[†]	Assassination of two members of the group Tamil Makkal Viduthalai Pulikal (TMVP) by the LTTE
April 2008[†]	Assassination of Highway Minister Jeyaraj Fernandopulle
January 9, 2009*	Government forces won the battle for Kilinochchi and retook the Elephant Pass
2009*	Government offensives won victory after victory as it forced LTTE troops into a smaller and smaller territory
May 18, 2009	Government declared victory over the LTTE
May 19, 2009	Government announced that Prabhakaran's body had been found
April 2011[‡]	UN declared that both the Sri Lankan government and the LTTE committed atrocities against civilians during the civil war and called for an international investigation
March 2012[‡]	UN Human Rights Council urged Sri Lanka to investigate war crimes. Sri Lanka argued this violates its sovereign rights.

Sources: *Keesing's World;* [†]Bhattacharji (2009); [‡]BBC News (2015a).

did. In part, this can be attributed to the Tigers' tendency to work to defeat rival Tamils.

Sri Lanka gained its independence from the United Kingdom (UK) in 1948. Since that time it has been plagued with violent conflict. As mentioned previously, the violence has centered on the relations between Sri Lanka's ethnic groups, the majority Sinhala (74 percent), who are largely Buddhist, and the minority Tamils (18 percent), who are predominantly Hindu. The country's religious fragmentation also includes about 7.8 percent Muslims, a group that has been targeted with discrimination and violence recently. The Tamils are further divided by the distinction between the Ceylon Tamils and Indian Tamils. Ceylon Tamils have a long history on the island, and many seek to have their ancestral territories turned over to them to establish an ethnic homeland (Eelam). The Indian Tamils were brought over to work on tea plantations in the nineteenth century and settled in the center of the country. They have exhibited limited interest in establishment of a homeland for Tamils and have not been prone to rebellion, in spite of the Sri Lankan government's refusal to grant them citizenship. Various factions of Sinhala and Tamils disagreed about strategies and the desirability of a mediated end to the fighting.

In elections, the Buddhist Sinhala identity was championed by political parties and student movements, culminating in the development of the Janatha Vimukthi Peramuna (JVP) in the 1970s. The JVP's tactics and importance varied over time. It attempted to overthrow the government in 1971 when it staged a major revolt. The participants in the movement were largely poor, rural Sinhalese who were frustrated with their lack of opportunity (Tambiah 1986). This action brought about a disproportionately brutal governmental repression resulting in an estimated twenty thousand deaths within a few weeks' time (CQ Press 2007b; Tambiah 1986). The group returned to prominence in 1989–1990, which is discussed in greater detail below.

The most important, powerful, and persistent Tamil group in Sri Lanka was the Liberation Tigers of Tamil Eelam (LTTE or Tamil Tigers), which formed in 1978 as a student uprising. Over the course of the conflict, there were other groups that emerged to champion the cause of the Tamil people. Some sought a political solution (Tamil United Liberation Front, or TULF, for example), while others fought for independence (such as the LTTE). Even among the groups dedicated to the concept of Eelam, however, there was disagreement about the strategies and tactics that were acceptable and the extent to which the LTTE should end up ruling the new state once it was achieved. There were additional factions between the native Tamils and those that immigrated to Sri Lanka from Tamil Nadu to work on tea plantations during the British colonial period. In later stages of the conflict, there was also a major divide between the eastern and northern Tamil factions, with the east complaining that the north was ne-

TABLE 4.2   Conflicts in Sri Lanka, 1971–2009

Conflicts	Groups participating	Primary geographic location(s)	Duration of conflict	Periods of outbreak of violence	Incompatibility
Janatha Vimukthi Peramuna (JVP)	JVP	Nationwide, with emphasis on Colombo	1971–1990	1971; 1989–1990	Government
Tamil Homeland	Liberation Tigers of Tamil Eelam (LTTE, Tamil Tigers); Tamil Eelam Liberation Organization (TELO)	Eelam (northern and eastern Sri Lanka)	1975–2009	1984	Territory
Tamil Homeland	LTTE; TELO; Eelam People's Revolutionary Liberation Front (EPRLF)	Eelam	1975–2009	1985	Territory
Tamil Homeland	LTTE; EPRLF	Eelam	1975–2009	1989	Territory
Tamil Homeland	LTTE	Eelam	1975–2009	1984–2001; 2003; 2005–2009	Territory

Source: UCDP/PRIO (2014).

glecting its interests. Singer argues that at the "height of Tamil militancy there were at least five major militant groups and at least 32 factions among them" (Singer 1992, 714). None of these challengers to the LTTE's power lasted long against dedicated LTTE resistance. Throughout the conflicts with other groups the leader of the LTTE, Velupillai Prabhakaran, decried the disunity as undermining the Tamil cause and claimed to be in favor of the various groups uniting (Pratap 1984; *Hindu* 1986; annual Heroes Day speeches). However, his actions to eradicate competing groups are not indicative of such a desire. It is possible that the Tamils could have fared better against the Sri Lankan government if the various Tamil factions had been able to engage in collective action rather than fighting among themselves (Lilja 2010). However, the divide between the eastern and northern Tamils and the fear some had of Prabhakaran's dominance kept such unity from ever developing.

The conflict was characterized by continued strikes and retaliatory attacks. Both the government forces and the rebellious groups seemed unconcerned about civilian casualties. The LTTE was an innovative group that engaged in a wide variety of guerrilla and terrorist tactics in its attempts to address the power asymmetry it had with the government. It pioneered (invented, per the

FBI [Bhattacharji 2009]) the use of suicide vests, engaged in suicide bombings as a strategic campaign, extensively involved women in the organization, had a small air force and navy, used chemical weapons at one point in an attempt to keep the government from increasing its capacity, deployed landmines in large numbers (estimated in 2002 to be over 1.5 million), and had an international system for fundraising and training. The group reportedly also trafficked in drugs to raise funds. The group was so sophisticated that in 2007 its air force carried out small-scale aerial bombing campaigns (Saddique 2007). All these actions were undertaken to increase group capacity relative to the government. The Sri Lankan armed forces engaged in numerous large-scale bombings and military campaigns geared toward isolating or eradicating the LTTE.

The LTTE attacked both Sri Lankan military and civilian targets. Within the civilian population it particularly targeted Sinhala and Muslim citizens. It has been argued that the LTTE occasionally did this in order to draw the government's fire, which it could then depict as repression in order to stimulate support in Sri Lanka and abroad (UCDP). It was also not uncommon for violence to erupt after elections (for instance, in 1958 and 1977) if portions of the society were concerned that the outcome of the election would disadvantage their group (Little 1994). The LTTE would also target Tamil civilians who were seen to be complicit to the government's cause or any Tamil group that attempted to become a peer competitor for Tamil allegiance. The LTTE has been accused of using children as soldiers, sometimes kidnapping them and compelling them to serve (U.S. Department of State 2009c).

Throughout the conflict, the government declared states of emergency on a fairly regular basis. During such times, rights of citizens were constrained significantly. In 1961, for instance, all citizens who lived in the Jaffna district, which was dominated by Tamils, were required to surrender all firearms to the government (*New York Times* 1961). Other common government tactics to control the violence included restricting the flow of information by rescinding freedom of the press, banning foreign media from the country, or engaging in extensive censorship in times of struggle (De Silva 1981). This complicates information gathering about the conflict and throws suspicion on casualty counts circulated by the government, as independent verification was not common. Disappearances, mass arrests, and the holding of prisoners incommunicado and without charges for lengthy periods of time were also common practices.

The Sri Lankan civil war began in 1983. Periods of attempted negotiated settlement of the conflict have included 1985, 1989–1990, 1994–1995, and 2001–2002 (Nadarajah and Sriskandarajah 2005). Throughout the conflict Prabhakaran would use talks to his advantage, using the time, and sometimes intentionally delaying the proceedings, to rearm and rebuild the strength of his forces (Ramesh 2007).

The number of people killed in the civil war is estimated at about seventy-five thousand (*New York Times* 2009). In 2009, government forces defeated the Tamil Tigers and then proceeded to punish Tamil citizens for the actions of the Tigers. Since that time the Tamil-related violence in the country has diminished considerably. However, it is impossible to determine whether the conflict is truly terminated or if it is merely in a lull, as so little time has passed between the defeat of the Tamil Tigers and the publication of this book, and the grievances of Sri Lanka's Tamils have yet to be addressed. While military defeat tends to bring about longer-lasting conflict termination, resurgence of violence after such a defeat is not unprecedented.

CONFLICT PROGRESSION AND DYNAMICS

The Sri Lankan civil war has been divided into four distinct periods, which are referred to as Eelam Wars I–IV (UCDP). Each period begins with an increase in violence and ends with a subsequent decrease. The discussion of rivalry progression and conflict dynamics is divided into sections accordingly, as the Eelam Wars correspond with periods of escalation and de-escalation.

Eelam War I (July 1983–1989)

From the time of independence the Tamil population became increasingly dissatisfied with their situation and their ability to achieve any remedy for it through the policy process. In the early 1970s, student groups championing the rights of the Tamils flourished in the country. From this student movement, as many as thirty-six militant Tamil groups arose. A political party, the Tamil United Liberation Front (TULF), emerged. After political actions for change produced no progress, the TULF began organizing militant groups, one of which was the Tamil New Tigers (TNT, 1972–1976). This illustrates the shifting of the group's goal from policy change and representation to the use of violence but was not yet a point where autonomy or independence was sought. Beginning in May 1976 the TNT was led by Velupillai Prabhakaran, who changed the group name to the Liberation Tigers of Tamil Eelam (LTTE) and began the process of eliminating competitors inside and outside of his group (B. Hoffman 2009). Essentially, Prabhakaran assassinated anyone he deemed to be too moderate in pursuit of the Tamil cause.

The creation of the LTTE was followed by the government's response in the form of the passage of the Prevention of Terrorism Act in 1979, which gave government forces the right to arrest, imprison, and hold incommunicado and without trial for up to eighteen months anyone accused of unlawful activity. Amazingly, the new law was applied retroactively, resulting in the abuse of many

FIGURE 4.2   Patterns of Violence in Sri Lanka, 1983–2009

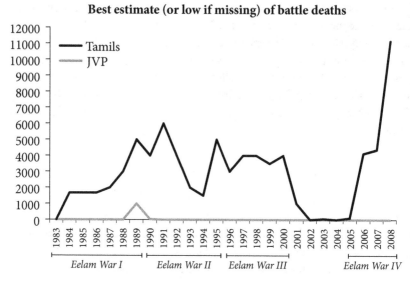

Best estimate (or low if missing) of battle deaths

Drawn from Lacina and Gleditsch (2005).

Tamils already in custody (DeVotta 2000). Beginning in the 1980s, numerous dissatisfied Tamil groups formed, with some supporting peaceful routes to change and others espousing the use of violence, but all had significant disagreements with the LTTE that were largely based on tactics and the perceived negative attitude about eastern Tamils held by those in the north. By the mid-1980s, there were almost forty identified groups devoted to the creation of a Tamil state (DeVotta 2009). At the same time as the LTTE was battling government forces, it was fighting against these groups to maintain its position as the sole voice of the Tamil cause. These conflicts were relatively short and limited in intensity. The LTTE's superior training, funding, weapons, and discipline allowed it to defeat these competing groups (UCDP; DeVotta 2009).

Tensions between Sinhala and Tamil entities grew through the end of the 1970s and into the 1980s. Singer has argued that "there were 'race riots' in 1956, 1958, 1978, and finally the worst in July 1983 in which 1,000 innocent Tamils were killed and tens of thousands made homeless" (Singer 1992, 713). This 1983 riot was essential in mobilizing support behind the LTTE and other Tamil militant groups. In July 1983, an LTTE landmine killed thirteen Sinhala soldiers, resulting in enormous backlash against Tamils in the country. Sinhala citizens rioted; burned Tamil houses, businesses, and property; and killed and injured thousands of Tamils. According to Spencer, in some cases entire suburbs of the capital city of Colombo were "razed to the ground" (Spencer 1990, 616). Tambiah goes so far as to refer to the Sinhala rampage as an "orgy of killing of Tamils in Colombo" (Tambiah 1986, 15). Estimates of the number of Tamils killed in the fighting range from five hundred to two thousand (UCDP). Thousands more Tamils lost their property and became refugees. Enough of these refugees settled in Tamil Nadu in India to cause Indira Gandhi to become concerned, perhaps more about their potential to destabilize the region in India rather than about the Tamil plight, and to commit her government to training and financing Sri Lankan Tamil militants (Little 1994).

In the 1983 civil war the Sri Lankan government forces not only were slow to protect Tamil civilians (as they had been accused of previously), but openly assisted the Sinhala rioters or saw themselves as mere observers (DeVotta 2000). Regarding the violence, Human Rights Watch (1995b) observed that police and military personnel watched while Tamils were attacked, and in some cases they carried out violence against civilians themselves. Government officials were accused of stimulating and coordinating the anti-Tamil violence. Four days after the riots ended, President J. R. Jayawardene made a statement in which he decried the violence perpetrated by Tamil groups rather than condemning the pro-Sinhala attacks (Human Rights Watch 1995b, 88–89). One of the government's responses to the beginning of the civil war was the passage of a controversial constitutional amendment in August 1983 that prohibited support or advocacy of independence that would threaten the country's territorial integrity (Nadarajah and Sriskandarajah 2005).

The LTTE used these events to their benefit, emphasizing the violence and government's disinterest in stopping it to recruit new members, raise funds domestically and with the Tamil diaspora abroad,[1] and purchase weapons. These were clearly efforts to increase the group's capacity. Throughout the conflict, the LTTE shifted funding and weapons sources as international actors altered in their backing of the group, which served to diminish the group's capacity. Typically the support came from entities within states that had a significant Tamil diaspora presence. Obtaining resources became increasingly difficult as more and more states deemed the LTTE a terrorist organization and prohibited trade and financing arrangements with the group. By August 1984, the LTTE forces had swelled in numbers, were using more sophisticated weapons, and were shifting somewhat from guerrilla tactics to sustained attacks (*Keesing's World*, September 1984, 33099). This fed an increase in the violence in the conflict as the LTTE's increased capacity allowed it to combat government forces more effectively.

Once the war broke out in 1983, the Indian government began to train and equip the Tamils, who had close ties to the Indian state of Tamil Nadu. The LTTE drew on support from this area of India for much of its existence (maintaining and increasing its capacity), though the sponsorship of these activities shifted from official Indian government support to that of the citizens of Tamil Nadu when, in 1985, peace talks between Sri Lanka and the LTTE failed and India began to push for peace along a different path. Hassan argues that this was, at least in part, due to India's desire to keep the Sri Lankan Tamil activities from stimulating dissent in Tamil Nadu (Hassan 2009, 7). The flight of thousands of Sri Lankan Tamils to Tamil Nadu to avoid the violence added to the Indian dilemma.

The 1985 peace talks were facilitated by Rajiv Gandhi but failed to make progress. Tamil political groups came together to form an umbrella organization to represent Tamils and agreed on demands that they should put before the government. These included recognition of Sri Lankan Tamils as a separate nationality, creation of a Tamil homeland by joining the northern and eastern sectors, and the right of all Tamils residing in the country to citizenship (which was denied to Indian Tamils at the time). The government refused to even consider these points as a start for negotiations. The Tamil United Liberation Front (TULF) then countered in December with an autonomy arrangement, which would have given the Tamils a high level of local autonomy, loosely based on the Indian model of federalism (Pfaffenberger 1987). While the government argued it could acquiesce to some of these demands, it refused to allow for the uniting of the northern and eastern regions or its designation as a homeland for the Tamil population. This undermined the negotiation process. While the moderate TULF found the government's position "reasonable" (Pfaffenberger 1987, 158), the more militant factions rejected it. Prabhakaran complained that the TULF was "retarding the liberation struggle," that it failed to take concrete steps, and that it was attempting to stifle the revolution (Pratap 1984, 2).

In 1985 and then again in October and November 1986, the government increased its arms acquisitions (Sislin and Pearson 2006). These purchases, which represent clear attempts by the government to increase its capacity, preceded the initiation of major government offensives against Tamil-held areas (Sislin and Pearson 2006). These included cutting the LTTE's supply lines (Hindu 1986).

Subsequent negotiations between the Sri Lankan and Indian governments led to the signing of the Indo–Sri Lankan Agreement on July 29, 1987. Shortly after the agreement was signed, thousands of Indian troops were engaged in Sri Lanka under the auspices of the Indian Peacekeeping Force (IPKF, numbering around eighty thousand troops). It is perhaps telling that the agreement involved the governments of the two countries, but not any of the rebel organizations. From the Tamil perspective, the most significant provision of the agreement was that it allowed for the northern and eastern provinces to be merged into a single administrative district and recognized those areas as the traditional Tamil homeland. In addition, the agreement provided for amnesty for political prisoners (Rupesinghe 1988). Prabhakaran reluctantly agreed to a ceasefire for a short time when it became clear the agreement was going to go ahead over his objections (Ghosh 1999). However, the Tamils soon took up arms to continue the fight for a Tamil homeland against the government, IPKF, and Tamils they identified as being complicit with the agreement.

India's involvement in both peacekeeping and conflict is explained by Carment and James (1996) as stemming from three main factors. First was the Sri Lankan refusal to offer permanent citizenship to the Indian Tamils who had lived in the country for generations, resulting in the more than 975,000 Indian Tamils being stateless people. Second was the Congress Party's need to maintain the support of two major Tamil Nadu parties in order to win the state. Third was the existing strong ties between the Sri Lankan Tamils and the citizens of Tamil Nadu, including military training camps (Carment and James 1996, 543–544). A fourth possible explanation is provided by DeVotta (2009), who argues that the Indian government was displeased by the Western-leaning tendencies of the Sri Lankan government and was seeking to undermine it (1029). From an outsider's perspective, the perplexing thing about this accord is that it was intended to restore peace to Sri Lanka but included no LTTE representation in its negotiations or implementation. The announcement of the agreement surprised many and, perhaps as a result, was met with mixed reactions (Rupesinghe 1988).

While the Indian troops were sent to Sri Lanka as a peacekeeping force, the situation devolved into an armed struggle, effectively intensifying the violence that was already occurring in the country. By October the LTTE was fully engaged against the IPKF. The Sinhala rejected the presence of the IPKF almost as intensely as the LTTE did. This resulted in the eventual collaboration between the Sri Lankan government, led at this point by President Ranasinghe Premadasa, and the LTTE to drive the Indian forces out of the country (Hopgood 2005, 49). This included talks with the LTTE, which had been weakened by its struggle against the IPKF (Little 1994). The situation strained relations between Sri Lanka and India, as a timetable for the removal of the Indian troops was difficult to agree upon and implement. Fighting throughout the time that the Indian troops were in Sri Lanka was fierce. According to Little (1994), the conflict with the IPKF had the unintentional consequence of strengthening the LTTE and extending the conflict.

The Indo–Sri Lankan Agreement, in particular its offer of amnesty to Tamil militants who denounced violence and engaged politically, also had the effect of turning some Sinhalese forces and left-wing actors against the Indian troops and Sri Lankan government (CQ Press 2007b). This brought about episodic violence as the JVP returned to prominence and gained strength in the aftermath of the signing of the agreement. The JVP "launched a death squad campaign in which backers of moderation among both communities [Sinhala and Tamil] were systematically targeted" (Sisk 2009, 154). Such violence from a group devoted to Buddhism seems out of character. However, the actions were undertaken as an obligation in defense of the faith. The violence has also been attributed to young, impoverished, extremist Buddhist monks who felt deprived within the Sri Lankan political system (Little 1994). By the end of the year, the group had significantly increased its capacity by amassing weaponry and was engaged in assassination of its competitors. This included the targeting of the families of prominent members of the Sri Lankan military. The government's response was repressive, with the ensuing conflict causing over a thousand fatalities before the end of 1989. The violence continued, though at a lower level (sixty-one fatalities), into 1990 (UCDP). Through the remainder of the conflict, the JVP stood in opposition to any peace settlement that devolved power or gave autonomy to Tamil regions. However, the group did so through its role as a political party rather than through violence.

The constant fighting and conflict with the Indian military as well as that of Sri Lanka had significantly diminished the capacity of the LTTE. This resulted in its willingness to seek accommodation and the signing of a ceasefire agreement in 1987 (UCDP). Another factor that contributed to the group's fatigue was the fact that during 1987 it was also engaged in armed conflict with the Tamil Eelam Liberation Organization (TELO). This was related to the north/east divide among Sri Lankan Tamils, the fact that Prabharakan wanted the LTTE to be the sole voice for Tamils, and his belief that other Tamil organizations were too moderate. TELO was the second most powerful Tamil group at the time but had poor discipline and leadership, leading to its defeat by the LTTE (J. Richards 2014). Though the LTTE emerged victorious, this additional fight divided its capacity between the conflicts with TELO and government forces, further diminishing its capacity.

Indian troops were finally withdrawn in March 1990. By that time, the combined fatality rate was over twelve thousand, with another five thousand wounded (Hassan 2009).

Eelam War II (Early 1990s)

In spite of the ceasefire to which Premadasa had reluctantly agreed, once the Indian forces withdrew from the country the LTTE reengaged in the fight with the Sri Lankan government. In general, the 1990s saw a shift in the nature of warfare in Sri Lanka from guerilla attacks on government forces to more traditional military offensives between territories controlled by either side (Nadarajah and Sriskandarajah 2005). In spite of the fact that the group had been weakened, it retained sufficient capacity to engage the government.

While the Sri Lankan Armed Forces enjoyed significant numerical superiority over the LTTE rebels in the 1990s (240,000 Sri Lankan Armed Forces versus about 10,000 rebels), the government attempted to further increase its capacity by promoting anti-LTTE paramilitary forces (Nieto 2008, 578). This may have been due to the poor preparation of the Sri Lankan Armed Forces. Several sources point to the limited training and equipment in the Sri Lankan Army as a contributing factor in government's inability to defeat the LTTE (Nieto 2008; Hopgood 2005).

In early 1990, the LTTE stepped up its attacks against Sri Lankan military bases and managed to seize control of the Jaffna peninsula in the north, which became the seat of power for the LTTE until 1995 (UCDP). In early June the LTTE launched a series of attacks on police stations. The government responded with massive bombing campaigns, which included the use of napalm. On July 22, a mass grave was uncovered by government forces. In it were as many as two hundred dead policemen who had been blindfolded and shot in the back of the head. They were believed to be from the more than six hundred who were captured during the LTTE police station raids. From June 11 to August 17, 1990, as many as 3,350 deaths were recorded as resulting from the conflict (Bandarage 2009).

Another important LTTE event in 1990 occurred when it surrounded a military encampment in East Kiran, a peninsula in the Batticaola district, on June 11. The LTTE continued to hold the camp under siege until June 21. The government succeeded in breaking the siege by successfully bringing in a column of troops by sea. The importance of the incident was the reaction of the LTTE to the impending arrival of the relief troops. According to Bruce Hoffman (2009), when the LTTE sensed that the advantage in capacity would shift to the government with the arrival of reinforcements, it deployed barrels of chlorine gas upwind of the besieged camp (469–470). Hoffman attributes the use of chemical weapons, at least in part, to the LTTE's diminished ability to acquire and import quality weapons at this time. This is a clear example of a group's shift in tactics based on a perceived impending shift in the relative capacity between itself and the government.

Violence during Eelam War II peaked with an estimated 6,400 fatalities in 1991 (UCDP). In the late 1980s, the Jayawardene government signed a proclamation that merged the northern and eastern provinces for administrative purposes, which was a stated goal of the Tamils. This created the North-East Provincial Council. In 1990, before the complete withdrawal of Indian troops, the North-East Provincial Council approved a resolution declaring independence for the region. In June 1990, Premadasa dissolved the council and called for new elections. In response, the LTTE engaged in a new wave of violence against both government and competitive Tamil entities (CQ Press 2007b).

In November 1993 the government suffered its worst losses to date when a single LTTE attack killed more than 500 soldiers and forced another 1,500 to withdraw from a base in Jaffna. This defeat, scandals that had weakened Premadasa, and his subsequent assassination in 1993 may have contributed to the government's willingness to enter into negotiations in 1994 and contributed to the lull in the conflict (Little 1994; Gargan 1993). Prabhakaran indicated that he hoped the new government would be amenable to talks but emphasized that the provision of autonomy was an important factor in whether he would find peace proposals acceptable (Prabhakaran 1994). This marked the end of Eelam War II.

Eelam War III (Late 1990s)

Chandrika Kumaratunga became president of the country in 1993. Her father had been the prime minister of Sri Lanka until 1959, when a Buddhist monk assassinated him. Her husband was assassinated in 1988, just as his political career had started to progress (Dugger 2000). She took office in an environment of national dissatisfaction with the costs of the continued conflict and a belief that military victory could not be achieved. She "came to power with a mass sentiment that through negotiation she would pursue an end to the war" (Sisk 2009, 154). Negotiations began again in 1994, resulting in a ceasefire on January 8, 1995. There was agreement that power would be devolved to the Tamil areas. However, the LTTE exited the talks in 1995, after which the government continued to negotiate with moderate Tamil groups in an attempt to marginalize the LTTE (Sisk 2009; Prabhakaran 1995). The peace process was, of course, opposed by Sinhala and Tamil extremists.

When the LTTE intensified its violence in response to the failure of the talks, the government shifted its policy for dealing with the group. It had been willing to negotiate a settlement of the conflict. Significant damages imposed on the government by the LTTE in April 1995 shocked it into action, and its goal shifted toward one of complete military victory (UCDP). The government felt the urgent need to increase its capacity versus the rebels (Saravanamuttu 2000, 156).

July 1995 marked the beginning of another massive offensive (Leap Forward) by the Sri Lankan government. The aim of the action was to weaken the LTTE in its stronghold of Jaffna and reinitiate peace talks with the group. The government mobilized over ten thousand troops along with air and sea missions in the Jaffna peninsula. The LTTE initially offered little resistance, but after five days it mounted a serious counteroffensive that included surface-to-air missiles and a large number of suicide missions (Bullion 1995). This was followed later in 1995 by the Riviresa offensive, which mobilized twenty-one thousand soldiers and heavy artillery in Jaffna. This effort caused over five hundred thousand refugees to flee the region and eventually trapped two thousand LTTE rebels in a single town. In November the government declared that military spending had increased by 33 percent to support its attempts to intensify military operations (Subramanian 1995). The Sri Lankan government was clearly emphasizing increasing its capacity by concentrating forces in problem areas and by prioritizing military spending.

A new agreement was released in August 1995. It gave significant autonomy to Tamil areas. The agreement failed to have impact, however, as some Sinhala felt it gave too much to the Tamils while extremist Tamil populations felt it gave too little. The LTTE responded with a major attack in Colombo, marking the resumption of hostilities.

In 1995 the Sri Lankan government achieved a major victory as it drove the LTTE from its long-term stronghold in Jaffna. By 1996 the government had achieved additional military victories, effectively driving the LTTE into the jungles and putting them on the defensive from 1996 to 1998. This defensive period coincided with the October 1997 U.S. Department of State designation of the LTTE as a foreign terrorist organization (FTO; U.S. Department of State 2009c). This U.S. action impacted the LTTE's ability to raise funds, acquire weapons, and gain concessions from the international system. During this time, the LTTE strategy in the north was primarily a conventional war against the Sri Lankan military. In the east the strategy was more focused on guerilla tactics, while in the south the group engaged in a bombing campaign (UCDP). This can be attributed to the fact that the Tamils in the north had a stronger capacity versus that of the government than those to the east.

In July 1996, the LTTE overran a government base at Mullaittivu in the northeast of the island, inflicting heavy losses on government forces. The government responded with a massive offensive against Kilinochichi, where the LTTE had relocated its headquarters after being driven out of Jaffna. It seems there were fewer than five hundred combined government and LTTE fatalities, but hundreds of thousands of civilians were displaced (Human Rights Watch 1997).

Two major attacks by the LTTE took place in the late 1990s. The first occurred when a four-hundred-kilogram bomb was detonated in the business district of Colombo on October 15, 1997, killing eighteen and injuring more than one hundred. Two possible motives have been given for the attack: that the group was attempting to raise morale after suffering losses in Jaffna or that the attack was a response to the U.S. State Department's designation of the LTTE as a foreign terrorist organization (De Rosayro 1997).

The second major attack was on January 25, 1998, when the LTTE used an explosives-filled truck to attack one of the holiest Buddhist temples in Sri Lanka, the Temple of the Tooth. The temple housed a tooth that is believed to be one of Lord Buddha's and was revered as the holiest Buddhist site on the island (DeVotta 2000, 55). It had, however, become closely associated with Sinhala chauvinism, as successive prime ministers gave speeches from the temple in which they emphasized the importance and dominance of Buddhism in the country (Little 1994). The Sinhala Buddhists believe that Sri Lanka is intended to be a country dedicated to the preservation of Buddhism (Pfaffenberger 1987, 157), making this a particularly despicable attack in their eyes. This sparked a major round of ethnic rioting as Sinhala and Tamil nationalists clashed, pushing fatality rates up to over 3,500 in 1998 as compared to the previous two years, when there were fewer than 3,000 battle deaths (UCDP). In response to the LTTE's attack on the Temple of the Tooth, the government outlawed the group. The government had previously avoided banning the organization, as that would complicate peace negotiations and any attempt to grant the Tamils autonomy (Human Rights Watch 1999b; *Economist* 1998). An outlawed organization would lack standing in such legal venues. These two attacks on civilian targets were likely the result of the LTTE's recent losses and associated reduction in capacity.

By June 1998, the government had banned all news coverage of the civil war by either local or foreign media (Human Rights Watch 1999b). The government claimed to have gained control of a number of key sites in September 1998, including the highway that serves as a lifeline for Jaffna. Over a thousand died in the fighting. On September 6, Prabhakaran called for talks with the government (Rotberg 1999).

The LTTE had halted the Sri Lankan Army's offensive and wiped out the gains they had achieved through their stepped-up operations by November 1999. The LTTE recaptured several military bases and the supply road to the Jaffna peninsula. On November 27, Prabhakaran called for the government to remove its forces from Tamil lands and enter into peace talks (Prabhakaran 1999). This was typical of Prabhakaran's tendency to attempt to negotiate from a position of power. While the government was engaged in track two diplomacy consistently, a formal round of talks did not emerge from Prabhakaran's call.

The late 1990s were a period of rearmament for the government (UCDP). It continued to seek weapons and counterterrorism training internationally throughout the early 2000s, with those activities becoming increasingly effective after the 9/11 attacks and the global antiterrorism actions that followed. The Sri Lankan government seemed at this time to be focusing on increasing its capacity.

Track two negotiations (e.g., typically behind-the-scenes discussions) had taken place in the 1990s and carried over into the early twenty-first century. These laid the groundwork for resumption of talks in 2000, with Norway agreeing to serve as mediator.

Fighting raged throughout 2000. By the end of the year, in spite of some significant military accomplishments, the LTTE was exhausted, sought negotiations, and declared a unilateral ceasefire (UCDP; Sisk 2009). This resulted in a de-escalation of the conflict and the eventual end of Eelam War III. The government maintained its insistence that the group agree to negotiate unconditionally, which hindered talks until 2001. Those talks, the subsequent ceasefire agreement, and the additional talks that followed are discussed further in the section on negotiations. Importantly, however, throughout the negotiations period the LTTE exhibited a willingness to accept an autonomy agreement rather than independence (UCDP), marking a significant shift in the group goal. Pressure was put on the LTTE by the 9/11 attacks, which caused the UK and other world powers to join the United States in designating the group a terrorist organization (Sisk 2009). The increased international activities to interdict the flow of weapons to terrorist organizations and block fundraising and the movement of money internationally significantly impacted the LTTE's ability to maintain its capacity level (Sisk 2009; Ganguly 2004). In addition to the troubles the LTTE was experiencing, "clearly one major incentive for both sides was that the war had reached the point of stalemate" (CQ Press 2003).

While there was a lull in the fighting from 2001 to the resumption of violence in 2005, there was a great deal of ongoing activity between the government and LTTE. A memorandum of Cessation of Hostilities was signed on February 22, 2002. The agreement, which was never very effective, included provisions for decommissioning weapons, opening the Elephant Pass road, and permitting civilian air traffic into Jaffna (Sisk 2009). One of its primary functions was to facilitate six rounds of talks from September 2002 to 2003. The focus of those talks was on humanitarian issues, reconstruction, normalization of relations, and, at least at one point in November and December 2002, a political solution to the underlying dispute (UCDP). Mayilvaganan (2009) has argued that these negotiations never bore much fruit due to the lack of sincerity on both sides (25). This negotiation process differed from others in that a peacekeeping mission was established to monitor the ceasefire. It was called the Sri Lanka Monitoring Mission (SLMM) and consisted of members from Norway, Sweden, Finland, Denmark, and Iceland (Hassan 2009). In spite of the ceasefire and the SLMM, neither side was willing to discuss or come to an agreement on the core issues of the conflict. The ceasefire was violated frequently, and the situation gradually returned to one of insecurity and violence. The SLMM withdrew in 2008, and the government launched renewed offensives against the LTTE. Funding to the military was increased, which allowed for a 40 percent increase in the size of the Sri Lankan Armed Forces (Hassan 2009).

By April 2003, however, the LTTE accused government negotiators of slow implementation of the agreed-upon reconstruction activities and "attempting to marginalize the organization" (UCDP). This resulted in a deadlock in negotiations and the eventual LTTE withdrawal, which marked an endpoint of effective negotiations in the country. While other attempts were made, they had little to no impact on either side's conduct, regardless of their content or intensity.

The situation was exacerbated by an important splintering event in LTTE history in March 2004. LTTE Colonel V. Muralitharan (known as Karuna) wrote to

Prabhakaran to express his dismay at what he felt was the mistreatment of the eastern Tamils by the LTTE and requested that the eastern wing be permitted to function separately (Ratnayake 2004). He argued that the northern leaders of the movement treated the eastern members as second class and that eastern leaders were denied adequate representation in leadership positions (Sri Lanka Project 2004). Karuna also complained separately about eastern troops being deployed to northern battle areas, leaving their home territories unprotected (Ratnayake 2004). In a second letter, Karuna wrote to the SLMM and asked if he could arrange a separate truce for his troops. Karuna was subsequently expelled from the LTTE on March 6. He took with him five to six thousand fighters, or about a third of the LTTE's military forces (Ratnayake 2004). This move clearly diminished the LTTE's capacity, especially in the north of the country, from which Karuna's forces would have been drawn. Ratnayake (2004) argues that this rift was actually the manifestation of wealthy Tamil interests in the north and east attempting to negotiate the best possible peace for their region, at the potential expense of Tamils elsewhere. This may indicate that Karuna had doubts that the LTTE had the capacity to defeat the government. Lilja (2010) argues that while the LTTE had the leadership and capacity to mobilize its members for war, it lacked comparable skill to lead them toward peace.

Karuna's military battled Prabhakaran's LTTE for control of eastern territories and was largely defeated (CQ Press 2007b). He then shifted strategies toward one of seeking political accommodation for the eastern Tamils from the government. Karuna eventually started a political party and served in the Sri Lankan government. For the negotiations process, the Karuna split was important in that it exacerbated tensions between the LTTE and the government and seriously weakened the LTTE. The LTTE declared that the government was supporting Karuna's faction in an attempt to diminish the LTTE's power (Wax 2009). While this may not have been the government's intent, it certainly was one of the outcomes.

Eelam War IV (2005–May 2009)

The ceasefire of 2002 was frequently violated by both sides. While there had been hope that the 2004 Asian tsunami would create a more peaceful environment, this was not to be. In the immediate aftermath of the disaster, all sides seemed willing to put aside their grievances to respond to a true national tragedy. An estimated thirty thousand Sri Lankans were killed in the tsunami, with many of them in the contested eastern region. However, after this initial rapprochement, the tragedy became an additional bone of contention, as decisions about how to distribute international aid increased tensions and violence (CQ Press 2007a). It was June 2005 before a controversial deal could be struck that would allow the LTTE to have any share in the international funds pledged for tsunami relief efforts (Human Rights Watch 2006). Violence built significantly through 2005, and the ceasefire had collapsed completely by 2006. In particular, in April 2006 there was an LTTE campaign of suicide bombings against the military in Colombo,[2] attacks against naval installations, and in May an attack on a naval convoy. By June the LTTE and the Sri Lankan government were fully engaged militarily (Sisk 2009, 160).

In 2006, Sri Lankan president Mahinda Rajapaksa maintained a two-pronged policy toward the LTTE, seeking negotiations at the same time as retaliating for any damages inflicted by the group. However, as the year progressed, the government withdrew officially from the 2002 ceasefire, negotiations were abandoned, and fighting intensified. August 2006 saw an increase in the intensity of the violence as the LTTE undertook a large number of attacks. In October 2006, the LTTE sent peace monitors with the SLMM home to their respective EU countries. It has been argued that the LTTE's actions in the latter half of 2006 were designed to sidetrack talks that were to take place in late October in Geneva (CQ Press 2007a). In the aftermath of those talks, it seemed neither side was sincere in its desire to participate. Rather, international aid donors had pressured both into attending (Chopra 2006).

On June 19, 2007, President Mahinda Rajapaksa sought to increase government capacity through the expedited recruitment of fifty thousand additional troops in order to "maintain the momentum of military successes in the east" (Lanka Newspapers 2007). The expansion was to be funded through cutbacks in other government spending.

Sri Lankan government forces undertook major ground offensives against the LTTE in 2007, particularly in the east of the country, bringing "the eastern part of the country back under government control for the first time since 1994" (UCDP). Governmental offensives in 2007 significantly weakened the LTTE (UCDP), which certainly contributed to its tactical decision making as the war came to its conclusion. The LTTE's actions in the last phases of the conflict have been condemned (as have the government's, which are discussed below) by the United Nations and various humanitarian organizations. After the government created safe zones into which civilians could flee the fighting, LTTE actions denied civilians access to these secured areas. During this period, the LTTE has been accused of shooting civilians who were trying to leave conflict areas, firing artillery near known camps for internally displaced persons (IDP), using IDP and hospitals as shields for their camps and equipment, and continuing to carry out suicide attacks against civilians who were not in areas of active conflict (*Report of the Secretary-General's Panel* 2011).

On January 2, 2008, the government officially declared its abrogation of the 2002 ceasefire agreement. The agreement had been ineffective for a while, but neither side wanted to be seen as the one that had ended it, so it remained in place (UCDP). The conflict escalated significantly after the announcement. In September 2008, the Sri Lankan Army started a major offensive to capture remaining rebel territories in the north (UCDP).

In February 2009, the LTTE issued a call for a ceasefire. The government, which had by this time managed to overtake all of the group's strongholds and was close to a military victory, ridiculed and dismissed the ceasefire request (Fuller 2009). Fighting leading up to the government's victory in May 2009 was intense and claimed thousands of lives (UCDP). The government captured the town of Kilinochichi, retook the Elephant Pass so it could supply Jaffna, captured numerous LTTE camps, and drove the group into an increasingly smaller area to the east. According to the International Crisis Group, almost all of the LTTE's political and military leadership was killed in the fighting (UCDP).

As mentioned previously, the government's ruthless execution of the last phases of the war has been decried by the United Nations and many international human rights organizations. In response to the international community's concerns over the plight of civilians in conflict areas, the government set up safety zones to which they could flee. The Sri Lankan government is accused of using large-scale shelling against various areas during the last phases of the conflict, including the safety zones. Like the LTTE, the Sri Lankan government has been accused of significant human rights violations in the conduct of the conflict, especially at these late stages. It fired into the safe zones established to protect civilians and shelled humanitarian relief areas including a UN hub and International Committee of the Red Cross and Red Crescent ships. The government stands accused, in fact, of causing the majority of civilian casualties toward the end of the conflict through its indiscriminant shelling campaigns (*Report of the Secretary-General's Panel* 2011).

The capacity of the LTTE organization plummeted with the death of Prabhakaran in May 2009. Not only had the organization's numbers been decimated by the government's onslaught, but it also lost the central figure of the group's capacity to mobilize support at home and abroad. His leadership style was totalitarian and consistent with Weber's definition of charismatic leadership, which emphasized that the leader's personality is fundamental to the group's existence (Jordan 2009, 726; Weber 1964, 358). Leadership of the LTTE was so closely tied to Prabhakaran that, according to Hoffman, members pledged their allegiance to him each day rather than to the country or the cause (Hoffman 2009, 466). Both Nieto (2008, 583) and Sisk (2009, 160) predicted that peace would not be possible until Prabhakaran either died or stepped down from power.

After the cessation of hostilities, in 2010, the European Union ended Sri Lanka's preferential trade relationship with it based on the human rights abuses committed by the government during the war. In April 2011, the UN argued that both sides had committed atrocities against civilians and recommended an investigation into war crimes. This was followed in 2012 by a resolution of the UN Human Rights Council, which called for the Sri Lankan government to investigate its abuses, which was met with resistance from the Sri Lankan government, which argued that the demand violated its sovereignty. The UN's calls were essentially rejected by the government, which said in August 2014 that a UN delegation sent to the country to conduct an independent investigation would not be allowed to enter the country (BBC News 2015a). In February 2015, the United Nations agreed to defer release of its report on potential war crimes after the Sri Lankan government argued that the country was experiencing a new era of cooperation. The United Nations agreed to delay the release of the report based on the government's assurance that it would cooperate with the continued investigation and conduct a credible domestic investigation as well (Sengupta 2015).

Meanwhile, in the north and east of the country the Tamil National Alliance, an ethnic Tamil party, was consolidating political power. In 2011 elections, the group won two-thirds of the seats in local councils in the former war zone. In September 2013 elections, the Tamil National Alliance won seats in a semi-autonomous northern provincial council, with 78 percent of the vote (BBC News 2015a).

CONCLUSIONS

Relative capacity was clearly an important element in the continuing rivalry between the government of Sri Lanka and the LTTE. Both sides actively courted external support for funding, training, and weaponry. The tactics employed by the LTTE were impacted by its perception of its capacity, with more terrorism and guerrilla tactics being employed when it was at a disadvantage and more traditional tactics of warfare being used when it felt superior. In one remarkable instance, it even attempted to use chemical warfare to keep the government from expanding its capacity in a specific geographic location.

Intervention also impacted the patterns of violence. Indian intervention mobilized both the JVP and the LTTE into higher levels of violence as both sides objected to the presence of Indian forces on the island. Foreign diplomacy also was an intervening factor. The U.S. inclusion of the LTTE on its list of foreign terrorist organizations may have triggered an escalation of LTTE violence. It certainly constrained the group's fundraising and weapons acquisition activities. The events of 9/11 further hindered the group's ability to increase its capacity. In the aftermath of that terrible incident of terrorism, countries around the world increased their restrictions on dealings of all types with designated terrorist organizations.

One of the relatively distinctive aspects of this case as compared to others in the book is the incredible importance of charismatic leadership on the rivalry.

Quality of leadership is a factor in capacity. Prabhakaran's personal power and charisma emboldened and strengthened the LTTE. Group members reportedly felt aligned with him against the government, rather than feeling allegiance to a cause or the country. This benefited the group so long as he lived, but it became a serious weakness upon his demise. No reports were found that indicated he was grooming a successor. If he were, it likely would have been among his top generals, however, and many of those were killed or captured along with him in 2009. The group's capacity was so tied to the personal power of Prabhakaran that it is unclear if the group could have continued under different leadership.

In the Sri Lankan case we see both sides seeking to negotiate when they have the advantage as well as when they are at a disadvantage to their competitor. Prabhakaran preferred to negotiate from a position of power, but when his group faced truly dire circumstances, he might also request talks.

This case also illustrates a progression in group goal. Initially, when there were student riots, the goal was to gain awareness for the unfair treatment of the Tamils and to gain policy change to help alleviate their plight. When such policies were not forthcoming, the TULF and subsequently LTTE sought various autonomy arrangements with the government. The JVP's vigorous objection to any arrangement that might have benefited the Tamils kept autonomy agreements from coming to fruition.

As mentioned previously, at the time of publication of this book it is still too early to determine if the rivalry has indeed terminated. Government forces managed to damage the LTTE organization profoundly with the killing of Prabhakaran and most of the other group leaders in 2009. However, as Hassan (2009) argues regarding Sri Lanka and others have argued more generally, military victory did nothing to address the underlying grievances that drove the Tamils to violence in the first place. In contrast, others argue that military victories, though violent, lead to longer-lasting peace than negotiated settlements. The fact that Karuna and representatives of more moderate Tamil groups have received seats in government may help to satisfy some Tamils that their voices are being heard. It may also be that the group capacity of the LTTE was so devastated by the government that it cannot resurge in the future. It is simply too early to tell if the rivalry is truly over. However, there were no reports of Tamil violence found for 2015, which could indicate that Tamils are currently satisfied with trying to have their grievances redressed through representation and policy change rather than through the use of violence.

CHAPTER 5

A Case of Enduring Rivalries
Myanmar

Myanmar has experienced eight different intrastate conflicts (Gleditsch et al. 2002) and over thirty armed factions or rivals (Ballentine and Nitzschke 2003) in its short history, making it a country with a very complicated conflict history.[1] It involves both ideological and identity-based rivalries. Despite the repressive nature of the ruling military junta (which has changed over the country's history), the central government has never actually achieved control over its entire polity at any point, although it has certainly done better in this regard lately. The trajectories of the conflicts involved have been significantly impacted by the role of external actors, as well as intergroup collaborations. As a result, it is an ideal candidate to examine conflict dynamics when the state is faced with violence from multiple potential foes.

GEOGRAPHY AND HISTORICAL CONTEXT

Myanmar stands out among the cases examined elsewhere in this book. Not only has conflict been lengthy and enduring in Myanmar, but the relationships that exist among the many conflict actors intertwine as interconflict collaboration unfolds or collapses. The country of Myanmar is situated in Southeast Asia bordering Thailand, Laos, China, India, and Bangladesh, which made cross-border activity with neighboring countries and rebels a major challenge. This access had a significant influence on the capacity of many nonstate actors and the choice of tactic employed by the groups involved. Grundy-Warr (1993) has suggested that political and military conflicts in Myanmar are best explained in light of the country's cross-border space. First and foremost, the ability for rebels to find sanctuary from army pursuit allowed for some groups to employ hit-and-run tactics for long periods of time successfully. Thailand, in particular, provided consent for some of Myanmar's rebel factions to establish bases on its soil beginning in 1954. This permission was revoked in 1988 when Thailand negotiated logging rights with the Rangoon government (Human Rights Watch 1998). Both decisions changed the capacity of rebels to wage their war against the government. Similarly, Bangladesh served as a sanctuary for others fleeing from governmental offensives several times over the country's history. More

FIGURE 5.1 Myanmar

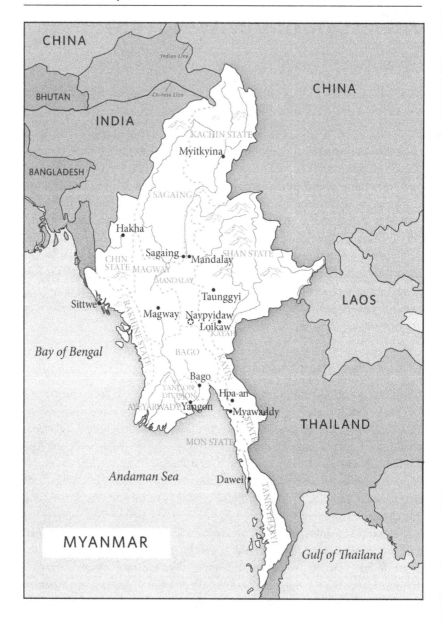

recent decisions to close that border to refugees have led to a humanitarian disaster. In the north, the border with China benefited several Myanmar rivals through assistance and safe havens as well. In light of the country's location relative to its neighbors, it is not surprising that this case involves more conflicts of the enduring nature than others examined in this book.

In addition, Myanmar's terrain is ideal for groups engaged in guerrilla warfare. In particular, the central Irrawaddy delta, which is sandwiched between steep, rugged mountainous regions and jungle terrain, is well suited to such tactics. Guerrilla warfare is indeed the most prevalent form of violence employed by all rebel factions in the country. This terrain has allowed rivals to take and hold territory, effectively creating rebel group strongholds. The territory in the northeastern portion of the country bordering Laos is also ideal for growing poppies. Rebels have been able to capture this resource, increasing their capacity in the process. The money generated from the drug trade has also changed the nature of some groups from those engaged in identity-based secessionist movements to profit-driven splinter groups that have subsequently shifted their tactical choices.

The historical and cultural experience of Myanmar has also played into the trajectory of conflict within its borders. The terrain discussion is relevant to this experience. The lowlands and highlands of Myanmar are not only conducive to rebellion, but they also involve spatial dichotomies (Grundy-Warr 1993). The ethnic majorities that live in the highlands are distinct from the national majority Burman in the lowlands. These differences were exacerbated during colonialism, when the British decided to administer the Shan States and northern Burma, ethnically different areas from Burma proper, as separate, distinct entities (Taylor 2008; Holliday 2008). Divide-and-conquer techniques were employed in Arakan, with Rohingya Muslims receiving preferential treatment over Buddhist Rakhines. As independence approached, the leaders of the Shan States, including the Shan, Da-nu, Pa-O, and Wa, along with representatives from the Chin, Kachin, and Karen, met and formed the Supreme Council of the United Hill Peoples (SCOUHP). When they met again in February 1947 they did so with revolutionary leader Aung San, who agreed to full autonomy for the frontier areas and equality for all races, resulting in the Panglong Agreement (Ethnic Nationalities Council 2007; Silverstein 1997). Aung San was a leader whom other minorities could trust to fulfill this promise. However, he was assassinated in July of the same year. Given the historical animosities and cultural differences that were exacerbated during colonial times, the new Burman leaders that emerged were unable to establish that same relationship, nor did they fulfill the promise of the Panglong Agreement. The fact that it existed became a focal point for minorities living in the frontier areas whenever negotiations were introduced. In fact, the Ethnic Nationalities Council, located in Chaing Mai,

TABLE 5.1 Timeline of Key Events in Myanmar's Conflicts, 1946–2003

Date	Event
February 5, 1946	Karen National Union established
February 22, 1946	Red Flag splintered from the Communist Party of Burma (CPB)
March 1946	Burmese Army began first counterinsurgency operations
January 4, 1947	Burma became independent
March 1947	Mon National Defense Organization established
April 4, 1947	CPB and Rangoon government experienced first bout of violence
August 9, 1948	Rebellion in Karenni states
December 1948	U Nu invited CPB leaders to peace talks, which were rejected
April 6–8, 1948	Inconclusive peace talks with Karen National Union (KNU)
January–March, 1950	Chinese Kuomintang (KMT) crossed into Burma from China
February 1951	Burmese Army and KMT fight
March 1954	Thai authorities allowed Karen and Mon rebels to set up camps along Thai border
January 20, 1956	CPB indicated it wanted to discuss peace
June 1956	U Nu resigned
March 1, 1957	U Nu returned as prime minister
September 26, 1958	U Nu announced new government led by Ne Win
October 28, 1958	Ne Win formed new government
January 1960	Ne Win visited China and signed a mutual nonaggression pact
May 1960	CPB again indicated it was willing to negotiate
March 2, 1962	Ne Win took control and jailed U Nu, as well as Shan and Karenni leaders
March 3, 1962	Constitution was suspended, and Parliament was dissolved
April 1, 1962	National amnesty provided for all rebels followed by talks with Mon, Chin, Karenni, Kachin, CPB, and Shan
July 7, 1966	China indicated its disapproval of Ne Win regime; suspension of aid followed
January 1, 1968	CPB launched new attack with Chinese support
January 15, 1968	Kachin and CPB leaders agreed to military cooperation
December 15–18, 1973	Shan State Army established link with CPB. Both Shan and Karen rebels visited China.
January 3, 1974	New constitution adopted without autonomy provisions
June 29, 1974	United States and Burma signed antidrug agreement
November 11–15, 1975	Ne Win visited China, resulting in nonaggression agreement
July 5–6, 1976	Kachin Independence Organization and CPB agreed to end their intergroup conflict. Kachin began purchasing weapons from China.
February 11, 1978	Government offensive in Arakan resulted in massive refugee flows into Bangladesh

TABLE 5.1 Continued

Date	Event
July 12, 1979	Aid agreement between China and Burma announced
November 19, 1979	China reduced its support for CPB
September 23, 1980	CPB proposed peace talks
October 17, 1980	Peace talks began with Kachin Independence Organization (KIO)
May 9, 1981	Government called off talks with KIO
March 12–18, 1988	Student unrest in Rangoon
July 23, 1988	Ne Win resigned. Sein Lwin takes power.
August 12, 1988	Sein Lwin resigned. Replaced by Dr. Maung Maung. Protests continued.
September 18, 1988	State Peace and Development Council established
December 14, 1988	Thailand and Burma agreed to logging rights
February 20, 1989	CPB leaders encouraged to retire in China
April 17, 1989	Wa troops captured CPB headquarters
May 27, 1989	Burma became Myanmar
September 2, 1989	Ceasefire signed with Shan State Army (SSA)
January 1990	KIA faction made peace with government
March 27, 1990	Pa-O rebels signed agreement with government
April 21, 1990	Palaung rebels signed agreement with government
1994	Ceasefire agreement with Karenni National Progressive Party
1995	KNU headquarters taken by Myanmar Army
2003	KNU signed ceasefire with government

Source: Lintner (1994); UCDP.

Thailand, and representing the Arakan, Chin, Kachin, Karen, Karenni, Mon, and Shan States, still proclaimed "Long Live the Spirit of Panglong!" on its website commemorating the sixtieth anniversary of the agreement.

The groups that make up the armed identity-based conflicts are distinct in culture and language from the politically dominant Burman. While the Panglong Agreement seemed to embrace diversity within the newly forming state, subsequent administrations have either undermined that position or, worse, moved in the direction of attempts at assimilation. President U Nu's 1960 "Burmanization" campaign, which communicated his intent to make Buddhism the national religion, serves as an example. The Kachin, the leadership of the Karen, and the Muslims in Arakan took exception to this policy. Neither the Karen nor the Arakanese were in any position to escalate conflict at that point, but the Kachin Independence Army (KIA) was formed in response. Despite efforts to force assimilation, changes in cultural identity were slow to occur and certainly were resisted. The region's colonial and historical background regarding its various identities challenged such a shift even more so. This experience of unfulfilled promises as the country achieved independence has fed into the enduring nature of the conflicts examined here.

BURMESE CONFLICTS

Communist

The largest, most successful campaigns against the Rangoon government took the form of Communist insurrection. Communism emerged early in Myanmar's history. After a history of colonial exploitation and animosities over its status relative to India, the independence movement took on a nationalistic fervor aimed at ridding the newly emerging state from external economic intervention (Thompson 1948). As a result, Burma's revolutionaries (the Anti-Fascist People's Freedom League, or AFPFL) had leftist-leaning ideologies. The socialist faction of the movement, however, emerged as the country's leadership upon independence, having expelled the Communist Party of Burma (CPB) in 1946 (Thompson 1948). At this point, the Burmese Communists could have elected to present a united opposition to the AFPFL. Instead, the CPB expelled Thakin Soe, a more radical Communist (Lintner 1994). He went on to set up the Communist Party (Red Flag), which itself supported the Rohingya separatists in the Arakan conflict presented below. Thakin Than Tun emerged as the leader of the CPB, also referred to as the White Flags, a much larger faction. Both groups waged war with the central government of Burma until 1989, when the Communist insurrection disintegrated (UCDP/PRIO 2014) as a result of diminished group capacity. The AFPFL, originally led by revolutionary hero Aung San, included its militia or People's Volunteer Organization (PVO). A large portion of the PVO emerged as a rebel faction opposed to the new government along with the Red Flags and the larger CPB. All of these organizations together are considered part of the Communist conflict.

Wa

The breakup of the CPB resulted in the Wa emerging into their own right with about twelve thousand troops that formed into the United Wa State Army (UCDP/PRIO 2014). The UWSA took over the CPB headquarters at Panghsang and much of the CPB drug trade, including agricultural fields and strategic trade routes. The group was permitted to administer this territory upon the signing of its own ceasefire in 1989 (globalsecurity.org n.d.).

TABLE 5.2   Conflicts in Myanmar, 1948–2011

Conflict	Dyads	Duration of conflict	Episodes of armed conflict
Government	Communist Party of Burma; Communist Party of Burma—Red Flags; People's Volunteer Organization	1948–1988	1948–1988
Arakan	Arakan People's Freedom Party; Arakan People's Liberation Party; Arakan Rohingya Islamic Front; Harkate Jihadul Islam; Mujahid Party; Rohingya Patriotic Front; Rohingya Liberation Organization	1948–1994	1948–1961 1964–1978 1991–1992 1994
Kachin	Kachin Independence Army	1949–2011	1949–1950 1961–1992 2011
Karen	Democratic Karen Buddhist Army; Karen National Union; Karen National Defense Organization; Karen National Liberation Army; Karen National United Front; Karen National United Party; Karen People's Liberation Army; Kawthoolei Armed Forces	1949–2011	1949–1950 1961–1992 2011
Mon	Mon National Defense Organization	1949–1996	1949–1963 1990 1996
Shan	Noom Suik Harn; Shan State Independence Army; Shan National United Front; Shan State Army; Kokang Revolutionary Front; Shan United Revolutionary Army	1959–2011	1959–1970 1972–1973 1976–1988 1993–2002 2005–2011
Wa	United Wa State Army	1997	1997

Source: UCDP/PRIO (2014).

Karen

The remaining conflicts in Myanmar were and are identity-based in nature, although several factions within the conflicts were either sympathizers with the CPB or entered into convenient coalitions with larger, well-connected rebel groups. Armed insurrection by the Arakan and Karenni began almost immediately after independence in 1948, and the following year the Mon and Kachin also rebelled. The most effective of these groups appears to have been the Karen. They are an ethnically distinct group located in the Irrawaddy delta and along eastern Myanmar. The Karen National Union (KNU), and its militia (Karen National Defense Organization, or KNDO), emerged early in the conflict following the massacre of Karen by the pro-Japanese Burma Independence Army, launching its first offensive at independence in 1948 (Lintner 1994). The majority of Karen are Buddhist (60–70 percent), with the remaining members adhering to Christian or animist religions. The rebel leadership, however, was predominantly Christian, which became a factor facilitating group splintering in 1994 and the creation of the Democratic Karen Buddhist Army (DKBA) (Minorities at Risk 2009).

According to its 1949 manifesto, the Karen were waging a war for the right to self-determination, equal rights, and democracy (Rajah 2002). Other Karen insurgent groups include the Karen National United Party (KNUP), the Kawthoolei Armed Forces (KAF), the Karen National United Front (KNUF), the Karen People's Liberation Army (KPLA), and the Karen National Liberation Army (KNLA) (Lintner 1994). Collectively, these groups comprise the Karen conflict.

Arakan

Another rivalry that emerged early in Myanmar's history came from the Arakan State (currently Rakhine) in western Myanmar near the East Pakistan (now Bangladesh) border. The majority of Arakan are Rohingya Muslims of Arab, Persian, and Moorish descent. Their citizenship has been questioned repeatedly by the Rangoon government through several immigration and citizenship laws implemented over time, resulting in various human rights violations (Human Rights Watch 2012). Immigration enforcement in Arakan has involved military operations, mass arrests, and forced relocation. These operations and interethnic violence have resulted in significant refugee flows into Bangladesh. The Rangoon government has also denied the Rohingya property rights, educational opportunities, and more recently, has targeted birth control policies aimed at limiting population growth (*Guardian* 2015). There were two main rebel groups in the Arakan rivalry: Arakan Rohingya Islamic Front, the more moderate faction, and the Rohingya Solidarity Organization (RSO). The Rohingya Patriotic Front, Rohingya Liberation Army, Arakan People's Freedom Party (APFP), and the Harkate Jihadul Islam were also active, but smaller in size (Lintner 1992). The Arakan People's Liberation Party (APLP) was a Buddhist faction that sought independence for Arakan as well.

Shan

The Shan rebellion in northeastern Myanmar emerged about ten years after independence. Under the newly independent government, the Shan operated with the understanding that they would be able to secede if they chose to do so after ten years. The Shan share a common religion with the dominant Burman but are culturally and linguistically different (Minorities at Risk 2009). In 1958, the Rangoon government refused to accept Shan secession, which led to the creation of the Noom Suik Harn (Young Warriors) with fewer than 450 men, and began the Shan rivalry with the state. In 1960, the Shan State Independence

Army (SSIA) emerged as a splinter group that took refuge in the northern Wa hills and recruited new members (Lintner 1994). The Shan National United Front (SNUF) was also created at this time from the Young Warriors. A coalition was formed in 1964, creating the Shan State Army (SSA), which included the SSIA and SNUF as well as the Kokang Revolutionary Front (KRF), a rebel group from a Chinese-dominated portion of the Shan States. From this coalition, the Shan United Revolutionary Army (SURA) branched into its own splinter faction.

The Chinese Kuomintang (KMT) was also active in Shan territory, although certainly not part of its enduring rivalry. Both the Shan and the KMT, however, found it lucrative to engage in the drug trade, which made for an unfriendly alliance. Interestingly, the Shan also cooperated with the CPB, which allowed them to also receive weapons from China. This decision caused a rift in the Shan rebellion. Although the Shan continued to engage in intrastate warfare, several warlord-type factions emerged, driven more by profit than political concessions (Lintner 1994), including the SURA and the Shan United Army (SUA), which eventually formed a coalition and became the Mong Tai Army (MTA) in 1985 (UCDP/PRIO 2014).

Kachin

The Kachin are involved in another intrastate conflict in Myanmar. Similar to the Karen, the Kachin are largely Christian and are culturally and linguistically distinct from the Burman majority. They reside in the northern-most territory bordering China and India, distant from the Burmese capital. Economic and insurgency challenges early in Myanmar's history resulted in underdevelopment and resentment in this region. Following U Nu's "Burmanization campaign" in 1960, the Kachin Independence Organization and its rebel army, the Kachin Independence Army (KIA) formed. Unlike in other conflicts discussed, the KIA did not experience dramatic intragroup shifts in the form of splintering. It did, however, form a coalition with the CPB. Initially, the two groups fought one another as the CPB extended its influence in northern Burma, but by 1976, the two were working together against their common enemy (UCDP/PRIO 2014). As of the time of writing, the KIA continues to exist and has once again been identified as an insurgent organization by the government of Myanmar (UCDP/PRIO 2014). Fighting continues, but so too are negotiated efforts to resolve the conflict.

Each of the conflicts examined in this chapter is enduring in nature, having engaged in a conflict trajectory that extends over much of the country's history since independence. The groups identified and described above are by no means the only armed factions or even the only ethnic insurgents operating in Myanmar, however. The Karenni, the Pa-O, the Kokang, and the Lahu are among other smaller groups that have worked alongside those mentioned in opposition to the government. In order to examine the theoretical framework presented, however, analysis is limited to the larger, more persistent conflicts.

CONFLICT PROGRESSION AND TACTICS

Clearly, Myanmar involves a complex set of interactions across a range of actors engaged in a number of armed conflicts. While each of the conflicts examined here has its own conflict trajectories, these histories parallel each other at times and intersect at others. Tactical decisions by armed rebels in Myanmar are similar, however, and are heavily influenced by the same set of factors.

First and foremost, conflicts in Myanmar, whether ideological or ethnic in nature, are heavily influenced by outside actors. At times, countries such as China and Thailand have provided military support, aid, safe havens, and other resources, allowing groups such as the Communist Party of Burma, the Kachin Independence Army, and the Karen National Union to battle the government from a bolstered position. Under such circumstances, it is not surprising that those groups shied away from negotiation tactics, choosing instead to pursue an armed campaign designed to capture territory with the ultimate goal of secession or revolution. When that outside support shifted toward the Myanmar government, the position of these groups faltered. Negotiations were then possible, but with a much improved position for the government. This is evident throughout the conflict progressions presented below.

Some groups in Myanmar relied less on outside support and more on generating their own resources, while others were able to gain from both. Success in controlling drug routes or the ability to sell timber to Thailand gave groups in the Shan, Wa, and Karen conflicts access to resources. While timber trade allowed the Karen to resist negotiation attempts, access to the drug trade led some groups, such as those involved in the Shan and Wa conflicts, to accept the negotiation terms offered by the government in the early 1990s because it allowed them to continue to have access to that stream of revenue and control of the territory.

Myanmar conflicts have also been heavily influenced by intergroup dynamics. When groups such as the CPB and the KIA worked together against the government, both with the support of the Chinese, they were able to make significant progress in gaining territory. In such situations, again, negotiations were much less likely, while guerrilla and conventional warfare were pursued. When those arrangements either collapsed or were torn apart through decreasing outside support, the government was able to take advantage of the situation and target negotiations to one group at a time, thereby turning them against one another.

FIGURE 5.2   Patterns of Violence in Myanmar, 1948–2008

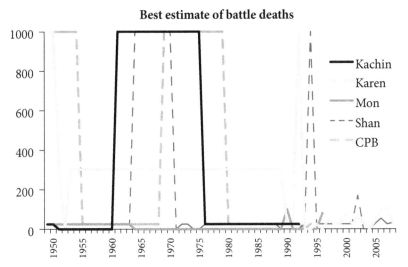

Best estimate of battle deaths

Drawn from Lacina and Gleditsch (2005). Arakan is not included in the diagram because it reached only the minimum battle death threshold for the years 1948–1988, 1991–1992, and 1994.

What follows is a discussion of the ebbs and flows of both the ideological and ethnic conflicts in Myanmar, illustrating how they unfolded over time and how they interacted with one another.

Ideological Rivalry

The Communist insurrection is the only ideological conflict in Myanmar. The expectation is that this type of conflict would be the most threatening to the Rangoon regime and, therefore, the most likely to experience high levels of intensity and sustained violence. It did indeed last forty years. Armed conflict involving various factions of the Communists and the Rangoon government emerged in April 1948 as the government launched a full-scale attack against the rebels from Rangoon to Mandalay (*New York Times* 1948). The insurrection was undertaken by members who had been a part of the country's independence movement led by the "30 Comrades." Not only had they participated in an armed rebellion against a colonial regime, but they were active participants (fighting on behalf of the British) in the Second World War. As a result, the leftist-leaning faction that emerged to become the Communist conflict was well equipped, at least initially, to engage in conventional warfare, which is what it did. When U Nu approached Communist rebels in late 1949 requesting negotiations, the rebels, given their size, responded with an emphatic "no."

As discussed in chapter 1, the number of rebels that any one conflict can claim is only part of the group capacity picture. It is obvious, having reviewed the number of armed factions present in Myanmar's history, that the cohesiveness of groups is also likely to influence their capabilities vis-à-vis the government. The message delivered to U Nu in early 1950 came from a unified force, as the various factions of Communist insurgents had met and responded as one. According to Lintner (1994), by 1950, the CPB claimed 15,000–18,000 fighters, plus an additional 1,500–2,000 Red Flags and 4,000 from PVO. Comparatively, U Nu's military had experienced significant defection as it was split along both ideological and ethnic lines. Defection levels for the Burmese military were to the point that the CPB had a clear advantage. U Nu's decision to seek negotiations made sense in light of this information. The unified Communist insurgency in the form of the People's Democratic Front (PDF) was short lived, however, and the tide began to turn in 1950. Amid a fractured PDF, the Burmese army that had been ravaged by mutiny was able to rebuild with massive assistance from neighboring India. This began a general theme in Burmese conflict history whereby escalation and de-escalation are closely linked to external support and the extent to which weapons were available. Early insurrections by the CPB, KNU, and others were made possible by weapons in the countryside that had been used to fight Japanese forces in World War II (Lintner 1994). This fact, along with the diminished capacity of the newly formed Burma military, allowed the CPB and KNU to make early advances. Those weapons, however, were either used up or required new ammunition over time, forcing rebels to capture weaponry in battle, which both groups were able to do at times, or seek outside support. The government, on the other hand, was able to make up through requests for outside assistance what it lacked in personnel and equipment. In 1950 the lack of progress for both the CPB and KNU rivalries was largely accounted for by the decisions of outside actors to supply the Burmese army (Lintner 1994).

The Rangoon government was the beneficiary at this time. Support from India was followed by military assistance from the United Kingdom and the United States in response to their larger regional concerns. Just when the Communist insurgency was experiencing its second bout of splintering, the government was consolidating. By the end of 1950, in a little less than a year, Rangoon was able to reestablish control over all towns seized by the Communist groups in the previous two years (Lintner 1994), creating a lull in the previously hot conflict that lasted until 1968. The Communists were certainly not defeated, but their effectiveness waned.

In 1953, the dominant Communist faction, the CPB, reached out for external assistance. The Communist revolution in China had succeeded, resulting in the fleeing Kuomintang taking up residence in northeastern Burma. The CPB sought assistance from China while, interestingly, offering to combine forces with Rangoon to defeat the KMT rebels (Lintner 1994). Both requests fell on deaf ears, although China was indeed sympathetic to the CPB's cause. At the time, however, the Chinese were not willing to risk alienating the Burmese government, which itself was battling the KMT.

The CPB shrunk significantly following government successes through the late 1950s and 1960s. However, the New Year's Day offensive in 1968, which was launched by the CPB from China, brought about a period of relative strength for the CPB, where it effectively gained control over most of northeastern Burma, including the Wa hills. The capacity of the CPB at this time included twenty-three thousand armed rebels. It was at this time that the Wa were incorporated into the CPB army (UCDP/PRIO 2014).

China made the decision to provide aid, weaponry, and training to the CPB in 1968, which led to the CPB offensive that proved successful until the Chinese again changed their view and policy regarding Burma. In the meantime, the new capacity of the CPB allowed them to challenge the Rangoon government successfully, to the extent that by the mid-1970s they controlled a twenty-thousand-square-kilometer section of northeastern Burma (Lintner 1994). Further, China was also willing to provide weapons to other groups, including the Kachin, as long as they recognized the CPB as the dominant insurgent group. Failing to make progress in northeastern Burma given the renewed strength of the CPB and its allies, the government shifted its attention to the floundering Red Flags in the Irrawaddy delta in 1970. Government troops forced the Red Flags to withdraw in 1975 (UCDP/PRIO 2014).

Rangoon, having experienced its earlier bout of military defection, worked to consolidate and grow its forces as well. In the mid-1970s, there was a rumored division within the armed forces of Burma between those operating against the ethnic insurgents in the frontier regions (led by General Tin U) and those operating in and around Rangoon. As a result, Ne Win purged the military of the pro–Tin U supporters, effectively consolidating the military and its loyalty even further (Lintner 1990; Maung 1990; Silverstein 1997; Schock 1999). In 1991, it appeared that Ne Win once again had some concerns over the loyalty of his military, resulting in orders to "shoot deserters on the spot" (Lintner 1991). This order came at a time when the government was engaged frequently with ethnic rebels and among some reports that local militias had joined the insurgencies (Lintner 1991). The Rangoon government also formed local militias, called the Ka Kwe Ye (KKY) or "home guards," to increase its numbers. The first KKY was set up in 1963 to combat the Shan (C. Brown 1999). In addition, the military had grown in size dramatically over time and became more pervasive in Burmese society (Lintner 1994). In the period following the pro-democracy movement, the army had grown to twice its earlier size, approximately 380,000 (*Economist* 2005). This, coupled with the junta's willingness to sacrifice civilians in its campaign against ethnic rebels, brought many groups engaged in armed conflict to accept ceasefires even without political concessions.

In 1979, the CPB was forced to find other avenues of funding when the Chinese decided to decrease their aid and assistance. This led the CPB to also take advantage of the lucrative opium trade, as their territory accounted for a significant amount of the opium fields (C. Brown 1999). Earlier CPB leadership had been against participating in the drug trade. The assistance of China was further reduced in the late 1980s. With the Burmese government courting investors and providing access to resources, China was anxious to take part. As a result, the CPB and Kachin leaders were pressured by their former financiers to retire to the Yunnan province inside Chinese borders. A CPB ceasefire with Rangoon was finally reached in 1989. This prompted the Kachin to follow suit, but not until a June 1992 Kachin offensive into northwest Burma had failed (Lintner 1993). With a significant loss in group capacity, both the CPB and Kachin were brought to the table. No political concessions were offered, but the offensive against them stopped.

The 1979 shift in Chinese policy resulted in a de-escalatory phase for the CPB, bringing about what appeared to be the ultimate termination of the conflict in 1989. A short-lived Communist-inspired All Burma Student's Democratic Front (ABSDF) took up arms against the government following nonviolent demonstrations in 1988 that resulted in government repression,[2] but this armed conflict with the government was terminated as many of their collaborators began negotiating agreements with the State Law and Order Restoration Council (SLORC).

The UWSA also claimed large numbers, having emerged from the CPB. According to the *Wall Street Journal* (2010), the Wa have a private army of as many as twenty thousand. The UWSA was able to take advantage of the splintering and then the demise of the CPB, as well as the surrender of the drug lord Khun Sa (Shan United Army), and expanded its operations (Cornwell 2005). The Communist armed rivalry may be terminated, but Wa activity continues.

Ethnic Rivalries

Despite theoretical expectations, ethnic conflicts have been long in duration and equally intense at times. Although the government has not been engaged in a battle for its survival (the only exception being the Karen's unsuccessful push toward Rangoon early in its conflict), it is clear that the animosities between various ethnic insurgents, the Karen and Rohingya (discussed further below) in particular, served as fuel for the fire. The military's willingness to target civilians as a tactical choice has demonstrated such. The length of these rebellions in light of the nature of the conflicts can also be attributed to the country's terrain, which was addressed previously. Each of these ethnic insurrections was able to take advantage of the mountainous and jungle terrain that they call home.

Karen. The Karen National United Party emerged in the delta working closely with the CPB, sharing the Rangoon government as a common enemy (UCDP/ PRIO 2014). The first period of escalation coincided with that of the CPB and Red Flags in a display of intergroup collaboration, where they effectively took over parts of eastern and central Burma where much of the Karen population lived. The KNDO, which also gained experience fighting in World War II, began with the same conventional warfare approach as the CPB but shifted to guerrilla warfare after losing a May 1949 battle over Insein (Lintner 1994). Following a few years of heavy fighting, a lull emerged until 1955, when the KNU of eastern Burma experienced a renewed campaign by Rangoon against their remaining strongholds (Lintner 1994). By 1956, it appeared the Karen were close to defeat along with the CPB, although it was at this point that the Karen (and the Mon) were able to establish rebel camps in neighboring Thailand. The conflict continued, however, and escalated again in 1971 as the KNUP, an armed faction within the Karen conflict, cooperated with the CPB. With the conclusion of the Communist hold in the delta in 1975, the KNUP was forced to reunite with its KNU counterparts in the east.

A subsequent government offensive in early 1984 led to another period of escalation for the Karen conflict (Lintner 1994). What followed was a series of government offensives, with the army capturing more Karen territory. The Myanmar offensive against the Karen began in 1989 and brought about the fall of Manerplaw (Rajah 2002). Fighting between ethnic insurgents and the Rangoon government was the norm during 1991. Pursuing rebels gave the government something of a diversion from repressing political dissent in Rangoon and elsewhere. What seemed to have shifted at the time, however, was the location of fighting, which was taking place in the Irrawaddy delta (ironically, where much of the fighting took place early in the CPB and Karen conflicts), not in the border areas (Lintner 1991). This shift was the result of a Karen offensive to break out of their limited Manerplaw stronghold and extend their influence west toward Rangoon.

In 2004, the KNU was engaged in discussions with General Khin Nyunt, preparing to settle on a ceasefire arrangement. He was relieved of his duties at that time (which appeared to be the result of division within the government), and the KNU returned home (*Economist* 2004). Conflict escalated dramatically around 2005 when the military moved the capital to Pyinmana (Mullany et al. 2008), and the SLORC began a violent campaign of forced removal of Karen from eastern Burma (Human Rights Watch 2005).

The KNDO, KNU's militia, boasted large numbers as well (nearly twelve thousand in the early 1950s according to Lintner [1994]). It too began with conventional warfare and, for the same reason, moved to embrace guerrilla warfare around the same time as the CPB, although not entirely. Having once established a base of operations in Manerplaw, they continued to employ conventional warfare tactics until the fall of that base in 1992 (Rajah 2002). As one of the last ceasefire holdout groups, the Karen were able to draw popular support from the civilian Karen population, numbering 2,122,825 (6.2 percent of the total population), according to the government's 1983 census (Silverstein 1997).[3]

The cohesiveness of the Karen, or lack thereof at times, had also impacted the conflict and its progression. Although several Karen groups emerged early in its history, particularly as the Karen resistance was split between those in the eastern hills and those in the Irrawaddy delta, the factions continued to collaborate against the central government. This geographic split, later involving a political orientation division as well, meant that the government could focus in either one direction or the other. In other words, the Karen power in numbers was indeed diminished because the force was not concentrated. This is what the government did when it focused on the Karen in the Irrawaddy delta (along with the Red Flags) in the early 1970s. The KNU forces were compelled to flee and join their KNU counterparts in 1975.

A more significant splinter, however, occurred when the Buddhist elements in the KNU perceived their Christian leadership as unrepresentative of all Karen and defected to the Burma military following a decision to build sacred sites, pagodas in particular, in Karen-held territory (Hayami 2011). Later this group created the DKBA (1994), which agreed to a ceasefire with Rangoon the following year. Before this, however, the Buddhist Karen led the Myanmar military through the minefields surrounding Manerplaw, leading to its fall (Rajah 2002). After the ceasefire of 1995, the DKBA also aligned itself with Rangoon and actually took up arms against their Karen brothers of the KNU.

In addition, the inability of the central government to control the frontier areas allowed insurgents to set up tollgates gathering revenue by taxing trade on jade, teak, and opium, among other resources (Ballentine and Nitzschke 2003). As mentioned, the drug trade has been a significant revenue generator for many rebel groups. Although the KNU did not participate in the drug trade (Grundy-Warr 1993), the Shan and the Wa did. The ability to participate in the drug trade within the Golden Triangle has allowed rebel groups to purchase weapons to continue their conflicts, but it has also created divergent interests. Khun Sa, for example, reached the top of the wanted list of the U.S. Drug Enforcement Administration (DEA) for his participation in the drug trade. Although the SUA, Khun Sa's Shan United Army, had the appearance of an insurgent group in pursuit of political goals, the interests of Khun Sa and those around him became increasingly led by the motive to increase profits (Cornwell 2005). Several of the armed conflicts have been transformed in this regard with insurgent armies, warlords, and the state benefiting from continued violence (C. Brown 1999).

Myanmar has been the benefactor of outside assistance many times through its history (Holliday 2005). Often this assistance has come at crucial times. This occurred early on with India, but also more recently in the post-1988 election

debacle.[4] Trade and support from its regional partners provided the central government with the resources it needed to continue to repress dissent and wage
warfare against those groups that have fought ceasefire arrangements. The recent
development of a pipeline from Arakan through Myanmar to China's Yunnan
province is expected to provide the Myanmar military with at least $29 billion
over the next thirty years (Jagan 2009). It has also benefited the government
in that it drew China's support of a UN Security Council veto of a measure that
would have required the country to release all political prisoners, engage in dialogue, and end widespread human rights abuses (UN News Centre 2007). The
Myanmar army continues to receive and purchase weapons from China, Russia,
Ukraine, and Singapore (Jane's 2012), which has allowed the army to increase
its capacity.

The 1989 timber agreement between Burma and Thailand was a serious blow
to the KNU rebels, who had been operating in the previously rebel-friendly Thailand (Grundy-Warr 1993). The Karen and Mon (a conflict not covered here) had
been able to operate from bases in Thailand and purchase weapons since 1953,
which had dramatically increased their capacity. While Thailand continued to
push its neighbor to come to talks with the rebels because of its history with
these groups, the change in policy also gave permission for the Burmese army
to pursue those rebels across the border. Thailand further moved to assist its
neighbor in 2003 with the repatriating of refugees and illegal immigrants in an
agreement that also promoted cooperative trade and drug eradication activities
(Yin Hlaing 2004).

Because of the resource opportunities and the Association of Southeast Asian
Nations (ASEAN) policy of constructive engagement (Holliday 2005; *Economist*
1992), the SLORC named Thailand, China, Pakistan, and Singapore as its supporters. Even Japan, which originally suspended aid in light of the 1988 uprising, refused to join in the Western boycott because of its interests in the country
(Schock 1999). Demonstrating that this support has changed over time, however,
both Thailand and China helped to foment rebellion in Myanmar with the arm-
ing of rebel factions and providing safe havens at earlier times. When they did
so, those rebellions did well. A shift in their policy and their alliances changed
the trajectory of those conflicts significantly.

Arakan. An additional conflict was initiated in western Myanmar, by the Arakan People's Liberation Party but joined by the Mujahid rebellion in 1948. The
groups worked closely with the Red Flags, although that group was itself the
smaller of the Communist factions. The groups did well early on in their campaign. By August of that year, the Rangoon government could claim very little
territory in the western region bordering Bangladesh (UCDP/PRIO 2014). However, most of the territory in northern Arakan was recaptured as the numbers

of Mujahid dwindled from several thousand in 1948 to "just a handful" in 1950 (Lintner 1994). For the most part, the rivalry seemed to enter a lull at this time, although in 1954 some political concessions had been offered (Lintner 1994), suggesting that resolution might have been possible. One-sided violence reignited, however, in 1978, when the government initiated Operation Naga Min, a massive offensive effort to identify illegal immigrants (Kamaluddin 1992). The government effort caused more than two hundred thousand refugees to flee to Bangladesh (UCDP/PRIO 2014; Lintner 1994). The implementation of a citizenship law in 1981–1982 also contributed to the flight of people across the border (Minorities at Risk 2009). The mass exodus of refugees brought international attention and ultimately forced the Rangoon government to repatriate the refugees following negotiations with Bangladesh. A similar exodus occurred in 1992 following a renewed operation in Arakan by the Myanmar military.

In 1989, the Rohingya were permitted to form political parties and managed to get four members elected. That permission was revoked by General Ne Win in 1991, however, and two of those elected were arrested and tortured (Silverstein 1997). More recently, intercommunal violence and government policies have resulted in Rohingya fleeing or being forcibly removed from their homes. With Bangladesh and other regional states unwilling to allow for the same mass of refugees as in the past, Rohingya were confined to makeshift camps with little to no resources or have taken to makeshift boats in the hope of finding sanctuary, generating large-scale humanitarian crises in the process (*Atlantic* 2015). The armed conflict that existed early in Burmese history has been in large part replaced by one-sided violence by the government and communal violence between the generally Buddhist Rakhine and the predominantly Muslim Rohingya.

The original armed insurrection led by the APLP involved some two thousand rebels who worked closely with the Red Flag portion of the Communist rivalry. This allowed them to do well in their war against the government early on, but their numbers could not withstand government offensives. As a result, the rivalry was one of fairly low intensity, with the rebels unable to sustain their efforts much beyond 1978. Compared to other conflicts examined here, the Rohingya have been unorganized and lack international networks to bolster their position vis-à-vis the government (Parnini 2013). Further, the level of one-sided and communal violence was notably pronounced in this case. Although the Myanmar government has been quick to accept civilian casualties in its campaign against ethnic insurgents throughout the country, that is particularly the case in the Arakan conflict. The animosity many Burman feel toward the Rohingya helps explain the brutal nature of the interactions between the government and the Rohingya people of Arakan State. Rohingya are frequently referred to as Bengali, which suggests that they are seen as primarily recent refugees from

Bangladesh rather than long-term residents of Myanmar, which has led to the types of exclusionary policies identified above. These views are exacerbated by concerns that the Muslim community is growing too quickly and "threatening to take over" (*Guardian* 2015). Not surprisingly, this is the only conflict examined that did not involve some form of negotiated outcome in the late 1980s, despite the brief permission for Rohingya political parties. Much of the armed aspect of this conflict had been replaced by repression and intercommunal tension, although the Arakan Army continues to operate amid the instability. As of 2016, the Myanmar government has vowed to eliminate the group (Radio Free Asia 2016).

Shan. The Shan rivalry emerged later than those examined above because they had been promised a referendum on independence ten years following statehood. When that did not happen as expected, armed rivalry emerged. The Shan benefited from large numbers and significant demographic support. Although the Shan rebellion did not emerge until 1958, they were five to six thousand strong in the 1970s. They also benefited from a Shan population of nearly three million (as of 1983) (Silverstein 1997). Their numbers had increased dramatically through collaboration with the MTA (although its leader, Khun Sa, was ex-KMT). The MTA claimed between eighteen and twenty thousand members (Lintner 1994). The capacity of the Shan had been diminished, however, with the splintering of groups and its participation in the drug trade, which is ironic given that the revenues generated in the trade also increased its capacity in another regard. The splinter factions of the Shan have not always cooperated and, in fact, have fought one another at times, particularly when some of these groups became more defined by the drug trade and their profit motive than their desire for independence or autonomy. The ceasefire and surrender of some groups, such as the SSA and the MTA, was made possible because the government allowed these groups or their leadership to continue to engage in such business ventures.

When the CPB disintegrated, many Shan factions signed ceasefire agreements or joined the MTA. By late 1995, the Shan State National Army (SSNA) and even Khun Sa of the MTA were forced to negotiate a ceasefire with the government. The splinter SSA-South continued the fight, however, and proved to be fairly effective in gaining control of several areas of the Shan States (UCDP/PRIO 2014).

Kachin. The success of the Kachin insurrection can also be attributed to its links with the CPB. The KIA was composed of six to seven thousand members by the early 1990s (UCDP/PRIO 2014). As indicated earlier, it was also a cohesive unit. Although the Kachin population was only approximately 1.4 percent (Silverstein 1997), splintering was not evident in its history. They are located in the far reaches of northern Burma, making it a challenge to reach them for the

Myanmar army. The length of the Kachin conflict can be explained in large part by its location and its close cooperation with the CPB. After its emergence and coalition with the CPB, the trajectory of the KIA mirrored that of the Communist conflict, with a ceasefire reached in 1993. The ceasefire agreement with the KIA collapsed in 2011 over exploitation and the forced displacement of Kachin surrounding the Chinese Myitson Dam project. However, the KIA and Myanmar government continued to engage in dialogue over the dispute.

The Panglong Agreement could have paved the way for a more inclusive, less violent Burma. That agreement was abandoned, however, leaving the lasting impression that the government could not be trusted, which explains why groups held on to secessionist and autonomy goals. As discussed earlier, the goals of ethnic rebels in Myanmar began with calls for independence and the right to determine their own governments. Early success by the Karen, coupled with behavior of the Rangoon government toward the Karen insurgents and civilians, left them clinging to the hope they could achieve at least some political autonomy. For the most part, rebels in Myanmar refrained from employing terrorist tactics, with only a few exceptions (kidnappings in 1975 by the KIA and 1983 by the KNU, for example). Terrain in this case made for lengthier conflicts as groups were effectively able to evade capture or defeat over long periods of time. As the conflicts endured, and victory remained elusive, groups were more willing to accept autonomy instead of independence. These shifts in group goals made negotiation a more likely scenario. Negotiations did indeed occur with the CPB, Red Flags, Karen, Mon, Shan, and Kachin rebel armies in 1963 (Lintner 1994). The government, not surprisingly given its position vis-à-vis its rivals at the time, was unwilling to provide political concessions and set the precedent that it would provide concessions. It was, however, willing to discuss these groups' surrender. This pattern was repeated time and again. It was not until group capacity waned in relation to the government's, along with the promise that groups could maintain some of their territories and privileges within, that ceasefires emerged.

Intrastate conflicts in Myanmar have been dominated by guerrilla warfare on the part of the rebels and repression on the part of the government, coupled with calls for outside assistance to continue the fight. For the rebels, pursuing guerrilla warfare as a tactic allowed them to survive even as the Myanmar military became larger. The government, for its part, continues to employ repression because this tactic keeps it in power. Its approach, as a result, was consistent, and it increased in intensity over time. In the mid-1960s, the government began to implement the "Four Cuts" approach to dealing with its ethnic rivals. The military worked to cut off the supply of food, funding, information, and recruits to the rebels. "Free fire" zones were also established in areas heavily populated with Karen, Karenni, and Mon. The policy forced villagers into the jungles, becoming internally displaced (Lee et al. 2006). The Four Cuts policy continued to foment anger and mistrust among Myanmar's minority groups, as it confirmed once again that civilians were fair game. It also communicated to the rebels that the government was perfectly willing to target civilians to achieve its goals.

The Four Cuts policy failed to defeat Myanmar's intrastate armed factions completely. As a result, a new phase of the policy emerged in 1989. The military regime encouraged ceasefire agreements with insurgents using a carrot-and-stick approach. If groups were willing to agree to a ceasefire, insurgent leaders were provided business concessions allowing them to benefit from trade in their area (legally), or the government would tolerate their participation in the opium trade (Ballentine and Nitzschke 2003). Agreeing to those concessions meant they were also aligning themselves with the central government in opposition to insurgents who continued the fight. Refusing to come to ceasefire terms would mean extra pressure would be placed on that group's civilian population (Silverstein 1997). The goal of this approach was to lessen the number of active armed dyads for the government, as well as reduce the chances of rebel group coalitions forming. When the government adopted this policy, fifteen insurgent groups accepted the ceasefire (Silverstein 1997). During these ceasefire discussions, political concessions were not on the table, but the promise to participate in a national convention was. These promises have yet to amount to much. As a result, subsequent negotiations followed, including the October 2015 Nationwide Ceasefire Agreement (NCA) involving half of the country's rebel factions. Those that did not sign the agreement called for the government to end its military offensives and create "good opportunities for national reconciliation" (Radio Free Asia 2015).

CONCLUSIONS

Myanmar clearly involves a complex set of armed conflicts that have changed significantly over time. The theoretical framework put forth has proved to be an effective tool for understanding how and why they have changed in the way they have. Static factors, such as terrain, cultural aspects, and historical experiences, have created an environment conducive to guerrilla warfare that can persist, despite the increasingly repressive tactics employed by the government. It is also evident that the capacity of groups relative to that of the government has influenced conflict trajectory. When groups benefited from large numbers in comparison to those of the government, they were able to do well on the battlefield. When outside assistance was provided, it allowed groups to survive and sometimes flourish, even when a growing military was on the offensive, as did intergroup collaborations. When the tide of outside intervention shifted, however, insurgencies were diminished and intergroup fighting emerged.

Rebel groups' capacities have been significantly influenced and improved through intergroup collaboration to an extent not seen in any of the other cases examined here. Although coalitions did form in the Republic of the Congo, the extensive sharing of resources, collaboration in battle, and the merging of groups into larger entities appears unprecedented. This allowed smaller groups to persist and larger groups to expand. In fact, despite the number of conflicts that existed and the divergent number of issues involved, intergroup collaboration was the norm, and intergroup conflict was fairly uncommon early in the Myanmar conflict histories. This changed, however, when the government actively pursued eliminating rivals through its Four Cuts policy. By breaking down intergroup collaboration, actively pursuing groups, promising economic opportunity to group leaders, and limiting external support to rivals, the government was effectively able to decrease the number of active armed conflicts that existed. Of course, the democratization movement emerged during this time, which served to perpetuate violence in Myanmar.

CHAPTER 6

Challenges of a Heterogeneous Population
Indonesia

Indonesia has seemingly been plagued by instability for much of its history. Its geographic position along a major trade route made it attractive for colonization and violent exploitation. World War II resulted in the displacement of Dutch colonial rule by Japanese occupation, followed by a postwar independence struggle against the Dutch as they attempted to reassert control. Subsequent disputes arose as to what the nature of the newly independent state should be: Islamic or secular, unitary or republic, one or many states. Since that time, instability has been rather pervasive, complicating attempts to study it. The Indonesian government has been persistently challenged with secessionist movements, ethnic and religious disputes, communal clashes, and coup attempts. Governmental response has typically been repressive. It is rare that the government has the luxury of addressing one incident of violence at a time. This is further complicated by the geography of the country, which results in a dispersal of violence across the archipelago's many islands.

This chapter examines violence in Indonesia and the factors that influence its dynamics. The analysis examines diverse cases of violence, including ideological conflict that occurred nationwide against the Darul Islam Movement (1953–1961), Permestas (1958–1961), and the Revolutionary Government of the Republic of Indonesia (Permerintah Revolusioner Republik Indonesia, or PRRI) (1958–1961), and the identity-based conflicts in the regions of the South Moluccas (1950), West Papua (1965–1984), East Timor (1975–1998), and Aceh (1989–2005).

GEOGRAPHY AND HISTORICAL CONTEXT

Indonesia is an archipelago of 17,508 islands, fewer than half of which are inhabited. The combined size of its territories is about three times the size of the state of Texas. The largest of the islands are Java, Sumatra, Borneo, New Guinea, and Sulawesi. The terrain that would be encountered by combatants varies by

FIGURE 6.1 Indonesia

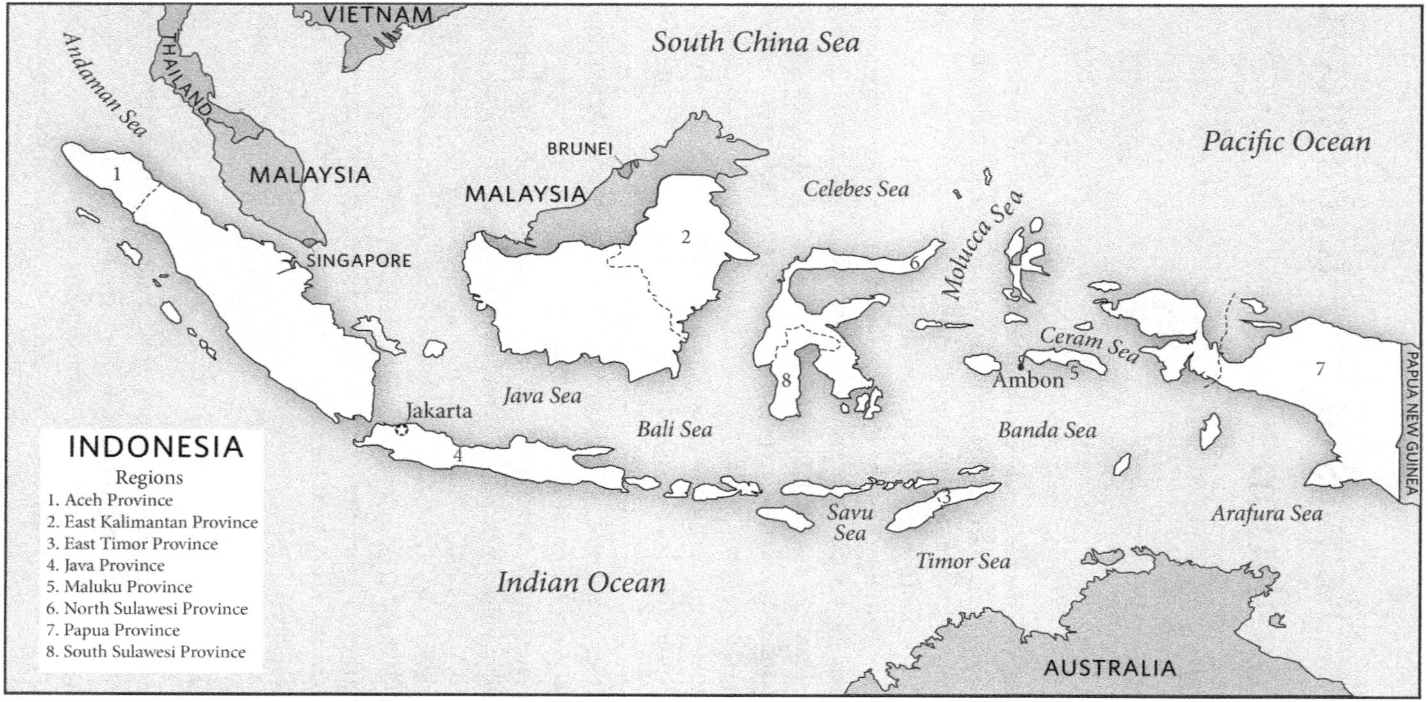
INDONESIA
Regions
1. Aceh Province
2. East Kalimantan Province
3. East Timor Province
4. Java Province
5. Maluku Province
6. North Sulawesi Province
7. Papua Province
8. South Sulawesi Province
Andaman Sea
THAILAND
VIETNAM
MALAYSIA
SINGAPORE
South China Sea
BRUNEI
MALAYSIA
Celebes Sea
Molucca Sea
Pacific Ocean
Ceram Sea
Ambon
Jakarta
Java Sea
Bali Sea
Banda Sea
Savu Sea
Timor Sea
Arafura Sea
Indian Ocean
AUSTRALIA
PAPUA NEW GUINEA
1
2
3
4
5
6
7
8

island and specific location on each island. Most of the islands that constitute the country are largely tropical lowland regions, with some of the larger islands also having mountainous highlands. The archipelago is located along the Ring of Fire, resulting in several of the islands being volcanic and relatively frequent earthquakes. Each island within the chain has its own sociopolitical makeup, cultural groupings, and economic characteristics, all of which contribute to the country's diversity. One author has commented that "many of [Indonesia's] problems still looked insurmountable [at the end of 2006], mostly because of the nearly impossible archipelagic geography and its implications for state organization" (Kingsbury 2007, 161). Thus, even in modern times, the country's island makeup creates challenges for governance. One of the most important implications of the geographic dispersal of the country is that the government has been challenged, at times, by multiple foes at the same time but on different islands. These opponents differ in character, grievances, strategies, tactics, and demands.

The country's islands are situated in the Indian and Pacific Oceans and are near the contentious South China Sea. Among the countries in relative proximity are Australia, Papua New Guinea, Malaysia, the Philippines, Vietnam, Cambodia, Thailand, and Myanmar. Given the neighborhood in which it is situated, it is not surprising that Indonesia was impacted by the Vietnam War and the growing importance of communism in the region. Furthermore the many different conflicts experienced within countries of the region have impacted Indonesian government and society.

Each island has its own religious, ethnic, and cultural identity. The country has been faced with numerous secessionist movements; some violent, others bloodless. In a few cases, these have been long-term activities that started at, or even before, independence. Examples of these would be the secessionist movements in Aceh and East Timor. A key division in Indonesian society, regardless of the specific island, is between the Javanese and those from other areas of the country who share the perception that the Javanese are unfairly advantaged in the system. The Javanese comprise nearly half of the country's population and are seen as being unfairly benefited in the system. They control most of the country's major government seats and corporate interests (Weatherbee 2002).

This is further complicated by the uneven distribution of natural resources in the country. The areas richest in natural resources are Aceh, Papua, Riau, and East Kalimantan (Tadjoeddin and Chowdhury 2009, 39). People in many regions were unhappy with the "New Order" policy of the Suharto government (1966–1998) that monopolized the use of resources in many regions of Indonesia. "People outside of the Island of Java . . . were particularly frustrated with the centralistic government. They felt that they had never enjoyed the benefits of development and probably never would because the people in Jakarta were 'taking and eating most of the fruit'" (Ananta 2006, 3).

Natural gas and oil deposits have been exploited and controlled by the central government, with the associated revenues largely remaining in Java. Each of the resource-rich regions has attempted to secede from Indonesia in what Tadjoeddin and Chowdhury (2009) refer to as an aspiration to inequality, or a desire for the resource-rich areas to retain their economic superiority. The anger over the loss of control of their local wealth has been exacerbated, in most cases, by the control of the resources by nonlocal representatives. Typically, Javanese citizens have been sent to develop the natural resources of other areas and to manage and work in the industries that arise. This has resulted in the presence of very wealthy, well-educated "foreigners" or "others" in the resource-rich areas. Furthermore, under the Suharto transmigration policies, many Javanese and other groups moved to these regions, with the perception that the natural resource wealth would mean better jobs and higher incomes. Some of the resource-rich regions have compromised with government on their secessionist demands in exchange for the return of a greater proportion of the revenues generated by their natural resources. Aceh has achieved the most significant benefit from its struggle, with a peace agreement promising the return of up to 70 percent of the wealth generated through the sale of the region's resources (Weatherbee 2002).

Religion has also played a role in instability. Indonesia has the world's largest Muslim population, with over 86 percent of its citizens practicing Islam. Because of this preponderance, one of the persistent debates in the country is the role that Islam should play in governance. Through its recent history, the national government has varied between efforts to restrain the role of Islam and times when it sought to promote its interests. As the country has moved toward a more federal system in the post-Suharto era, one of the major factors in the quest for local autonomy and in the ceasefire agreements has been the role of Islam in local governance. Christian/Muslim violence is not uncommon; however, religion is not the predominant source of conflict in the country.

Violence in Indonesia is so pervasive as to have caused some to hypothesize that it is inherent in its culture (for a discussion see Varshney 2008; Coppel 2006; Collins 2002). There have even been arguments that Indonesian culture and human rights are irreconcilable (Asplund 2009). Violence permeates the country in various ways, including communal unrest, government repression, coup attempts, religious conflict, harsh police tactics, and deadly vigilantism. While it may be an exaggeration to refer to Indonesia as having a "culture of violence," it must be admitted that the people of the country tend to be accepting of violence as a means for addressing problems. Some say this can be traced back to the colonial era, when corporal punishment was used by the Dutch to ensure compliance (Colombijn 2002, 51).

The country declared its independence from the Netherlands on August 17,

1945, but it was December 27, 1949, before it was officially recognized. The intervening years were strife ridden, as Indonesian groups fought the Dutch presence on the island, and each other in many cases. Indonesia's postcolonial experience was tumultuous. Even during the struggle for independence, there were some in Indonesia, including many Dutch members of the military, who felt that the country should remain part of the Dutch sphere of influence. In contrast, the independence movement united others against the common Dutch enemy. Once the country was free, the differences among groups came to the forefront, sometimes resulting in independence movements. These often resulted in violence and the need for the newly formed Indonesian government to fight battles on multiple fronts and on several different islands at the same time, spreading resources thin and diluting its capacity.

Many of Indonesia's conflicts come from the immediate post-independence period. When the Dutch, under pressure from the international system, agreed to relinquish Indonesia, an agreement called the Round Table Conference of 1949 was signed. This specified that Indonesia would be a federal republic, and that each territory had the right to join the republic or not. However, shortly after independence was granted, on August 17, 1950, Sukarno declared Indonesia a unitary state (Yaeger 2008, 216; Horikoshi 1975, 72). The state's identity-based conflicts arose from regions' desires for independence. The country's one ideology-based conflict emerged after independence, as debates about the role that religion would play in the new government stimulated conflict. There were some in the country who had thought the new state would be Islamic and were disappointed at the new government's secular nature (Arifianto 2009, 73–75).

The Dutch had also initiated policies designed to alleviate poverty in Java and Madura. Javanese were essentially paid to move to one of the less populated islands. The migrants were sometimes compensated with land rights or used the funds given to them by government to buy property (Tajima 2008, 458–459). These policies were resurrected by the Suharto administration's *transmigrasi* policies, which were intended to alleviate overcrowding and poverty. By one estimate, by 1990 as many as four million were resettled "to Kalimanta, Sumatra, Sulawesi, Maluku and West Papua" (Djuli and Jereski 2002, 43). The areas of the country that were attractive to the Javanese varied depending on what territories offered the best opportunities for the migrants; this could mean available land, employment in resource extraction or other sectors, or a perception that the area was safe. Families of migrants who have lived in the host territories for generations are frequently still treated as outsiders by those indigenous to the islands.

Lethal violence was also cultivated by the government at various times (including the independence movement and the purge of Communists in the mid-1960s) when it suited its purposes. In many cases where communal violence has taken place seemingly without a government role, it has later been found out that government provided support to one side or the other. The country is remarkably diverse, with cleavages dividing people in many ways: religion, ethnicity, region of the country, language, socioeconomic status, and urban versus rural dwellers. People are also divided along the lines of major political decisions facing the country, including the desirability of independence (national movement or for any region), the value of democratization, the role that the military should play, desirability of secular government, distribution of national wealth, the value of decentralization, and natives of a region versus those who have moved there from elsewhere in Indonesia. At one time or another, in various regions across the country, each of these issues has resulted in bloodshed. This incredible heterogeneity led Wirajuda to observe that "Indonesia is a multi-ethnic state-nation, which means that the state plays an instrumental role in creating the nation—rather than the other way around" (Wirajuda 2002, 17).

An important factor in the civil-military relations in the country is the violence that occurred in 1965–1966. After an attempted coup was blamed on Communist actors, the Indonesian government and citizens went on a large-scale purge of Communists, resulting in the massacre of an estimated five hundred thousand (Collins 2002; Bertrand 2008). Discussing the events that occurred at that time remains largely taboo, even in the media (Collins 2002). The lasting impact is a general distrust of government and the military due to their role in the carnage. An additional challenge experienced regarding the military was the doctrine of *dwifungsi*, which established a dual function for the country's military, adding domestic political stability and economic development to the more traditional role of the military as a protector from external aggression. This policy stood until 2000, when parliament dictated that the police be separated from the military (Tajima 2008).

Religious disputes have also been part of Indonesia's identity-based conflict history. Where Christians have tended to believe Muslims are attempting to shift Indonesia to an Islamic state, Muslims have accused Christians of campaigning to convert Indonesians to their faith (Arifianto 2009, 74). Because of the preponderance of Muslims in the country, Christians have been accepting of authoritarian administrations that have tended to be inclusive of all religions. They fear the treatment they would receive under a democratic regime or, perhaps worse, in an Islamic state. Muslims, on the other hand, witnessed the mass conversion of Muslims to Christianity after the Communist purges of the late 1960s after which Muslims were accused of having been aligned with the Communists (Arifianto 2009, 81). All of these issues, in addition to the shifting preferences the Dutch and subsequent Indonesian administrations showed toward the two faiths, combined to create deep distrust and animosity. A series of religious-based conflicts erupted at the end of the Suharto regime in 1998, which resulted in nearly ten thousand deaths (Tadjoeddin and Chowdhury 2009, 38). It should be noted that the degree to which these conflicts were truly religiously motivated is debatable. Because of the many cleavages among the combatants, some may be more accurately identified as ethnic, but that may be a difficult determination to make.

The long history of violence in the country, both communal and between groups and government, has left the people of Indonesia untrusting and feeling insecure. Distrust between societal groupings is the norm, with each fearing that the others are getting more from the system or are colluding with perceived enemies. Interpersonal violence ranges from episodic to sustained campaigns. Low-level fighting between individuals is so prevalent that scholars and citizens differentiate "everyday" or "routine" violence in the Indonesian context as that which is not tied to a major, sustained violent outburst (Tadjoeddin and Chowdhury 2009, 43–44). Government participation in massacres, extrajudicial killings and other forms of violence, and human rights violations have led to public distrust of both its intentions toward them and its ability to resolve local conflicts.

Vigilantism is prevalent in the country, and the penalty for thievery is often death at the hands of villagers. This was reportedly tied back to the colonial code of Indonesia, which permitted the killing of thieves (Hefner 2003, 1005). Historical government practices may have reinforced the public tendency toward fatal vigilante justice. The most remarkable period of time in this regard was 1982–1985, when government-sponsored forces killed between five and ten thousand petty criminals and left their bodies on public display to discourage crime and foster order (Colombijn 2002, 52). This was under an "Elimination of Crime" policy program, which is sometimes referred to as *Petrus*, a contraction derived from indigenous words for "mysterious" and "shootings" (Pemberton 1999, 196). The public practice continues today and, in fact, has increased in the post-Suharto era, as some citizens perceive government as being unwilling or unable to address problems. Through time, bands of *premans* (thugs) have roamed areas of the country providing security at a cost to villagers. The *premans* then give over a portion of their earnings to local government officials. Post-Suharto, there has been an increase in anti-*preman* violence (Giblin 2007, 521).

A related phenomenon occurred in Indonesia in 1998 when the country moved from the New Order of the Suharto regime to the *reformasi* regime of President Habibie. Part of this, under international pressure, was an emphasis on increasing human rights protections in the country. While it would seem that this would result in improved security for the people, in some cases it led to increasing human rights violations among the citizenry. In at least some regions and among some people, the perception developed that HAM (Hak Asasi Manusia, a translation of "human rights") interfered with the ability of government to do its job (Herriman 2006, 378). For example: "When a Muslim man who would later form an ad hoc militia asked an army officer why the military did not intervene, he replied that with only ten ill-equipped soldiers, they lacked the capacity to repel a mob of hundreds of Christians and that the military 'could not kill the [fighters] because of human rights'" (Tajima 2008, 466). Police and military personnel could no longer, for instance, kill suspected sorcerers, so it was now up to the citizenry to punish those accused of wrongdoings (see, for example, Herriman 2006). In other cases, local militias formed to address perceived problems because human rights placed restraints on the extent to which the military and police forces could act (Tajima 2008).

An additional observation about the nature of the groups in Indonesia is that the cleavages among the people have been reinforcing, rather than crosscutting. In Aceh, for instance, traditional Acehnese have tended to be agrarian, poor, and uneducated and to support secessionist movements. In contrast, the Javanese who moved to the area under *transmigrasi* are more likely to be employed in industry, wealthy, educated, and in favor of Aceh remaining part of Indonesia. Aside from potentially sharing a faith, which may not even be the case, there is little held in common among many of the disparate groups that make up Indonesian society.

All of these characteristics of the history of Indonesia and its current practices combine to create a cultural context for conflict that is both accepting of and expecting violence. There is societal distrust of government and the intentions of other groups. This combines with a lack of faith that government or any of its actors will protect individuals or groups to create a society where violence is the norm rather than the exception.

INDONESIAN CONFLICTS

There have been five conflicts in Indonesia that have met the UCDP threshold of at least twenty-five battle deaths per year. One of these was ideological, centering on the role that Islam should play in the country. The other four were identity-based conflicts in the South Moluccas, West Papua, East Timor, and Aceh. The most significant group challenging the government in the ideological conflict was the Darul Islam (DI) Movement, though the Permestas and the Revolutionary Government of the Republic of Indonesia (PRRI) also participated.

Darul Islam

The Darul Islam Movement emerged after independence as groups within society fought for different forms of government. In this case, the contention was about whether Indonesia would remain a secular state or transition into an

TABLE 6.1   Timeline of Key Events in Indonesian Conflicts, 1512–2005

Date	Event
1512–1602	Portuguese and British join the Dutch colonization of the country
1602	Establishment of the Dutch East Indies Company. Dutch became the dominant colonial power.
1825–1837	Dutch policy of religious neutrality shifted to favor Christians after Islamic-inspired rebellions (Diponegoro in Java, 1825–1830 and Padri in West Sumatra, 1823–1837) (Arifianto 2009, 76–77)
World War II	Japanese occupation
Post–World War II	Aceh: Acehnese initially embraced Indonesian independence but then grew restive as the new country seemed too secular (G. Brown 2005, 2)
August 17, 1945	Indonesia declared independence
1948	Darul Islam (Islamic rebellion; DI) Movement in West Java (Ricklefs 2003, 49)
1949	Aceh: Subdued by Indonesian forces
December 27, 1949	Indonesian independence recognized
April 25, 1950	Republic of South Moluccas: Rebels declared its independence
1953	DI movement engaged government in a short-lived conflict
1956–1965	President Sukarno's era of "Guided Democracy"
1958	DI, Revolutionary Government of the Republic of Indonesia (PRRI), and Permesta: Joined to engage in conflict with government
1959	President Sukarno dissolved the Constitutional Assembly and declared the 1945 Constitution without the Jakarta Charter (Arifianto 2009, 80)
1961	DI, PRRI, and Permesta: Conflict ended
1962	Aceh: Aceh received special region status, so it could govern its own religious affairs; Papua: Dutch handed the region off to the UN
September 30, 1965	Five top generals were kidnapped and killed. The Indonesian Communist Party (PKI), likely with Sukarno's help, attempted to seize power but failed. This was followed by a purge of Communists and ethnic Chinese, resulting in 500,000–1,000,000 deaths.
1965	Papua: Organization for a Free Papua (OPM) initiated conflict with government
March 1968	General Suharto removed Sukarno from power and was appointed president
1969	Papua: Referendum on independence (likely rigged) was held
1970s–	Aceh: Transmigration program brought many Indonesian immigrants to Aceh
1971	Aceh: Oil and natural gas was found in Aceh, increasing its importance to Indonesia (G. Brown 2005, 3)
1975	East Timor: FRETILIN engaged government in conflict

(continued)

TABLE 6.1 Continued

Date	Event
1976	Aceh: Formation of the separatist Free Aceh Movement (GAM); East Timor: Indonesian military invaded
1981	Papua: Operation Clean Sweep undertaken by government forces
1984	Papua: OPM conflict ended
1982–1985	Petrus killings: 5,000–10,000 petty criminals were rounded up and killed, their bodies left in public places as a warning by military personnel
1989	Aceh: Dispute with GAM reached conflict level
1966–1998	Indonesia's New Order period. Governed largely by Suharto, who was reelected repeatedly in uncontested elections. Suharto's transmigration policy encouraged those living in populated areas (particularly Jakarta) to migrate to less populated areas, encouraged with land grants to migrants.
1990s	Aceh: Another peak in transmigration to Aceh from other areas of Indonesia
1997–1998	Indonesian economic crisis
1998	Suharto regime fell, followed by violent conflict; East Timor: Conflict ended
1998–1999	B. J. Habibie president
April 1, 1999	Police force separated from the armed forces
October 1999–August 2001	Abdurrahman Wahid president
June 26, 2000	Moluccas: A state of emergency was declared for Maluku and North Maluku
August 2000	Ambon: International and national pressures resulted in the creation of a special joint battalion of troops to deal with problems in the region. Yon Gab troops arrived on this date, but they failed to bring about peace and, in fact, engaged in the violence against civilians (Azca 2006, 440–443).
September 2001	Papua: OPM entered talks with government
2001–2004	Megawati Sukarnoputri president
2001	Aceh: 1,500 died in the violence. This year also saw the most substantial efforts to negotiate a peace (Djuli and Jereski 2002)
Mid-September 2001	Aceh: Call to declare the GAM an enemy of the Indonesian state ignited violence
January 2002	Aceh: Special autonomy agreement for region went into effect
First 10 weeks of 2002	Aceh: More than 300 died in violence
February 2002	Aceh: A new military command approved for Aceh, and a decree authorizing a military campaign in the region was extended (Dalpino 2002, 89)
May 2002	Aceh: Laskar Jihad (LJ) troops sent to Ambon to support Muslim fighters against Christians. The LJ forces were supported by the military (Azca 2006, 439, 444).

TABLE 6.1   Continued

Date	Event
May–November 2003	Aceh: Indonesian Aceh campaign. Military killed about 900 GAM members and 300 citizens, arrested more than 1,800 (Charlé 2003, 22).
October 20, 2004	Election of Susilo Bambang Yudhoyono as president
December 2004	Asian tsunami disaster. Aceh: Devastated.
August 2005	Aceh: Indonesian government signed peace agreement with separatist Free Aceh Movement (Cochrane 2012)

Islamic one. It was an effort to change the Indonesian state's form and function, rather than to secede from it (G. Brown 2005, 7). According to Horikoshi, one of the most significant factors contributing to the movement was the "personal ambition and charismatic leadership of the DI leader, Kartosuwiryo" (Horikoshi 1975, 60). He reportedly believed that the area of the Indonesian republic was *daru'l-harb* (the abode of war) and that it was the duty of Indonesian Muslims to engage in jihad (holy struggle) to transform it to *Daru'l-Islam* (the abode of Islam) (Soebardi 1983). Kartosuwiryo's leadership was an important aspect in the capacity of the group. He was believed to have mystical powers, and his followers circulated the word that he was selected by "God to become the Imam of the World Caliphate" (Horikoshi 1975, 74). The DI adapted a traditional oath in which the faithful vowed to obey and support their religious leaders so that its members were promising obedience to and sacrifice for the movement and Kartosuwiryo himself (Soebardi 1983). He was not only his followers' military commander, but also their Imam and a person they believed was vested with magical powers. This mystic perception allowed him to mobilize the poor and faithful Muslims of Indonesia behind the DI.

Colonial experiences contributed to the religious conflict between Christians and Muslims. Early Dutch policies focused on equitable treatment of the peoples of different faiths in the country. This practice ended after a series of Muslim-led independence movements in the 1800s. After that, the Dutch openly favored Christians, granting them powerful positions in government. The conflict between the groups continued at independence. The Jakarta Charter was a set of clauses proposed for inclusion in the Indonesian Constitution. One clause read that Indonesia would be organized as "a Republic founded on the principles of the Belief in One God, with the obligation of adherents of Islam to practice Islamic law (Shari'a)" (Arifianto 2009, 79). Indonesian Christians were upset by the proposed inclusion as they thought it indicated an impending shift to an Islamic state. When the Charter was removed, Muslims were

TABLE 6.2 Conflicts in Indonesia, 1953–2005

Conflict	Groups participating	Primary geographic location(s)	Duration of conflict	Periods of outbreak of violence	Incompatibility
Darul Islam Movement	Darul Islam Movement; Permesta Movement; Revolutionary Government of the Republic of Indonesia (PRRI)	Throughout Indonesia	1953–1961	1953; 1958–1961	Government
North Sulawesi	Permesta Movement	North Sulawesi	1958–1961	1958–1961	Government
Military Leaders versus Government	Revolutionary Government of the Republic of Indonesia (PRRI)	Throughout Indonesia	1958–1961	1958–1961	Government
Organization for a Free Papua (OPM)	Organization for a Free Papua (OPM)	Western Papua (Island to the east of Indonesia)	1965–1984	1965, 1967–1969; 1976–1978; 1981; 1984	Territory
Revolutionary Front for an Independent East Timor (FRETILIN)	Revolutionary Front for an Independent East Timor (FRETILIN)	East Timor	1975–1998	1975–1989; 1992; 1997–1998	Territory
Free Aceh Movement (GAM)	Free Aceh Movement (GAM)	Aceh (northwest tip of the island of Sumatra)	1989–2005	1990–1991; 1999–2005	Territory

Source: UCDP/PRIO (2014). The table includes periods during which battle-related deaths exceeded 25. The Republic of South Moluccas conflict was not included in the table, as the number of fatalities did not exceed the threshold of 25.

offended and became distrustful of Christians and secular intentions for the country (Arifianto 2009, 79). Indonesia's Muslims formed their own political party, Masyumi, with the hopes that they could bring about an Islamic state through the political process, but that failed to emerge (Soebardi 1983). The DI was a country-wide undertaking, but there was limited coordination across the country's many regions. There were, for example, uncoordinated rebellions in West Java, Aceh, and South Sulawesi.

In 1959, after failed negotiations of the Constitutional Assembly, Sukarno re-instituted the 1945 Constitution without the Jakarta Charter and established authoritarian rule in the country. Conservative Muslim leaders were arrested (Arifianto 2009, 80). The most significant time period for this conflict was 1958–1961.

Permesta

The Permesta conflict emerged from the rebellious period of the late 1950s in Indonesia. Weakness in the central government had stimulated many regions to seek autonomy. In March 1957, an army commander for Sulawesi and East Indonesia proclaimed regional independence, resulting in conflict from that point to 1961 (Formichi 2012, 166).

PRRI

By February 1958, the Pemerintah Revousioner Republik Indonesia (PRRI) had emerged as another rebel organization. This one, however, brought together members of the military and groups that were previously seeking a political solution to the movement for Indonesia to be an Islamic state. The PRRI mobilized Masyumi, an Islamic political party. Frustration over the failure to resolve the question of the role of Islam, general mayhem in government, and poor economic performance contributed to the PRRI's formation (Formichi 2012, 166).

Ethnic conflicts have also occurred as regions of the country with distinct identities fought for independence from the government they perceive as being dominated by the Javanese. These movements overlapped chronologically, resulting in the government facing more than one foe at a time. Major groups associated with the ethnic conflicts include the Republic of South Moluccas (RSM), Organization for a Free Papua (OPM), the Revolutionary Front for an Independent East Timor (FRETILIN), and the Free Aceh Movement (GAM).

Republic of South Moluccas

The Republic of South Moluccas was declared independent by rebels on April 25, 1950. Fighting was relatively short-lived, lasting only about a month, and never escalated to the point of war. During Dutch occupation, the South Moluccas had been given special autonomy and were protected by the Dutch. Once the colonial power departed, the Indonesian military moved to absorb the islands into the new state. The fiercely independent Moluccans rebelled against what they saw as Indonesian colonialism.

West Papua

West Papua was a Dutch colony until 1962, at which time it was handed over to the UN and then to the Indonesian government (UCDP). One of the stipulations of the handover, referred to as the "Act of Free Choice," was that Indonesia had to hold a referendum in West Papua to determine if the population wished to remain part of Indonesia or become an independent state. Many citizens in West Papua felt that their culture was not shared with the rest of Indonesia and that they would fare better as an independent state rather than as a minority group in Indonesia. The referendum finally occurred in 1969 with the result being that the region would remain part of Indonesia. The process was designed and controlled by the Indonesian government, which permitted 1,025 elite Papuans to vote to reaffirm Indonesian sovereignty (Djuli and Jereski 2002, 39). This outcome stimulated violence in West Papua as pro-independence forces (Organization for a Free Papua, or OPM) clashed with those who wanted to remain part of Indonesia (UCDP). The violence in the area spanned from 1965 to 1984.

West Papua (also referred to as Irian Jaya in the literature) is the western portion of the island of New Guinea, while the eastern portion is Papua New Guinea. The area is natural resource rich, resulting in interest from the Dutch when it was a colony and from Indonesia after independence. It also was a destination for many Javanese during the Indonesian *transmigrasi* program, which led to local resentment of the resettled people. The natural resources came to be controlled by the Javanese migrants. The money generated from exploiting the resources was not distributed among the local citizens, but instead went back to the capital and enriched the government and Javanese. This exacerbated tensions. The island itself is separated from Australia by the narrow Torres Strait. Because of this geography, both Papua New Guinea and Australia participated in resolution attempts. Papua New Guinea was impacted by the conflict as the OPM crossed the border to set up bases and launch attacks, which led to some conflict between Indonesia and Papua New Guinea as Indonesian forces followed rebels into Papua New Guinea's territory (UCDP). Flows of refugees fleeing violence also entered Papua New Guinea, creating challenges for that government.

East Timor

The region of East Timor received its independence from the Portuguese in 1975. This was followed by violence as citizens who wanted to become part of Indonesia clashed with those who wanted independence. In spite of the fact that the majority of the Timorese did not favor annexation by Indonesia, military actions by the Indonesian government resulted in it becoming a province of the country in 1976. It occupies the eastern portion of Timor Island, which has natural resource wealth on its territory and surrounding seas. The Indonesian government feared that East Timor would become a Communist country. This led to twenty-four years of occupation (1975–1998), with East Timor finally gaining independence in 2002 (UCDP). The rebel group in East Timor was the Revolutionary Front for an Independent East Timor (FRETILIN).

Aceh

The Aceh region is located in the far northwest tip of Sumatra, the largest of the islands that constitute the country. It has been plagued by warfare since the termination of the Acehnese sultanate, with its fight against the Dutch alone raging from 1873 to 1942 (Kurlantzick 2001). It has been one of the most strife-ridden areas of the country (Tadjoeddin and Chowdhury 2009, 39). At the end of World War II, the leaders of the region supported the formation of Indonesia but were soon dissatisfied as it became clear the new state would be secular. Aceh was subdued by Indonesian forces in 1949, which led to its participation in the Darul Islam Movement in the late 1950s.

Discovery of oil and natural gas in Aceh in the 1970s increased its importance to the country. This served as a catalyst for later rebellion. Aceh is so resource rich that by 1992 it accounted for 15 percent of Indonesia's total exports (UCDP). By 1998, 40 percent of Aceh's gross domestic product was based on the oil industry. However, while the region was prospering from the oil resources, its population was suffering. Poverty rates in Aceh increased 239 percent from 1980 to 2002, during which time Indonesian poverty rates overall actually fell 47 percent (G. Brown 2005, 3). The people of Aceh have been frustrated by several factors: the government's failure to share proceeds of the province's oil sales adequately with the citizens of Aceh; Javanese control of the country's politics, to the disadvantage of minority groups; and military repression (Biswas 2009, 132; Bertrand 2008, 441). "Like other peoples in regions outside of Java, the Acehnese resent the fact that Javanese and other migrants seem to enjoy the greatest benefits from prosperity brought by oil and natural gas development in the province" (Weatherbee 2002, 28–29). As has been the case with other regions, the *transmigrasi* policies of the country have influenced the region's instability. Javanese were sent to the area to manage government interests in natural resource extraction. By 1990, Javanese born in the region accounted for 56 percent of the domestic population. Indigenous Acehnese (as compared to descendants of Javanese migrants) have dramatically lower incomes, lower educational levels, higher unemployment, and significantly smaller land holdings (G. Brown 2005, 2–7).

CONFLICT PROGRESSION AND DYNAMICS

Darul Islam

As mentioned previously, the Darul Islam Movement grew from the discontent among many of Indonesia's Muslims at the country not becoming an Islamic state after independence. The government faced a real challenge in dealing with the threat posed by the DI. The ideal of an Islamic state had great appeal to many Indonesians, and the government could not openly speak out against it (Vandenbosch 1952, 183). This conflict is unique as it spread across all of Indonesia while the others were geographically concentrated. In fact, there were occasions when the DI rebels would join with the regional secessionist groups (particularly those in Aceh and South Celebes) in struggles against the government (Weatherbee 2002; Van Bruinessen n.d.). The DI was a national-level movement that consisted of supportive groups in the many different regions of the country. It was particularly powerful in West Java. At times, DI would turn its violence on the citizenry, killing Christians, Communists, or Indonesian nationalists as they marauded through the country. On August 7, 1949, Kartosuwiryo refused to put his DI troops under governmental command and declared the creation of an Islamic state. He argued that the government was committing crimes against Islam, as they had failed to develop an Islamic state at independence. DI evolved to have regional political and military commands in Aceh, Sumatra, Kalimantan, Sulawesi, East Java, Central Java, Jakarta, West Priangan, and East Priangan, and two in West Java (Singh 2004, 50). At this point, the government was too weak to stop the DI's activities or even to understand the extent to which it posed a threat (Elson and Formichi 2011).

From independence to 1953, the discontent simmered and DI-on-civilian violence continued, but violence and casualties in the dyad between government and the DI were relatively limited. Throughout the time that the DI was powerful, it was supported by the Council of Indonesian Moslem Associations (Masyumi), an umbrella political party for the many Islamic organizations in the country that was fostered by the Japanese during their occupation (Horikoshi 1975, 65). Masyumi was a powerful force in Indonesia. Throughout the 1950s it pressured

FIGURE 6.2   Patterns of Violence in Indonesia, 1975–2009

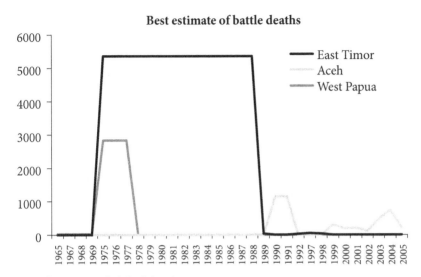

Best estimate of battle deaths

Drawn from Lacina and Gleditsch (2005).

the government to refrain from an oppressive drive against the DI. It feared that if the DI lost power, the Masyumi itself would lose support among Indonesian Muslims and fail to win elections. From 1950 to 1953, the DI's power peaked as the Masyumi sought negotiated settlement of the dispute, and the military remained reluctant to use force against the group. The Masyumi lost power in 1953 as nationalists and left-wing groups formed a political coalition, disempowering Masyumi and diminishing their ability to support the DI (Horikoshi 1975, 77). Violence by the various DI groups increased in 1953 but still remained at the minor conflict level as DI bands around the country burned homes and other buildings, assaulted rail lines, and destroyed farmland. West Java was particularly prone to instability at this time. Communists and nationalists there held demonstrations demanding that government declare all-out war on the DI and protect the citizens from lawlessness. However, other DI activities were taking place, with varying levels of intensity, in Aceh (which declared itself part of DI) and Celebes. In an August 1953 speech, Sukarno declared DI a threat to Indonesia and called for its destruction by any means necessary (Formichi 2012, 160).

    The next period of violence for the DI, which was preceded by an assassination attempt on Sukarno, began in 1958. During this period, the DI was joined by the PRRI and Permestas in their activities against the government (van der Kroef 1958b, 73). In January 1958, the Sukarno government was challenged as his top military personnel, many of whom were members of Masyumi and had regionalist tendencies, demanded that he replace his handpicked cabinet (Feith and Lev 1963, 34–35). Discontent spread throughout the country as Sukarno's legitimacy was challenged. The objection to the cabinet centered on Sukarno's inclusion of pro-Communists, which was consistent with his program of "guided democracy" policies in the country. Muslim groups in Indonesia were particularly against what was seen as rising influence on government by the Communists.

The problems were exacerbated by the conflict with the Dutch over West Papua (then West Irian Jaya) (van der Kroef 1958a, 59–61). In response to the disagreement, Indonesia moved to nationalize Dutch assets in 1957. Part of this effort included merchant marine assets, which Indonesia was eventually compelled to return to their Dutch owners. The loss of those ships decreased Indonesian shipping capacity and created a bottleneck in shipping that reduced both imports and exports (van der Kroef 1958b, 79–80). This caused economic deterioration in the country, which, combined with the costs of ongoing conflict, resulted in some areas of the country suffering near-famine conditions and water shortages (van der Kroef 1958b).

In February 1958, several generals (referred to at this time as the Padang group) demanded that the cabinet resign, that either Hatta or the Sultan of Jogjakarta form a new government, and that Sukarno return to his constitutionally mandated position (Feith and Lev 1963, 35). The government refused. In response the Padang group declared the PRRI as an alternate rebel government. The fact that the Padang group consisted of military personnel, some of whom were supportive of a role for Islam in governance of Indonesia, as well as being regionalists helps to explain the complexity of the conflict that ensued. Its main actors were the new PRRI, the DI (Islamic state), and the Permesta movement (regionalist separatists). The differences among the participants, however, proved more powerful than their similarities.

The DI was active in fighting that was taking place in outlying areas in support of the PRRI. During this time period the Indonesian military was spread across the islands, and many of its personnel were poorly armed. Concomitantly, the troops supporting the PRRI also lacked the capacity to fight the government (*New York Times* 1958). This was in spite of reports that the United States had dropped arms into West Sumatra in support of the rebels (Feith and Lev 1963, 36). The DI played a role in carrying out attacks in support of PRRI activities in West Java and South Sulawesi, as well as elsewhere. This was an important factor in diminishing the government's capacity to fight the DI in the many places it was operational. It was reported that at one point Premier Duanda's government ordered West Java officers to send troops to Sumatra but was refused on the grounds that they were already all engaged in the West Java conflict with the DI (van der Kroef 1958b, 73).

However, the rebellion failed to become a coordinated effort against the government, as DI in particular proved unwilling to commit its troops, and it lacked internal coordination of its activities (van der Kroef 1958a, 74). One example of this is the failure of the DI leader in Aceh to provide support. At the time Aceh had a special autonomy arrangement with the government, and it was feared that overt support for DI would end that (van der Kroef 1958a, 74). An additional challenge was that some of the PRRI leaders did not support the DI goal of establishing an Islamic state. There was also internal dissent within the DI about tactical issues (van der Kroef 1958b, 74). Furthermore, there was personal dislike among many of the key leaders of the rebellion and disputes over the distribution of arms among the many rebel entities and regions (Feith and Lev 1963, 38). All of these divisions within the rebellion kept it from developing the capacity it could have had if they had merged more effectively. So while the government's capacity was divided as it was facing varying levels of resistance from region to region, the failure of the rebels to unite deterred them from achieving the capacity necessary to defeat the government. Furthermore, as time wore on, though the DI was gaining support, its troops were fighting further and further away from their communities, weakening their resolve and perception that they were fighting for their own people and interests (Liong 1988, 876).

In April and May 1958 the government managed to retake Padang and Bukittinggi and encountered little resistance from the PRRI. By the end of May the tactics of the rebellion had shifted from traditional warfare to guerrilla activities on the part of the PRRI. By the end of July there were no significant towns left in rebel hands (Feith and Lev 1963, 36). However, the conflict continued. The poor performance of the PRRI and others in the rebellion in early 1958 has led some to speculate that their declaration of independence was a bluff, and the government successfully called it (Feith and Lev 1963, 36).

The rebel groups managed to coordinate more effectively in 1959 and 1960. Initially, this took the form of radio negotiations among actors (in particular, PRRI and DI) about closer cooperation. These eventually led to a declaration of a new governing arrangement called the Indonesian Federal Republic (Republik Persatuan Indonesia, or RPI). This new federation contained ten states, each of which would be permitted to choose whether it wished to engage in Islamic governance or not, which alleviated one of the major points of contention between the rebel groups (Feith and Lev 1963, 39). This cooperation coincided with the increase in violence in 1960 from minor conflict levels to war. The violence likely emerged from the combined groups' perception of increased capacity versus the government. The rebels were now able to confront government more effectively.

Supply issues continued to plague the rebel alliance, however. In particular, ammunition was in short supply, with rebels in some areas receiving a daily ration of only ten bullets by 1961. A major factor in the short supplies was the U.S. decision to stop providing support to the rebels in 1960. Low supply levels led to low morale, which further diminished the rebel capacity (Feith and Lev 1963, 40–41). Government offers of amnesty undermined group capacity as young rebels left to return to their normal lives (41). The combined rebellion of DI, the Permesta movement, and the PRRI ended in 1961 with the surrender of many of the rebels. Feith and Lev (1963) indicated that the ratios of arms to men in the conflict were between 1:2 and 1:4, which clearly limited the capacity for the rebels, regardless of how numerous, to effectively confront the government.

Negotiations for conflict termination were carried out by government (first by the army, then by a variety of representatives of government) and varied from region to region. The terms of the agreements were relatively forgiving, allowing rebels to return to civilian life (sometimes with three months' severance), and some leaders were permitted to return to their roles in government or the military if they swore allegiance to Sukarno (Feith and Lev 1963, 44–46). The DI continued to exist. On June 4, 1962, Kartosuwiryo and most of his top leaders were captured. Violence associated with DI subsequently decreased below the level of minor conflict (Singh 2004, 50). The collapse of the movement was largely due to its link to the charismatic leadership of Kartosuwiryo. However, another important factor was that, without support of the other groups to boost its capacity in the many regions in which it existed, the DI lacked the capacity to challenge the government effectively.

While the DI, Permestas, and PRRI are no longer organized groups that are threatening Indonesia, the country faces continued threats from Islamists and extremists who want it to become a Muslim state. Among the many groups that have been active recently are the following:

- Jemaah Islamiya (JI) was declared an FTO (foreign terrorist organization) by the U.S. Department of State in 2002. It has carried out numerous bombings and other styles of attacks since 2001. A number of Islamist groups have splintered off of JI and engaged in campaigns of violence.
- Jemaah Ansharut Tauhid (JAT) is one successor group to JI. It formed in 2008 and has attacked government members, police, military, and civilians. JAT has also robbed banks and committed other crimes to pay for its activities.
- Mujahidine Indonesia Timur (MIT) has been referred to as Indonesia's most active terrorist organization and has been linked to ISIL (Islamic State in Iraq and the Levant), JI, and JAT (U.S. Department of State 2015). MIT is based on Sulawesi but has been tied to terror attacks throughout Indonesia (Zenn 2013). It is a relatively small group, with only about sixty members (Alifandi 2015). It was designated a terrorist organization by the U.S. State Department on September 21, 2015 (Kerry 2015).

In addition to these groups, there are a number of supporters of the international Islamist groups, Al Qaeda and ISIL. An estimated four hundred Indonesians are thought to have traveled to Syria and Iraq to join with ISIL. In addition, the country's recent attempts to end rebellions peacefully includes the release of more than six hundred terrorist prisoners ("Discourse" 2015).

This should not be taken to mean that all Indonesian Muslims are extremists or terrorists. In fact, the vast majority are not. The largest Muslim group in Indonesia is Nahdlatul Ulama, with over fifty million members, which is part of an anti-extremism campaign and has publicly rejected overtures from both Al Qaeda and ISIL (Varagur 2015). A dynamic struggle continues in the country. At present, it is unclear whether extreme or moderate Islam will dominate in Indonesia, but given the large population, it is likely the religion will continue to have influence.

South Moluccas

The next conflict in the chronology for Indonesia was over South Moluccas. At the time of independence, many citizens of South Moluccas, including the approximately one thousand military personnel stationed there, thought they would become an independent state. When it became clear that this was not acceptable to the Indonesian government, the military personnel led the revolt, which was carried out through guerrilla warfare tactics (Nawawi 1969, 939). Their proclaimed basis for their actions was the government's failure to uphold the terms of the Round Table Conference (Yaeger 2008, 216–217). Additional motivations included fear that the military personnel would be targeted for retribution (in particular by Indonesian nationalists) for their role in fighting in favor of the Dutch in the war. The rebels also complained of economic deprivation. Part of the concern centered on the replacement of the Dutch-supported military troops on the island with Indonesian military forces, which would result in unemployment for many of the former military personnel. There were also fears about how the South Moluccan Christians would fare if the country became a Muslim state (Nawawi 1969, 943). Indonesian forces were landed on Ambon, the most prominent island of the region, to bring an end to the rebellion.[1]

Rebels on Ambon declared that they would negotiate with Indonesia under the auspices of the UN Commission for Indonesia. The rebel capacity was boosted by the support for their cause by citizens of the region, many of whom had served in the Dutch military. The Indonesian government imposed a blockade with the intention of reducing rebel capacity and threatened troop landings if the rebels did not relent. There were between 1,500 and 5,000 trained rebel troops on Ambon alone (*Mercury* 1950). Negotiations facilitated by the Dutch were unsuccessful. By July 1950, the government had started increasing its capacity in the region by moving troops to islands around Ambon, with a goal of surrounding it. The force assembled by the government was estimated to be 15,000 troops, clearly exceeding the capacity of the rebels, though they were well armed and trained. The Indonesian government initiated amphibious landings, but in spite of their preponderance of power, the rebels on Ambon continued to fight. By October, the UN Commission for Indonesia was bringing international pressure to bear on the government to end the fighting, but the Indonesian government continued to send more equipment and troops into the region. By the end of 1950 the leaders of the rebellion had been captured or killed, which impacted rebel will to fight, an important element of capacity. While fighting continued until 1952, it was not sufficiently intense to meet the battle death threshold of twenty-five (UCDP). Nothing in the research indicates that this conflict has recurred since 1952.

West Papua

West Papua was given to the Indonesians in 1962 by the United States and the United Nations after the United States brokered an end to an Indonesian campaign to wrest control of the region from the Dutch (Weatherbee 2002, 30). The inhabitants of the region, which is rich in natural resources, were not given an option for independence. The OPM was formed in 1965 by Nicolaas Jouwe, with the intention to "oppose Indonesia and disturb the security of eastern Indonesia's territory" ("Papuan Leader" 2014). Because of the natural resource wealth of the region, it was a desirable location for people to move to during the Suharto transmigration campaign. The result has been the marginalization of native Papuans, the destruction of their rainforests, and exploitation of the resources of the region (Weatherbee 2002, 30).

The typical tactics employed by the OPM included guerrilla-style attacks on both government forces and industrial sites, which were typically controlled by transplanted Javanese migrants. The OPM was not a very well organized, equipped, or trained rebel force. The Indonesian military repressed the movement with indiscriminate violence, targeting both OPM members and civilians. Tadjoeddin and Chowdhury attribute this relative lack of capacity to both the tribal diversity in West Papua, which undermined efforts to create a united OPM, and the fact that there was not a Papuan diaspora community that could provide funds and other support to the movement (Tadjoeddin and Chowdhury 2009, 40).

Violence met the warfare threshold of more than a thousand fatalities in 1976 and remained at that level through 1978. This followed Australia granting Papua New Guinea independence in 1975, which created concerns in Indonesian government that West Papua would increase its agitation toward independence. The Indonesian government stepped up its activities to expedite development and natural resource reclamation in the region, though none of the benefits achieved from this were shared with the local population. By 1980, the Indonesian government had determined that the Papuans were incapable of managing the oil industry in the region. It removed all Papuans from jobs in that industry and replaced them with Javanese personnel it deemed more skilled (Brundige et al. 2004, 26). When Indonesian authorities did permit locals to have jobs in the oil industry or forestry, they were paid poorly, or even sometimes forced to work for no pay.

In 1981 the Indonesian military engaged in a military initiative called Operation Clean Sweep, in which families and friends of OPM members were targeted with violence. In some cases entire families were killed. The goal of the campaign was to diminish and deter support for OPM activities. Government forces reportedly went so far as to use napalm and chemical weapons against Papuans, which accounted for many of the fatalities (Brundige et al. 2004, 29). The campaign created a major spike in the number of fatalities, which are estimated to have been between 3,500 and 14,000 (UCPD; Brundige et al. 2004, 29). In many ways these activities were focused on diminishing OPM capacity through reduction of the number of rebel troops, diminished public support, and interference with its ability to recruit and fundraise locally. As a result of this campaign, OPM lacked the capacity to challenge the government effectively, and violence levels dropped to below 25 fatalities per year until the late 1990s (UCDP).

During the mid-1990s, violence centered on the copper and gold mines in Freeport. The government has accused the OPM of hindering the economic development of the region. The OPM objected to the fact that the wealth generated by the mines ended up benefiting wealthy Javanese and members of government, with very little of it remaining in West Papua (Australia West Papua Association 1995). In 1998 Suharto stepped down under intense pressure to do so, at least in part due to the economic situation in the country, which was associated with the Asian market problems more generally. The OPM stepped up its activities in the aftermath of his departure, given the perception that the government was significantly weakened (reduced capacity). The Wahid administration (1999–2001) may have increased the level of violence in Papua when, in 1999, he allowed locals to raise the Papuan Morning Star flag, supported changing the name of the province, and promised the area freedom of speech. Locally based armed forces were angered by these moves and created the Papuan Presidium Council (PDP), which was made up of police, academics, and other elites. OPM activities received a boost in support (capacity) from the success East Timor (discussed below) had in gaining independence in 1999. Some saw this as a sign that the government would be more willing to grant independence elsewhere. In fact, a much higher level of autonomy was granted to West Papua in 2001, but this was not enough for the independence-minded Papuans.

In September 2001, the OPM entered into talks with the Indonesian government, which offered an autonomy agreement that the OPM rejected (Djuli and Jereski 2002, 40). The OPM claimed that the people were demanding separation "because of the central government's discriminative treatment against [Papuans], also human rights abuses and the wide disparity between indigenous locals and migrant people" (40). However, the negotiated settlement was the 2001 Special Autonomy Law for Papua, which went into effect on January 1, 2002, regardless of the locals' rejection of it (Tadjoeddin and Chowdhury 2009, 41; Weatherbee 2002, 30–31). The PDP declared the area sovereign in June 2002, resulting in an exacerbation of the violence by some members of the military against the civilian population (Djuli and Jereski 2002, 39). One of the fundamental problems of both the Aceh and the Papuan autonomy agreements was the provisions that grant the locals a greater share of the wealth they generate. The problem here relates back to the transmigration process and policies. While the agreements gave more money to the provinces, the control of those funds was vested in the elite, migrant population. The migrants to these areas have tended to gain control of the revenue-producing areas and assets, while the locals have continued with traditional farming activities. Transmigration has made it so that the majority population in both regions is not a local, indigenous population but the Javanese and Madurese migrants (Weatherbee 2002, 31).

In 2015–2016, the Indonesian government focused on a more positive approach to responding to separatist movements, including negotiations, granting of amnesty, and the unconditional release of political prisoners (including some high-profile individuals who had been in prison for over ten years). This approach was implemented in Papua, where the government began working with people and trying to build trust. At the same time, the government threatened the use of force if rebels continued committing acts of violence (Parlina 2016). The threat resonated with civilians, hundreds of which lived in a forest for more than a month in fear of arrest after rebels killed a military officer in 2015 (Somba 2016). The government's move toward peaceful strategies to resolve separatist problems is a positive one, likely stimulated by both the costs and failures of its previous military approach and the serious international backlash over the human rights abuses committed during those campaigns.

East Timor

The situation in East Timor began shortly after it gained independence from the Portuguese. The people of East Timor rejoiced in their independence, though not for long. Indonesia declared that the region lacked the capacity to govern itself and offered the East Timorese the opportunity to join the republic. The citizens of East Timor refused. This resulted in violence in East Timor, as those who wanted independence clashed with those who wished to merge into Indonesia. In 1974, the Timorese Social Democratic Association (ASDT) formed as a political party and began mobilizing East Timor's citizens to struggle for fair wages. The Indonesian government saw this dispute as further evidence that the area was not ready for self-governance, so in December 1975 Indonesia invaded. Large numbers of Timorese citizens fled into the mountains to avoid the Indonesian troops. In July 1976 the region was declared to be an official province of Indonesia (UCDP). FRETILIN, whose primary leader was Xanana Gusmão, formed as the ASDT transitioned itself into a national liberation movement.

Gusmão had started out as an information officer in the ASDT in 1974, became an armed resistance leader in 1978, and became the president of FRETILIN in 1981 (Cormick 1994). He understood that his meager forces were no match for the Indonesian military. Some of the regional groups in FRETILIN had to resort to taking the uniforms and weapons off dead Indonesian soldiers as a means of supplying the effort (Blenkinsop 1998). Gusmão said, "Militarily, we are very realistic, we don't dream of great military offensives. Our strategy is conditioned by the occupier's strategy. That's why our motto is: 'to resist is to win'—and not 'to annihilate is to win'" (Cormick 1994).

FRETILIN declared East Timor to be an independent democratic republic on November 28, 1975 (Capizzi, Hill, and Macey 1976). Fighting between government and FRETILIN resulted in at least a thousand fatalities for each year from 1975 to 1978 (UCDP). The Indonesian *transmigrasi* policy increased tensions as the East Timorese objected to the presence of the largely Javanese migrants and the unfair distribution of the revenues from the new industries.

The Indonesian government has been accused of committing large-scale human rights violations against the Timorese people. Its actions were so violent as to subdue the citizenry, which drove the fatality rate down below fifty per year from 1978 to termination in 1998 (UCDP). Both the United States and Australia supported the Indonesian policies for East Timor as they shared concern that the region would become Communist absent the Indonesian leadership (UCDP). The Portuguese supported the Timorese independence movement, especially after the human rights violations of the 1970s became known. The United Nations began to offer its good offices to mediate the conflict in the 1980s. Guerrilla warfare continued throughout.

After years of fighting, Gusmão was captured in November 1992, tried, and sentenced to jail. He continued to coordinate the actions of FRETILIN from prison, in spite of the harsh conditions under which he was kept (Blenkinsop 1998).

The Asian economic crisis in 1997 and Suharto's removal from office brought about an environment conducive to UN mediation, with the Portuguese and Indonesian governments participating. FRETILIN never had direct negotiations with the Indonesian government. However, both sides had reasons to support a ceasefire. For the Indonesian government, international actors were putting pressure on them to find a peaceful settlement for the situation. They also were facing domestic unrest elsewhere in the country and needed to resolve the problem in East Timor so they could focus elsewhere. FRETILIN needed to be freed up from fighting in order to raise funds, mobilize more Timorese in support of the group, and reorganize. The group also felt that the international involvement in the talks was a victory for them (Kammen 2009). In 1999, under the watchful eyes of the United Nations, a referendum was held in East Timor over whether they should remain part of Indonesia or become independent. The result of the vote was that 78.6 percent of Timorese (of which over 98 percent participated) voted in favor of independence (UCDP). The one-sided government violence that followed was some of the worst in Indonesia's brutal history (UCDP). Many blame the human rights violations that occurred on the Indonesian government, which is accused of having utilized local *premans* to carry out campaigns of terror against the citizens of East Timor (Tanter, Ball, and Van Klinken 2006; UCDP). A UN peacekeeping mission arrived in the country in 1999 and remained until 2005.

East Timor became independent in 2002, at which time Gusmão became its first president, as a representative of the FRETILIN government. Gusmão later became prime minister in 2007 as the head of his own National Congress for Timorese Reconstruction Party (CNRT) and served in that role until February 2015, when he stepped down ahead of the scheduled 2017 elections, in the interest of letting a younger cadre of leaders advance. Elections in 2015 resulted in Gusmão's CNRT forming a majority unity party by joining with FRETILIN. The position of prime minister was taken over by former FRETILIN member Rui Araujo ("East Timor President" 2015; *Jane's Intelligence* 2015). The potential for political instability had arisen again by the end of 2015, however. The president of East Timor, Taur Matan Ruak, was accused of being in the process of developing a new political party to challenge FRETILIN and the CNRT. East Timorese presidents are not permitted to be involved in a political party, according to their constitution. However, Ruak was argued to have been instrumental in the formation of the Peoples Liberation Party (PLP) with the intention of running for prime minister in 2017. In addition to the PLP, the Bloku Unidade Popular (BUP), an East Timorese political party, has formed as a coalition of five smaller parties. The PLP and BUP argue that FRETILIN and the CNRT are characterized by nepotism and corruption (McDonnell 2015). This competition in government is largely positive, however, as it illustrates that groups in East Timor are thus far content to resolve their differences through the political process rather than resorting to violence.

While domestic and international communities cheered the end of hostilities in East Timor, the negotiated settlement created major challenges for the Indonesian government. Many other regions, including Aceh, Riau, and Papua, saw the peace agreement as a sign of government weakness or willingness to compromise. This is believed to have stimulated separatism, which supports arguments in the theoretical literature about civil wars stating that governments with heterogeneous populations may be reluctant to negotiate settlements and set such precedents.

Aceh

At independence, Aceh was given a great deal of autonomy, but this was withdrawn in August 1950. From these early days the Acehnese rejected the formation of a secular government in Indonesia. According to Schulze, Aceh differs from the rest of Indonesia in that it was an independent sultanate until the Dutch invasion, in its ethnic and regional identity, and its "radical adherence to Islam" (Schulze 2004, 1). This led to its support of the Darul Islam Movement (discussed previously). The Acehnese also became increasingly resentful over time of the migration of people from other areas of Indonesia into Aceh, in particular those that were not Muslim or that came to profit from the oil and mineral wealth there.

In 1976, in response to increasing frustration and government repression, the Free Aceh Movement (GAM) was established. Its primary leader was Hasan di Tiro, who was a descendant of a family that was prominent in Acehnese government. He remained committed to the independence of Aceh and argued that Aceh existed before Indonesia, the Acehnese sultanate was conquered by the Dutch, Indonesia did not exist when the Netherlands withdrew in 1942, and that there was no Indonesian presence in Aceh in 1949 when the Dutch transferred sovereignty of the region to Indonesia (Schulze 2004). GAM's targeting included Indonesian political structures, the Indonesian economy (which it targeted to increase the state's fragility), Javanese civilians (which it saw as representatives of the colonial Indonesian will), and the Indonesian military and security forces (Schulze 2004). Di Tiro saw all of GAM's activities as being defensive military action, which included preemptive self-defense (Schulze 2004, 40).

Most of the leadership exhibited by di Tiro and other GAM leaders was done from abroad, as they lived in exile around the world. The top leadership therefore led through middle-level members of the group's hierarchy (Schulze 2004). They began a low-level rebellion in 1989 with attacks on military and police assets. It was 1990, however, before the conflict reached the twenty-five battle deaths threshold. This was achieved through the government's brutal use of force against members of GAM and Acehnese civilians. As predicted by the literature (Bueno de Mesquita 2005; Bueno de Mesquita and Dickson 2007), the government's repression actually served to increase support (and GAM's capacity) for the rebels from both the citizens of Aceh and the international community

(Biswas 2009). Government tactics ranged from traditional military maneuvers to disappearances and deaths. The period is known as DOM (Daerah Operasi Militer), which has been referred to as a systematic terror campaign that the government hoped would keep people from supporting GAM (Schulze 2004). This round of violence lasted from 1989 to 1991, at which point GAM was believed to be defeated by the government's preponderance of power. The organization survived because its leadership was in exile, GAM members fled to Malaysia and continued to train in refugee camps, and a new generation of recruits developed because of the brutal tactics of the government. Reaction against DOM was so negative that the territory controlled by GAM actually expanded (Schulze 2004).

As with East Timor, however, the 1997 economic crisis and subsequent departure of Suharto increased instability in the region (UCDP). Both sides were also influenced by the 1999 independence for East Timor. Government was further impacted by subsequent domestic and international pressure to maintain the integrity of the country. Hasan di Tiro became convinced at this time that all GAM had to do was hold their own and wait for the Indonesian state to fail. A GAM fighter once stated that they "don't have to win the war, we only have to stop them from winning" (Schulze 2004, 34). The government's heavy-handed treatment of the Aceh rebels was influenced by its desire to avoid another East Timor and to build a reputation of acquiescence to rebellions (Biswas 2009, 132–133, 141). During the late 1990s GAM was more successful than previously in its attempts to seize and hold territory in Aceh, resulting in an increase in capacity as the group was able to raise funds in the dominated areas and ransom kidnapped personnel from industrial sites.

However, GAM suffered from significant factionalization throughout its conflict with the Indonesian government. As mentioned, many of GAM's primary leaders lived in exile. Perspectives on strategies differed between the exiled leaders in Europe versus those that were in Malaysia or other Asian countries. This resulted in the most significant and persistent splinter in the group, when Majles Pemeritahan GAM (MP-GAM), a group led by Secretary General Teuku Don Zulfahri, who was in exile in Malaysia, broke with GAM. Another split in the group was between the relative level of secularity desired in the Acehnese government. Where MP-GAM followers argued for a Muslim caliphate, others preferred a more secular system of governance. There was reportedly another division within the group between the leaders in exile and the midlevel leadership on the battlefield, with those in exile taking the hard line about independence while those in-country tended to be more moderate (Schulze 2004). Finally, organizationally GAM divided Aceh into seventeen *wilayah*, or districts. Commanders in each *wilayah* had significant autonomy, and some even became warlords (Schulze 2004). GAM's leaders were united, however, in their desire to keep the factionalization of the organization secret. This arrangement held until it became clear that di Tiro's health was failing (about 1999), and a power struggle emerged among those who wanted to take his place (Schulze 2004).

While over time GAM participated in peace negotiations, it did not engage sincerely. Hasan di Tiro's goal in the negotiations was to internationalize the Acehnese dispute with Indonesia. About the negotiations, di Tiro is quoted as saying: "We don't expect to get anything from Indonesia. But we hope to get something from the U.S. and UN. I depend on the UN and the U.S. and EU. . . . We will get everything. I am not interested in the Indonesians—I am not interested in them—absolutely not" (Schulze 2004, 52). He believed that large numbers of casualties would cause members of the international community to intervene on Aceh's behalf, creating a scenario where pressure on the Indonesian government would be coming from above and below. Because of this, di Tiro interpreted international calls for negotiations, the willingness to hold the sessions outside of Indonesia, and the presence of prominent international advisers to the process as signs of international support for the GAM agenda (Schulze 2004). Both the Indonesian government and GAM continued to engage in violence during periods when peace talks were occurring. Each side feared that laying down their arms would cause them to lose leverage in the negotiations. In addition, both sides had significant factions that believed military victory was the only acceptable solution. The persistent problem was that many in GAM believed that independence was the only acceptable resolution to the matter, while many on the government side rejected independence for Aceh as a possible solution (Schulze 2004). Furthermore, on the few occasions when there was a cessation of hostilities, GAM used the time to recruit, fundraise, train, and acquire arms. This was particularly true during the "Moratorium on Violence," which was a ceasefire negotiated through the good offices of the Swiss nongovernmental organization (NGO) the Henry Dunant Centre for Humanitarian Dialogue that held from mid-January to July 2001 (Schulze 2004). Indonesian Army chief Ryamizard Ryacudo announced that the cessation of hostilities allowed GAM to grow from 3,000 to 5,000 men and from 1,600 to 2,150 firearms (Schulze 2004).

By 2001, both sides in the conflict realized they could not win. The GAM found itself in a changed environment (due to the international antiterrorism campaigns that followed 9/11) with dwindling support, which reduced its capacity to fight. GAM also felt that there was little support in the international system for further breaking up Indonesia after the loss of East Timor (Biswas 2009, 133). From the government's perspective, the international system was placing pressure on it, especially as the human rights abuses inflicted in East Timor came to light, to find a peaceful solution to the Aceh situation (Biswas 2009). Both sides became willing to engage in mediation. Crackdowns from the Indonesian military continued as negotiations were being undertaken. The Henry Dunant Centre for Humanitarian Dialogue mediated a ceasefire between the two sides in 2002 (Biswas 2009, 131). On January 1, 2002, a special autonomy agreement, referred to as the legislation of Nanggroë Aceh Darussalam (NAD), was signed by President Megawati and went into effect for Aceh. The autonomy agreement gave the region a much higher level of self-rule and a 70 percent share of the oil and natural gas revenues generated by the region. It also included a provision that Aceh be permitted to enforce Sharia law within the province (Weatherbee 2002, 29).

In spite of this unprecedented level of autonomy, the struggle continued among those who saw full independence as the only acceptable outcome of the struggle for Aceh. GAM leaders argued that they had accepted NAD as a preliminary step, while full independence continued to be their ultimate goal (Schulze 2004). In February 2002, the government established a special military base in Aceh and sent in reinforcements for the troops, increasing its capacity in the region. Over a hundred people died, and human rights abuses were rampant in the violence after the autonomy agreement was promulgated, with even human rights workers and prominent people becoming targets for Indonesian forces (Djuli and Jereski 2002, 42). According to some scholars, fighting in Aceh continued because the autonomy agreement was crafted to satisfy international demands for peace rather than to address any underlying grievances, such as "repression and violations of human rights by the military and police, perception of profound economic justice, and the social change that took place as part of the *transmigrasi* policy" (Djuli and Jereski 2002, 41). Locals were distrustful that the funds promised will actually be delivered by the government. Furthermore, much of the wealth in the area was controlled by Javanese migrants rather than Acehnese locals, which meant even a 70 percent return of funds to Aceh might not result in any benefit to the indigenous Acehnese.

Due to the continuation of hostilities, the Indonesian government declared martial law in the region on May 19, 2003. The government further increased its capacity in Aceh by devoting over forty-five thousand troops to the region, versus the estimated three to five thousand GAM forces, in an action reportedly patterned after the U.S. "shock and awe" campaign in Iraq. This, combined with the failure of ongoing peace negotiations in May 2003, resulted in a spike in the fatalities associated with the conflict, reaching an estimated 478 in 2003 and 738 in 2004 (UCDP). Outside Aceh, both domestically and internationally, popular opinion was with the government (Kipp 2004, 62).

Mediation activities continued with the participation of a Finnish NGO, the Crisis Management Initiative. The talks were initiated before the tragedy of the December 2004 tsunami, which devastated the Aceh region, killing almost two hundred thousand. To the credit of the negotiators and the Indonesian government, the final agreement did not predicate the delivery of relief aid on the capitulation of the rebels in Aceh (Rajasingham-Senanayake 2009, 218–219). However, it must be recognized that the tsunami had a significant impact on both the capacity to continue the fight and the psychological will to do so among the Acehnese. Rajasingham-Senanayake argued that this was because the outpouring of support from the rest of Indonesia for the Acehnese, who had previously felt ignored and uncared for in Indonesia, alleviated some of the secessionist motivation (Rajasingham-Senanayake 2009, 229). Another important factor, however, was that the tsunami sapped the capacity of the Acehnese to fight. Furthermore, international aid was difficult to receive and distribute so long as the fighting continued, which it did, however, for the first few months of 2005, resulting in about 215 casualties. International aid donors put pressure on both the government and GAM to reach a negotiated settlement.

The final Helsinki Agreement built on previous rounds of mediation and included provisions for the demobilization of GAM and expanded the decentralization of power to the Aceh (Rajasingham-Senanayake 2009, 213, 230). The European Union and ASEAN were designated monitors of the peace agreement, under the auspices of the new Aceh Monitoring Mission. The agreement laid out a new relationship between Aceh and the Indonesian government in great detail. It included discussion of human rights, disarmament, political participation, and an external monitoring entity (Biswas 2009, 134). Another factor that influenced the outcome was the Indonesian government's desire to be seen more positively and as a democracy by the international community (141–142). A significant influence on the Indonesian government's ability to successfully pass the provisions of the agreement was the strong political position of the government of Susilo Bambang Yudhoyono. GAM disarmed in December 2005, and by January 2006 the Indonesian military presence in the region had declined (134).

In December 2015, a group of about 120 former GAM members who had hidden in the jungles of the province and carried out small-scale attacks surrendered to authorities. They had persisted in their resistance as they argued that the region's leaders, some of whom were former GAM members, were not doing enough to benefit the people of Aceh (Agence France-Presse 2015b). From 2012 to 2016, the group was blamed for several attacks, including the kidnapping and death of two soldiers ("Amnesty Request" 2016). The group finally surrendered after months of intensive negotiation with authorities. They asked that government pay more attention to the victims of the fight for Aceh, especially orphans and former fighters who are living in poverty (Agence France-Presse 2015b). The plight of the Acehnese was highlighted by Amnesty International in a 2015 report, which decried the plight of those affected by the conflict and the government's lack of action to do something about it (Amnesty International 2015). Subsequently the group of rebels formally requested amnesty, which the government said it would grant assuming the proper processes were followed ("Amnesty Request" 2016).

CONCLUSIONS

Clearly, in the case of Indonesia the historical context is of vital importance. Many of the challenges that the government has faced can be traced back to policies carried out by the Dutch a half century ago. The conflicts and disagreements that have taken place in the intervening years have undermined trust, exacerbated tensions between groups, and created a profound sense of insecurity in the country. The government's frequent engagement in violent repression and violation of human rights has pushed people to a point where they feel only they can defend themselves and their kin. In such an environment, conflict is bound to flourish. This, combined with the country's archipelagic geography, provides an excellent illustration of the importance of the static variables in understanding a country's conflicts. The country's colonial history set the stage for ethnic, religious, and ideological disputes. The isolation of the many islands and regions of the country from one another reinforced the differences among its people, hindered creation of a sense of nationalism, and spread thin its capacity to respond to challenges.

The Indonesian case highlights the challenges that governments may face if they have multiple groups agitating at the same time. Indonesia had ongoing instability in West Papua, East Timor, and Aceh at the same time. Two phenomena emerged from this. First, events in the country or international system played out across multiple conflicts, increasing the challenges to the government and its capacity. Both the 1997 Asian economic crisis and the departure from office of Suharto in 1998 impacted each of these conflicts, increasing the intensity of violence due to increasing dissatisfaction, and Suharto's departure, which was both a symptom of and catalyst for the loss of the government's legitimacy, opened a door for successful rebellion. A second factor was that the granting of independence to East Timor in 1999 was perceived by the other two groups as a signal that they could achieve the same. In many ways, it was seen as a precedent that others could follow. Biswas (2009) argues that Indonesia gained the reputation for granting independence, which encourages others with secessionist goals.

Of the cases in this book, the Indonesian conflict in the late 1950s and early 1960s exhibited the lowest levels of violence. In fact, it has been referred to as "history's most civil civil war" (Feith and Lev 1963, 42). Given the extreme violence experienced in the country's other conflicts, this is both unique and surprising. This lack of violence has been attributed to the relatively high level of cultural and social commonality among the rebel leaders and their desire to change the nature of the state rather than secede from it or destroy it. They continued to support the institutions of governance. In our theoretical terms, the rebels sought a change in representation and policy, which contributed to the relatively limited violence. It also facilitated the negotiated settlement. However, this was unique in the conflicts faced by Indonesia.

There was consistency across the ethnic conflicts that the state has experienced. First, each of them was influenced by natural resource wealth in the areas that were inhabited by the ethnic populations. Desire to control those resources had a great influence on the government's actions in the regions. These included the forced migration of Javanese managers to the outlying areas, the control of wealth remaining with these few Javanese and the government, lack of economic opportunity for the indigenous populations, preferential land ownership for the Javanese migrants, and the human rights abuses in which the government engaged as it tried to maintain control of the regions. There were elements in each conflict, then, of both greed and grievance.

The Indonesian case also provides good examples of the way that capacity can be increased by the charismatic leadership of individuals. In the case of the DI movement, in spite of the group's significant losses to government, some members continued to fight until their leader, Kartosuwiryo, was captured. In contrast, where Suharto had led with much charisma for most of his rule, political events of the late 1990s and the Asian economic crisis greatly diminished his popularity and power. His departure from office in 1998 increased violence in both East Timor and Aceh, as the perception was that government was significantly weakened.

CHAPTER 7

Rivals, Conflict, and Ideology

Peru

The country of Peru borders Ecuador, Colombia, Brazil, Bolivia, and Chile. Its terrain is diverse, including "western arid coastal plains, central rugged Andean mountains, and eastern lowlands with tropical forests that are part of the Amazon basin" (U.S. Department of State 2009a). As is the case in many postcolonial states, the legacy of imperialism has been felt in a number of different ways. Peru has experienced a tumultuous political history. After Peru fought for independence from Spain, which it received in 1821, the regime changed hands twenty-four times between 1821 and 1845 ("Military Reform" 1992). Political instability has remained a challenge. Ideological differences play a significant part in the rivalries that have formed and their resulting conflicts.

Strife has also been layered in identity. Amid a diverse topography, not surprisingly, lives a diverse population of people largely defined by race. Although the majority of the population is indigenous, such groups exhibit disproportionately higher rates of extreme poverty than those of European descent or of mixed heritage (i.e., mestizo) (McClintock 1989; Strong 1992). The colonial legacy, involving political instability and differing racial classes with preferential treatment, creates the backdrop in which multiple rivalries emerged in the post–World War II era. The case provides an in-depth look at both episodic and enduring rivalries, all of which have resulted in similar frustrations. Despite the shared set of grievances, rivalries that occurred at the same time never coalesced and even sometimes fought against one another. Infighting among rivals in Peru helps in part to explain the conflict trajectories and tactical decisions that are examined here.

GEOGRAPHY AND HISTORICAL CONTEXT

A state's terrain can provide refuge for groups engaged in armed struggle against their government. This is certainly the case in Peru. The more remote mountainous and jungle regions of the country are where the bulk of armed struggle has occurred. All conflicts examined in this chapter have emerged from or otherwise benefited from the country's terrain. Guerrilla warfare is the primary tactical approach employed by most of the conflict actors in Peru as a result. It is not

FIGURE 7.1   Peru

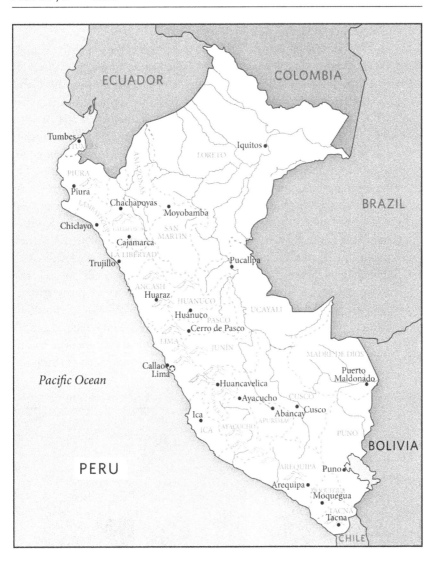

the only tactic employed, however. Why that is the case has to do with cultural cleavages that exist in Peru, as well as the ideological and organizational structure of the key rebel faction, Sendero Luminoso.

The armed struggle in Peru is also deeply a function of the country's cultural and historical experience. It has the most unequal land tenure system in Latin America (McClintock 1989). Further, poverty rates have been historically high. Some Peruvian regimes have made headway into this problem. In 2005, the national poverty rate was 55.6 percent. By 2013, it had dropped to 25.8 percent ("World Development Indicators" 1960–2014). As with land, the percentage of those at or below poverty is unequally dispersed geographically. Among the urban population, in 2012, the poverty rate was 16.6 percent, whereas among the rural population, the rate was an astounding 53.0 percent ("World Development Indicators" 1960–2014). This snapshot of poverty represents a clear gap between the progress of those in the coastal, more urban areas and those in the Sierras. Throughout Peru's history, as the country progressed it did so unevenly. This is illustrated in Figures 7.2 and 7.3. When the country experienced economic hardship, those in the lower socioeconomic strata felt the most drastic impact.

This gap emerged early in Peru's history but became worse in the 1950s and 1960s as agricultural production stagnated in the midst of continued population growth and import substitution industrialization policies took their toll (Kay 1983). This coincided with the shift of the dominant political party, American Popular Revolutionary Alliance (APRA), toward the right, which sparked the

FIGURE 7.2   Peruvian Urban and Rural Poverty Rates, 1970, 1980, 1986

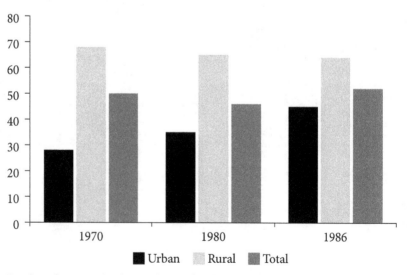

Data drawn from CEPAL (1990) reported in World Bank (1993)

FIGURE 7.3   Peruvian Urban and Rural Extreme Poverty Rates, 1970, 1980, 1986

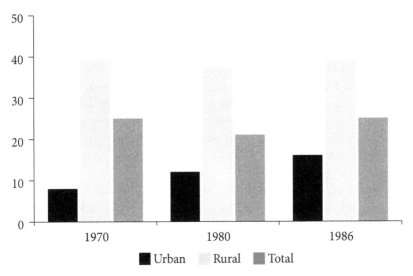

Data drawn from CEPAL (1990) reported in World Bank (1993).

first set of conflicts and elite-level rivalries analyzed below. As the figures indicate, Peruvians in the rural areas of the country have been significantly more likely to live at or below the poverty line over time. Nearly 40 percent were in situations of extreme poverty.[1] Poverty had increased for Peruvian urban populations over the time period examined here, but remained significantly lower than rural percentages. Further, by the early 1960s, 0.1 percent of the Peruvian population controlled 60 percent of the cultivated land (UCDP/PRIO 2014).

As was the case in many postcolonial, struggling countries, the poor migrated in search of work, which in part explains the increasing poverty levels in the urban centers illustrated in Figure 7.2. Migration to coastal cities brought with it the establishment of shantytowns. Governmental response to pervasive poverty and discontent in the Sierras involved efforts by the Belaunde government of the 1960s to provide modest agrarian reform and development projects in the high jungle (Crabtree 2002). These were ineffective and as a result failed to appease frustrated migrant urban youths or alienated peasants in the high country. Further, one of the initiatives to address underlying grievances had an even more problematic impact. In an effort to alleviate underdevelopment in the Sierras, the Peruvian government expanded educational opportunities for the poverty stricken. As a result, more universities were opened in administrative departments such as Ayacucho and Huancavelica.[2] Graduates of these schools, however, were unable to find employment as economies in these regions continued to be depressed and inequality remained, leading to further frustrations and political mobilization.

The Peruvian government made serious attempts to address this underlying inequality following the military coup of 1968 that deposed Belaunde. Under the leadership of General Velasco, Peru nationalized much of its industry, redistributed land, embarked on structural reforms, and more generally undermined the economic base of power of the old ruling classes (Champion 2001). These efforts, however, led to increased national debt and spiraling inflation. Attempts at austerity in the late 1970s gave way to renewed mobilization in the form of strikes and protest. Economic hardship continued through the 1980s, coinciding with the reintroduction of democratic leadership beginning in 1980. Inequality and inflation serve as the backdrop for a second set of rivalries that emerged at this time.

Inequality in Peru is complex. According to Strong, a tension exists between Western and Indian culture: "The idea that the vast majority of the population— Indian peasants, small merchants, miners, industrial workers, and wandering street vendors—is discriminated against racially is not even entertained. Yet their poverty, which stems from a history of economic stifling and exploitation by the whites, is dismissed as inevitable and their plight next to hopeless on the grounds of their race" (Strong 1992, 51).

Layers of identity in Peru involve where one lives, one's ancestry, and one's language, but in particular the indigenous Spanish identity is powerful, with significant implications for one's status in society. Ideology may be the mobilizing identity in the country, at least among the rivalries examined here, but the role of these other identities cannot be ignored. The animosities that exist between these varying identities may help to explain how ideological rivalries that appear ripe for guerrilla activity turn toward terrorizing civilian populations, the very people the leftist ideology sought to save.

PERUVIAN CONFLICTS

Peru has experienced four different armed conflicts with a short bout of violence in 1965 involving two factions and two more sustained intrastate conflicts that began in 1982 (Gleditsch et al. 2002). Each was leftist in nature and emerged over the same set of grievances. As a result, their histories are intertwined even when groups remained distinct from one another. Figure 7.4 illustrates how and when these groups emerged. The most well-known rebel faction to the Peruvian government is Sendero Luminoso, originally named Communist Party of Peru in the Shining Path of Mariátegui (i.e., "Shining Path"). Sendero's predecessor, however, was the National Liberation Army (ELN), which split from the Peruvian Communist Party in the early 1960s (Béjar 1969). In a similar fashion, the

TABLE 7.1   Timeline of Key Events in Peruvian Conflicts, 1945–1997

Date	Event
1945	Civilian government of Jose Luis Bustamante elected
1948	General Manuel Odria overthrew Bustamante
1956	Manuel Prado y Ugarteche elected with the backing of the American Popular Revolutionary Alliance (APRA)
1962	Military coup. APRA moved from leftist to moderate.
1963	Constitutional government formed by the Popular Action (AP) party. Fernando Belaunde Terry became president.
1965	National Liberation Army (ELN) and Movement of the Revolutionary Left (MIR) began their insurgencies. Neither survived longer than three months.
October 1968	Bloodless coup led by Juan Velasco Alvarado. Congress dissolved. Inca Plan in place socialized economy.
August 1975	Velasco overthrown by Francisco Morales Bermudez Cerruti
September 1975	Oscar Vargas Prieto replaced Morales Bermudez
January 1976	Jorge Fernandez Maldonado replaced Vargas
July 1976	Fernandez replaced by Guillermo Arbulu Galliani. State of emergency declared following unrest of austerity.
January 1978	Arbulu retired. Molina Pallochia replaced him. Constitutional assembly elected, paving the way for democracy. Belaunde Terry and his AP party won.
1982	Sendero Luminoso began operations in Ayacucho department
1984	Tupac Amaru Revolutionary Army (MRTA) began its armed struggle. Sendero's conflict intensified.
1985	Economic crises
April 14, 1985	APRA's Alan García Pérez won election. Economic crises continued. Government prematurely declared victory over Sendero. MRTA briefly suspended its campaign.
1986	MRTA renewed its campaign
1989	Victor Polay of MRTA captured, later to escape
July 28, 1990	Alberto Fujimori took office as president
April 1991	Sendero launched new wave of attacks
June 1991	Congress granted emergency powers to Fujimori
April 5, 1992	Fujimori dissolved Congress in self-coup
September 12, 1992	Abimael Guzman of Sendero captured
1993	Polay arrested
December 17, 1996	MRTA took Japanese embassy in Lima
April 22, 1997	MRTA embassy siege ended

Source: CQ Press (2009a).

FIGURE 7.4   Peruvian Rebel Group Tree

Peruvian Rebel Group Tree

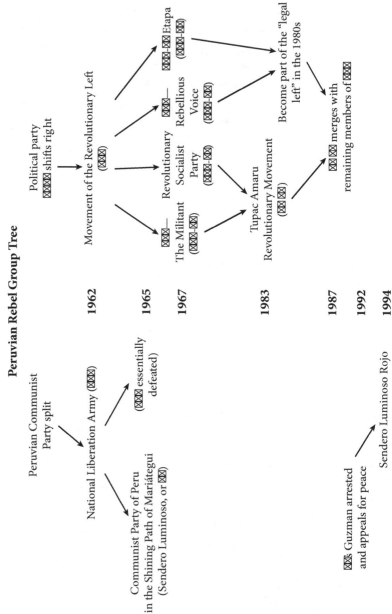

TABLE 7.2   Conflicts in Peru, 1965–2010

Conflict	Conflict dyads	Duration of conflict	Periods of armed conflict
Government	National Liberation Army (ELN)	1965	1965
Government	Movement of the Revolutionary Left (MIR)	1965	1965
Government	Sendero Luminoso	1982–2010	1982–1999 2007–2010
Government	Tupac Amaru Revolutionary Army (MRTA)	1989–1993	1989–1993

Source: Gleditsch et al. (2002)

Movement of the Revolutionary Left (MIR) emerged in response to the decision by the American Popular Revolutionary Alliance (APRA) to become more moderate in order to gain political power. In 1962, APRA decidedly embraced an anti-Communist and anti-Castro position. Further, APRA supported cooperation with the United States (*Keesing's World*, August 1962). Both the ELN and MIR mobilized in 1962 in response to the shifting political landscape and engaged in armed struggle beginning in 1965 (UCDP). MIR began its attacks from Cuzco and Junin, while the ELN emerged in Ayacucho. Despite the small size of these groups (discussed further below), each was able to survive for several months in the face of significant repression on the part of the government because of the terrain in which they operated. However, both were readily defeated by the Peruvian military, which appeared to bring these episodic conflicts to an end.

The ELN, however, had splintered when its leadership decided to take up arms in 1965. Abimael Guzman, along with a contingent of followers, broke away from the ELN, choosing instead to pursue a longer term, revolutionary strategy. Guzman became the well-known leader of Sendero Luminoso.

The MIR also splintered following the death of its leader during the 1965 outbreak of violence. Four separate groups emerged as indicated in Figure 7.4. The MIR, MIR—the Militant (MIR-EM), and the Revolutionary Socialist Party (PSR-MI) found more common ground in the 1980s, emerging as the Tupac Amaru Revolutionary Movement (MRTA) in 1983. A new armed struggle, and the fourth faction emerged. MIR was essentially defeated as an armed opponent in 1965. Those that continued to operate did so politically. In 1986, however, the remnants of the MIR merged once again with MRTA. Although both Sendero and MRTA were active during the same time period, and even shared the same leftist orientation vis-à-vis the government, they never coalesced. In fact, Sendero often targeted MRTA members and other leftist opponents during its campaign.

Both Sendero Luminoso and MRTA were engaged in more sustained conflicts with the state than the previous ELN and MIR factions. Although Sendero began mobilization in the aftermath of the 1965 armed conflict, it did not become an active rivalry until 1980, when it launched its guerrilla war against the government of Peru out of the Ayacucho region (*Peruvian Times* 1990). It is under the dire economic conditions of the Sierras, which were brought about by the inflationary policies of the administration described earlier, that this armed struggle took place. Although poverty levels and inequality in the Peruvian system have changed over time (in fact, recently national poverty levels have declined), the divide between the urban centers and the more rural territory of the country has remained. This division is central to the longest-lasting conflict involving Sendero.

Sendero Luminoso was organized first at the University of Huamanga in Ayacucho, a region that is isolated from the urban centers of Peru. As a result, the initial mobilization went largely unnoticed or was ignored (de Witt and Gianotten 1994). Later in the Sendero conflict, the group shifted toward northern Peru, focusing on the Huallaga Valley, where they were able to benefit economically from their role in the drug trade (discussed further below). The group built momentum during the early 1980s as the government failed to take it seriously. Conflict intensified in 1983 and 1984 as the Peruvian military turned its attention to the countryside in pursuit of Sendero rebels. By 1985 the government declared victory, albeit prematurely. Although numbers of casualties decreased during 1986 and 1987, Sendero presence continued to be felt among the indigenous population. Further, group activity spread to include attacks on Lima and areas bordering both Ecuador and Bolivia, as well as establishing a foothold in the Huallaga Valley, the center of coca production (UCDP). After this brief lull, Sendero renewed armed struggle in the late 1980s and early 1990s when the group's power peaked (Center for Defense Information 2003). In 1992, however, Guzman was captured. As a movement, Sendero continued beyond that time, maintained significant operational capacity (Palmer 1994), and even spawned the splinter group Sendero Luminoso Rojo. Its impact was significantly diminished, however. The group makes use of the dense jungle terrain in the Vraem region of eastern Peru, where the government estimates that 80 members remain in operation, though the rebels claim a force of 350 (Martel 2015).

MRTA officially began its armed struggle against the Peruvian government in 1984 (Center for Defense Information 2003). Unlike its predecessors, MRTA did not embrace rural guerrilla-based warfare. Its campaign began in Lima, located on the coastal flatlands. However, even in this case, the mountains provided sanctuary for the rebels. In fact, Victor Polay, the leader of MRTA, was first captured in 1989 in the Andean city of Huancayo along with forty-seven other group members (*Los Angeles Times* 1989). Prior to that, however, in 1985, MRTA had suspended its campaign following the election of APRA's Alan García, a childhood friend of Polay (Baer 2003). When it failed to experience the anticipated land reform, at least to the extent desired, MRTA took up arms again in

1986. The group was at its strongest, coinciding with the heyday of Sendero, in the late 1980s. Counterterrorism efforts of the Alberto Fujimori administration greatly diminished the power of MRTA by the end of 1993 (Palmer 1994), although not entirely. MRTA staged its last and most notable assault in 1996, when a group of MRTA members (numbering fourteen to twenty-five, depending on the source) stormed the Japanese Embassy in Lima and took approximately five hundred people hostage. The siege continued for 126 days, after which Fujimori, having refused any of the hostage takers' demands, used commandos to retake the embassy (CQ Press 2009a). All MRTA members were killed along with one hostage (Center for Defense Information 2003). The group continues to exist, although its armed approach appears to have ended. Its focus has changed in light of the 1996 embassy attack. Rather than engage in armed insurrection, members work to call attention to random arrests, decry human rights violations of those imprisoned, and seek the release of jailed MRTA leaders (Baer 2003).

Each of the conflicts that have occurred in Peru is ideological in nature, with various forms of identity woven throughout. This complicates the typical tactical choice assumptions that have been made to this point. Ideological battles over the state are likely to be particularly intense and enduring. That is certainly true for Sendero Luminoso, although less so for MRTA. It was not the case for the ELN or MIR. These groups, however, lacked the capacity of Sendero, which is discussed further below. The nature of these groups suggests that both the rebels and the government are less likely to compromise. This has certainly been the case. The intransigence may also be a function of the complex ideological/ identity nexus. Sendero Luminoso employed extreme views of identity, drawing a clear line between those on the side of the movement and those working against it. The us-versus-them dichotomy both helped and hurt group capacity building, as discussed below, but it also made terrorist tactics an option despite the typically natural combination of ideological causes and guerrilla warfare.

To understand the brutal tactics employed by Sendero more fully, it is essential to understand the foundation on which the organization is based and how it emerged. Guzman was prevented from joining the Communist Party in Peru as a student in Arequipa because he was not a child of a worker, which he explained was a "serious mistake" (Guzman 1993, 52). This would appear to be the beginning of Guzman's discontent with the policies and approaches of the Peruvian left, particularly those who aimed to work with reformist government leadership. According to Guzman, "I evaluated the party situation: Revisionism continued and we could make no progress unless it was wiped out" (56). By the late 1960s, Guzman thought it necessary to create this "Red Faction" utilizing revolution to bring a true government to Peru (Guzman 1993) without foreign interference. Guzman viewed all Peruvian governments since Spanish colonialism as illegitimate (Manwaring 1995). His 1975 trip to China solidified his approach, making Sendero Luminoso distinct by embracing Maoist ideology. He also maintained a steadfast unwillingness to compromise his ideals of a cohesive, revolutionary front led by him. According to Manwaring (1995), the primary objective of Guzman was power, and gaining that required discipline, intelligence, and motivation. The training of Sendero Luminoso revolutionaries was methodical and focused on creating a loyal set of followers with a centralized core that Guzman ruled through fear (Burgoyne 2010; Onís et al. 2005). His previous experience with leftist rivals and his lack of compromise in the area of ideology and loyalty made for an organization with a clear us-versus-them mentality. To not pledge loyalty to the organization made one an opponent and a threat—and, therefore, a target. Under such conditions, rival organizations, such as MRTA and unsupportive peasants, became targets.

The government, for its part, was quite willing to target civilians as well. Its disregard for the civilian population can be explained in large part by identity. Whether an individual was Indian, Quechua speaking, rural peasant, or leftist, all were considered fair game in the armed struggle against Peru's insurgents.

CONFLICT PROGRESSION AND CONFLICT DYNAMICS

Leftist opposition to the Peruvian government had a large population of sympathizers from which to draw membership due to the vast inequality in the system. Not all groups were able to harness this support and improve their capacity with numbers. The first two armed factions of Peru involving the ELN and the MIR were rather small in size and lacked organizational capacity (UCDP/PRIO 2014). Héctor Béjar (1969), a former leader in the ELN, examined his experience from prison shortly following the 1965 insurrection. Although the Peruvian army was fifty thousand strong, both the MIR and the ELN were working with small bands, as few as thirteen rebels. These were separated by distance, however, making communication between the various fronts difficult. According to Béjar, "when Lobaton [one of the MIR fronts] opened fire in June, de le Puenta [another front] was still not prepared and the northern front had not even begun its operations" (Béjar 1969, 79). This disconnect further handicapped these already small groups.

What the ELN lacked in armed members, it attempted to make up for with support among the community indigenous to the region in which the group operated. Having been exploited by fraudulent lawyers, judges, and landowners, the impoverished population of the Ayacucho region was indeed welcoming to guerrillas working to return communal lands. As Béjar indicates, wherever the rebels traveled in this region, they found friends. Rebels with significant sympathy among the population can potentially survive even if small in size. In order to grow and engage the government in larger battles, the ELN needed to convert

FIGURE 7.5   Patterns of Violence in Peru, 1982–2008

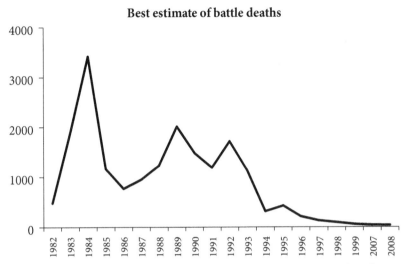

Best estimate of battle deaths

Data drawn from Lacina and Gleditsch (2005). Sendero Luminoso and MRTA are grouped together as one rivalry in UCDP/PRIO (2014). ELN/MIR reached approximately 138 battle-related deaths in 1965; neither is included in the diagram.

sympathizers into rebels. Identity differences between the city dwellers taking up arms and the indigenous rural peasant farmers they sought to protect were too great. Further, the ELN underestimated the government's willingness to re-press sympathizers. As Béjar indicates, "when the invasion finally comes, all of our supporters are tortured and shot" (Béjar 1969, 101). Although the ELN was able to work the mountainous and jungle terrain to its advantage somewhat, staying hidden in this region depends on secrecy. The Peruvian military readily utilized torture and repression on the indigenous population to find the rebels. Ultimately, these small bands of rebels were surrounded and exterminated or arrested. This experience helped form part of the historical memory for the indigenous peoples in the Andean region.

The MIR, operating simultaneously, suffered a similar experience. Neither the ELN nor the MIR was large enough or organized in a way that allowed for sur-viving the government's response to their mobilization. The two early factions never coordinated their activities to improve their organizational capacity vis-à-vis the government. Despite their size, both chose to engage the government in guerrilla warfare and were quickly surrounded. As a result, they were both short-lived affairs culminating in an estimated 138 total battle-related deaths in 1965 (Lacina and Gleditsch 2005).

Sendero Luminoso and MRTA were both better organized and larger in size than their predecessors. They were also able to draw upon available resources to ensure longer survival. Sendero was the largest of the rebel factions and, as a result, the most successful. Estimates of the size of Sendero Luminoso suggest the organization could claim as many as eight thousand armed members (Cunningham, Gleditsch, and Salehyan 2009), though other estimates suggest it was larger (Gregory 2009). It attacked towns and government forces in bands as large as seven hundred (*Keesing's World*, May 1983). Because it enjoyed significant numbers, it is not surprising that Sendero was the only faction in Peru that was able to engage directly in armed conflict with the government. It successfully employed guerrilla warfare early on, particularly as the government underestimated its strength and dedicated only a small fraction of its force to counter the Sendero threat.

Sendero Luminoso's relationship with the peasants it sought to save from the oppressive poverty discussed above has been complicated. Early in the campaign, Sendero enjoyed a significant amount of passive support (Berg 1994). Employing the indoctrination training mentioned above, Sendero was able to expand its membership well beyond its predecessors. Having formed at the University of Huamanga, the organization benefited from a significant number of sympathizers who, though educated, were unable to improve their lot in life. Unlike the experience of the ELN, some of these sympathizers took up arms and joined the cause. Of course, not all Sendero Luminoso supporters participated in the insurrection freely. The organization took a zero sum approach to its campaign. In the view of the rebels, indigenous peasants were either supporting the organization or the government, which made such traitors a target for reprisals in much the same way the government had done in past rivalries and would continue to do again in its battle to eliminate the Sendero rival. As a result, the conflict involved massive, well-documented human rights abuses. Membership and Sendero sympathy were also undermined by the group's ideologically driven efforts to transform indigenous societies. Rather than seeing themselves as participants in a revolution, the poor were once again victims of external aggressors (Isbell 1994). Despite a large amount of frustration on the part of the poor in Peru, the membership of Sendero, though large, was actually undercut by the group's policies and the atrocities it committed in the name of its cause. As was the case in the previous 1965 rivalries, the government contributed to this problem further. By the mid-1980s, indigenous peasants were organized into their own security forces to protect themselves against Sendero Luminoso. The government encouraged this to the extent that President Belaunde offered medals to peasants who killed terrorists (*Keesing's World*, May 1983).

At its height in the 1980s, MRTA was approximately two thousand strong (Baer 2003). Unlike the other armed factions in Peru, MRTA did not engage in guerrilla warfare. MRTA's tactics were carefully aimed at achieving its goals, which were "to create a new society in which all people were treated equally, enjoyed the same opportunities and level of prosperity, and shared ownership of all property" (Baer 2003, 4). MRTA leadership focused much of its activity on foreign, particularly U.S., interests that it blamed for persistent inequality and poverty in Peru. Its tactics have included bombing or small arms attacks on the U.S. embassy in Lima, hijacking food trucks that it then used to feed the poor, and, later, kidnapping foreign executives for ransom (Baer 2003). As a result, MRTA members did not require significant armaments. These tactics are clearly terrorist in nature. Interestingly, however, MRTA was careful to avoid civilian casualties by frequently calling in warnings of attacks and suggesting that buildings be evacuated. Rather than seeking to take over the government through force, MRTA aimed to gain attention for its causes.

Both MRTA and Sendero attempted to increase their strength in 1987 by shifting their area of operations. MRTA, which had emerged out of Lima, moved to embrace a "new strategy of rural guerrilla operations," paying homage to revolutionary leader Che Guevara (*Keesing's World*, February 1988). The organization, led by Victor Polay, raided the towns of Juanjui and San Jose de Sisa in the Upper Huallaga Valley. In the same year, Sendero Luminoso intensified its drive for political support by increasing its urban operations (*Keesing's World*, February 1988). The decision by MRTA to shift toward guerrilla tactics in the more remote Upper Huallaga Valley required additional resources. It has been suggested that it was here that MRTA members began to cooperate with coca producers. Sendero Luminoso already dominated this market by the time MRTA made its entrance, however.

Once again, a contradiction emerged in examining conflict involving Sendero Luminoso. The Peruvian government has benefited greatly from U.S. efforts to address the drug trade. The United States has trained antidrug agents in Peru, while providing assistance to destroy coca crops and encourage coca growers to substitute less lucrative options for drug crops. Although this assistance was intended to bolster the government's capacity, this was not necessarily what occurred. Efforts to eradicate coca and pursue rebels threatened peasant farmers' livelihood. In the end, the peasant farmers were willing to support whichever group would secure their economic livelihood (Gonzales 1994). As a result, a guerrilla-farmer security relationship emerged. Sendero was able to obtain the financial support its members needed, and the peasant farmers were protected from government efforts and policy.

Although the MRTA and Sendero factions coincided with one another, as was the case with the MIR and the ELN, the two never cooperated. To the contrary, the organizations worked against one another. MRTA took issue with Sendero policy of "selective killings," while Sendero Luminoso turned its back on, or targeted, all leftist groups that did not embrace its revolutionary, "ideologically pure" approach (*Washington Post* 1988).

Despite the lack of cooperation these rivals displayed, both were at their strongest in the late 1980s. Their success at this time coincided with a further deterioration of the Peruvian economy. Inflation, increasing debt, and loan defaults, along with crippling austerity programs, fed the population's dissatisfaction with its leadership. The Peruvian government appeared particularly inept at dealing with both the insurgencies and the economic crisis. This changed, however, with the election of Alberto Fujimori in 1990. Fujimori embarked on a severe austerity program that was able to rein in the triple-digit inflation and replenish government revenue (CQ Press 2009a). In addition, he launched a new counterterrorist effort that included a dramatic increase in its rural defense patrols (CQ Press 2009a) while introducing new antiterrorism laws (which were later ruled unconstitutional). This led to the capture of Sendero's Guzman in September 1992 and MRTA's Polay in 1993, along with other Sendero and MRTA leaders.

Both MRTA and Sendero Luminoso survived these arrests, but in significantly weaker states. The arrest of Guzman was particularly crippling for Sendero. The indoctrination training employed by the group provided a highly structured organization. Guzman was painstakingly careful in structuring the organization so that he would be the central figure of Sendero Luminoso (Gorriti 1999). This meant the group would benefit significantly from its cohesion. Rumors of potential splintering were rare (see *Keesing's World*, May 1990, as an example). But such a structure also meant that by arresting the rebel group's leadership the government had rather effectively decapitated the organization. Attacks by Sendero members continued, but at a dramatically reduced rate. It is at this time that Guzman and other Sendero members called for peace from their jail cells (*Keesing's World*, January 1994). This shift in tactics brought about a splinter faction of Sendero Luminoso, which refers to itself as the Red Faction, or Sendero Luminoso Rojo. Remnants of Sendero, approximately several hundred strong, continued to operate in the Upper Huallaga, Apurimac, and Ene River Valleys (Sullivan 2010). The armed conflict has not resulted in more than twenty-five battle-related deaths since 2010, however. This may be due in part to the group's shift in priorities. The region in which they reside is particularly suited for coca plantations. While still employing ideology as a tool of indoctrination, the rebellion has become more of a series of profit-seeking organizations proficient in money laundering for terrorist organizations (De Angelis 2015) than a revolutionary movement. In order to ensure continued survival, the group enslaved approximately two hundred people, particularly from the Ashaninka ethnic group. By using systematic rape and continued indoctrination of children born of rape, the group is literally growing its army. The government renewed its campaign, once considered dead, in 2015, capturing two Sendero leaders and freeing fifty-four slaves, thirty-three of which were children (Martel 2015).

The MIR, ELN, and Sendero Luminoso each sought to bring about revolution in Peru. The ELN was inspired by the Cuban Revolution, whereas the MIR was frustrated by the APRA's decision to reject communism entirely. It is not surprising that both groups took their fight to the rural, mountainous areas of Peru and engaged in guerrilla warfare. Sendero Luminoso also clearly wanted to bring Peru under Communist rule of its own making. It too took its fight to the mountains. Interestingly, however, despite Guzman's embrace of Maoist philosophy, the very people the Sendero group claimed to want to help became frequent targets. Mao claimed that to win the revolution, the revolutionaries needed to win the hearts and minds of the peasants. Guzman attempted to do this through indoctrination, often forced. The rebels' commitment to the Sendero ideology and its approach left no room for compromise. As a result, political avenues to address inequality in Peru were eliminated at the onset. Further, any leftist organization that attempted to do work politically, or any person who participated in elections, became an enemy. Rather than working with and embracing exploited workers and peasants, Sendero revolutionaries attempted to dominate them and impose their views and approach them often through force. Guerrilla warfare, as a result, relied heavily on terrorizing the Peruvian civilian population.

The theoretical model presented in chapter 1 suggests that groups and governments learn from their experiences and adjust their approaches in light of their successes or failures in previous interactions. Guzman appeared to have learned from the experience of the ELN and the MIR. Sendero took its time and effectively prepared to emerge as a revolutionary force. Its organizational capacity far exceeded that of its predecessor. What it did not overcome, however, were the various identity-based divisions in Peru. Sendero was able to find common ground with the peasant farmer in the Huallaga Valley, but for the most part, Sendero's tactical approach with the peasantry remained unchanged through the 1980s.

The shift by Sendero from an entirely rural approach to one that included an urban strategy appears to have come about by the limitations of the rural-only strategy. Competing leftist organizations, particularly MRTA, were making headway in the coastal urban areas. Ignoring this capacity-growing potential was to the detriment of each group's long-term goals. The same can be said of MRTA's shift toward the rural areas. What neither group could come to terms with, however, was overcoming their intergroup differences. Given the vast inequality in Peru, both historically and at the time of insurrections, the country was ripe for revolution. This is evident by the number of leftist groups that emerged over time. The differences among them and the fighting between them did not allow for cooperative endeavors.

There is evidence that the government learned from its mistakes, although its anti-insurgency campaigns were never truly successful. Under General Velasco, the military regime worked to address the issue of internal peace by implementing a series of structural reforms aimed at alleviating chronic poverty and underdevelopment in the mountainous regions where much of the indigenous population lives ("Military Reform" 1992; Champion 2001). The efforts were well received initially, at least by the poor and leftist groups, but they ultimately failed as a result of ineffective economic policy. The result was economic collapse, which only stimulated more insurrection. Subsequent efforts to alleviate the sources of intrastate conflict have been comparatively successful. The poverty rate in Peru in 2011 was 27.8 percent (*Peruvian Times* 2012). This has reduced the attractiveness of taking up arms and engaging in revolution, although the regional divide remains. The 2011 poverty rate for the rural population of Peru was 56.1 percent (*Peruvian Times* 2012).

The Peruvian government also shifted its antiterrorism tactics over time. The most notable was Fujimori's decision to strengthen antiterrorism laws. He also was able to improve intelligence, which allowed for the arrest or killing of key leadership of MRTA and Sendero Luminoso. Further, the 1992 Repentance Law allowed rebel group members to surrender for lenient or suspended sentences in exchange for turning over names of other guerrillas. The United Nations has indicated that 5,516 Sendero members and 814 MRTA members took advantage of the law (Human Rights Watch 1995a). The actions of these *arrepentidos* resulted in many arbitrary imprisonments, as those repenting did not have to provide much in the way of evidence, but it also significantly weakened both insurgencies.

CONCLUSIONS

Despite counterterrorist and poverty reduction efforts, Sendero Luminoso remains active primarily in the rural parts of Peru and seems more attached to the drug trade than its political goals (Skeen n.d.), while MRTA members continue to advocate for the more humane treatment of prisoners. The persistence of these groups can be explained in large part by the pervasive poverty and inequality in Peru. Despite the targeting of civilians by Sendero Luminoso, those suffering the most have not been able to trust the government either. Grievances remain. The failure of earlier factions to address this problem was a function of the lack of group capacity relative to the government. A terrain ripe for guerrilla warfare can actually be a detriment for groups that are too small to communicate effectively over large, dense terrain.

Unlike other cases examined in this book, intrastate conflict in Peru has not been influenced dramatically by outside intervention. Although the United

States does unknowingly benefit Sendero Luminoso when it helps Peru with crop eradication and substitution, diplomatic or military efforts by external actors appear to have been entirely absent. In this regard, capacity by armed groups is in large part dependent on what resources they can capture or whose sympathies they can garner. Sendero has done well in this regard, utilizing terrain to its advantage as well as capturing revenues from the drug trade. MRTA, in choosing not to target civilians, has been able to endure because of its tactical approach and the sympathy it has gained for its cause.

CONCLUSION

Civil wars are perplexing and complicated events, but as we have demonstrated here, they can also be viewed and examined as a series of actions and reactions over time. Using the theoretical framework presented in chapter 1, a disaggregated, systematic analysis of multiple conflicts within six countries has been presented. Doing so has demonstrated the value of looking beyond the state and focusing inward at the dynamic set of interactions occurring and the relationships evolving that collectively form something as destructive as a civil war. Group and government capacity is indeed dynamic in nature, as are the tactical decisions employed by conflict actors.

Reflection on the case studies in light of the theoretical arguments reveals findings that are both interesting and important. This chapter provides a summary of what has been learned and some examples of key arguments that were taken from the case studies. It is organized consistently with the theoretical framework that has been applied to each chapter and focuses on key findings in each area. The first section examines the relevant aspects of the conflict context. Special attention is paid to the conflict histories and how episodic or enduring violence has impacted the cases. The second section provides a summary of the dynamic factors, including previous tactics, leadership, and group cohesion, that were found to have influence over the patterns of violence in the cases. Finally, the chapter delves into the important aspects of tactical selections made by groups. This includes resorting to terrorism, international intervention, and conflict termination.

CONFLICT CONTEXT

The context of each of the conflicts studied influenced the actions taken by both groups and government. Terrain, timing, and the nature of the group rebelling were found to be largely as would have been predicted by the theory. A comparison of the impact of static factors on tactical choice across the cases is presented in Table C.1. Of the nineteen conflicts analyzed, five can be considered episodic in nature. These occurred in the Congo, the JVP in Sri Lanka, South Moluccas of Indonesia, and the ELN and MIR of Peru. Two of these were short lived but repeated, including the multiple political rivalries in the Congo and the JVP in Sri Lanka. In the short 1965 cases of Peru it seems evident that the

TABLE C.1   Comparison of Static Factors and Tactical Choices across the Cases

Country	Group	Static factors and tactical choice
Sierra Leone	RUF AFRC Kamajors	One of the most important static factors in Sierra Leone was geography. The presence of diamonds and shared border with Liberia had a profound impact on the tactical decisions made by both groups and governments. These conflicts were characterized at all times by violence against civilians carried out by the RUF and AFRC. During their period of junta rule, this transitioned to state-perpetrated violence against civilians.
Republic of the Congo	Cobras Ninjas Cocoyes Ninjas	Elite-led power struggle masked as identity politics (nature of group) led to appeals for international assistance (tactic).
Sri Lanka	JVP LTTE TELO EPRLF	Colonial history was an important static factor in Sri Lanka, where British favoritism shown to the Tamils resulted in significant backlash from the Sinhala when the country gained independence. Sri Lanka's geography was part of the basis of its conflict, in that the north and east of the country had high percentages of Tamils, focusing the fighting there. Another important static factor was the ethnic link between Sri Lankan and Indian Tamils, which influenced Indian intervention. Because of the identity-based nature of the conflict, terrorism emerged as a tactical option.
Myanmar	Arakan Kachin Karen Mon Shan	All ethnic rebels benefited heavily from their presence in the frontier regions distant from government forces, making guerrilla warfare particularly effective. Each of their insurrections were also informed by the legacy and promises of the Panglong Agreement signed at the time of independence. As a result, rebels continued to try and elicit the same promises through repeated attempts at negotiation over time.
	Communists	The Communist insurrection emerged at the time of independence as major political players fought to determine the direction the new country would take at independence. Having just fought in World War II, all groups were heavily armed, allowing for conventional warfare. The ideological nature of the insurrection led to successful appeals for international assistance from neighboring China.
Indonesia	DI Permestas PRRI South Moluccas OPM FRETILIN GAM	Two static factors were profoundly important in all conflicts in Indonesia. The first was the country's colonial history and independence, after which Muslim-based groups thought the country would be governed by Sharia law, and many of the country's regions thought they would receive independence. The second factor was the country's geography. In this huge archipelago, the government's ability to control outlying regions has sometimes been limited and impacted its capacity, particularly if it was fighting in two regions at once. In addition, the presence of valuable natural resources in some regions led to competition between the government and local actors. Where many of the conflicts began with the use of guerrilla warfare as a tactic, identity-based divisions in the conflict regions and the government's control of natural resource infrastructure often resulted in a shift to terrorism. Appeals for international assistance occurred at times when governmental violence peaked or group capacities versus the government were lacking.

TABLE C.1   Continued

Country	Group	Static factors and tactical choice
Peru	ELN MIR	Peru's mountainous terrain could have benefited these groups, but the lack of communication in the face of small numbers hurt their cause. Guerrilla warfare was the tactical choice in an effort to benefit from the terrain and hide within local peasant populations.
	MRTA	MRTA's anti-Western ideological stance and its urban location heavily influenced its tactical decisions. While terrorist tactics were utilized, the group was careful to avoid civilian casualties that would hurt its cause.
	Sendero Luminoso	Sendero's location in the remote mountainous region of Peru helped sustain its cause, making guerrilla warfare a good tactical choice. Its extreme ideological indoctrination resulted in the targeting of "unfriendly" civilian populations, however.

ELN and MIR simply lacked the capacity each needed to keep fighting. Despite the terrain advantage, and the sympathy of the Peruvian population in the high Sierras, neither group could overcome its numerical disadvantage. Further, the terrain actually became a detriment as the small bands of rebels lacked the ability to coordinate their attacks. As a result, they were easily defeated. In fact, in hindsight, launching such an attack at the time truly seemed premature, something Abimael Guzman had predicted. Although the ideology of the ELN and MIR would tend to move them in the direction of employing guerrilla tactics, which was indeed the course of action they took, their numbers would have suggested an approach more along the lines of strategic bombing or the targeting of specific governmental assets. Had they done this and stayed on the streets of Lima, their campaigns may have been more successful and the conflict more enduring. Perhaps their campaign was simply premature, as Guzman had suggested. The grievances that led to the 1965 conflicts in Peru were never addressed. In response, there was a more sustained, enduring set of conflicts that emerged later in the 1980s, one of which did choose this tactical path.

The JVP in Sri Lanka and the Republic of South Moluccas in Indonesia experienced an episodic conflict for similar reasons. In 1971 the JVP sought to overthrow the Sri Lankan government in an attempt to assure the prioritization of Sinhala nationalism over the Tamil cause. This brought about brutal government repression that terminated the conflict decisively. The independence movement for the Republic of South Moluccas began with a revolt over the failure of the Indonesian government to follow through on the promise that regions of the country would be allowed to vote for their independence. Again in this case, however, in spite of strong support and a significant number of trained rebel troops, a massive and coordinated government response brought the rebellion to a quick end.

Despite having the designation here as an episodic conflict, the JVP actually reemerged in the late 1980s over similar nationalist issues. In 1989 the JVP resurged to fight against Indian peacekeeping forces and the government that allowed them entry. Again, its campaign was short lived as the group found it could achieve its goals by working through its political party. As a result, the armed aspect of the conflict was terminated. There was a similar set of circumstances in the Republic of the Congo. Each rebel faction fighting for control of the government was elite led in nature with clear political goals. These objectives, however, were publicly presented as being derived from identity-based grievances. As a result, there were tactical decisions that involved terrorizing the civilian populations in Brazzaville as militias aligned with elite actors carved out their spheres of influence. These campaigns of terror were brought to an end in the first period of violence by a negotiated outcome. Opposition leader Kolelas and President Lissouba were able to come to terms as Kolelas was provided a position in the Lissouba government. Preelection violence renewed the conflict in the late 1990s, however, this time with the Lissouba government pitted against former president Sassou N'Guesso. It is possible that these elites could have again brokered their way to an agreement had it not been for the Angolan intervention, which decidedly tipped the power scales in Sassou's direction. A military victory for his Cobra rebels was guaranteed. Kolelas and Lissouba found themselves in exile as a result. Had Lissouba's pleas for international assistance been more successful and the regional alliances been more in his favor, the conflict may have been prolonged. That said, the tactical decision to ethnically cleanse Brazzaville alienated the Congolese population. Perhaps it is unlikely these leaders would have been able to generate the amount of support necessary to sustain guerrilla or conventional warfare as a result.

The remaining conflicts that were examined endured even in the face of sometimes significant power asymmetries. Their ability to do so seems to have been due to tactical decisions made by the actors, which is a function of group capacity versus the government. The longest of the conflicts occurred in Myanmar. The Arakan, Communists, Kachin, Karen, and Mon all emerged immediately post-independence. While the Communists fought to control the type of government the newly independent Burma would become, the other groups advocated for the right to self-determination. These groups were joined by the Shan in 1958 when they were unable to gain independence. Both the Communists and the Karen were able to employ conventional warfare tactics early in their campaigns as they benefited from their experience and the available weaponry their participation in World War II provided. These groups, and others, saw their capacities increase vis-à-vis the government when the Burmese army experienced a significant amount of desertion as individuals tied to one of these groups joined their ethnic or ideological kin. The Communists were clearly emboldened by their strength in the late 1940s and as a result were unwilling to negotiate an end to the conflict when such an offer was made by President U Nu. The strength of these groups waned over time, forcing them to employ other tactics, particularly guerrilla warfare.

The nature of conflicts seemed to vary across episodic and enduring cases. The MIR and ELN of Peru were ideological in nature, as was the JVP in Sri Lanka. All three were unable to endure or to achieve their goals. The Republic of South Moluccas in Indonesia suffered a similar fate, although that conflict was identity based. The elite-led conflict in the Republic of the Congo seemed to have different dynamics. The dyads that occurred in that case emerged almost entirely due to elite aspirations, which could more easily be negotiated. The intervention by Angola, of course, changed that possibility and brought about a military victory by Sassou instead. Among the more enduring conflicts there are both identity-based and ideologically based motivations.

DYNAMIC FACTORS

Intrastate conflicts are indeed dynamic. Among the more enduring conflicts examined here, different trajectories emerged. Some conflicts ebb and flow, involving varying intensities, while others seem to maintain a fairly consistent level of violence. What accounts for these differences can be discovered, as has been demonstrated, by disaggregating the conflict and examining the tactical decisions made by the actors involved. A comparison of the key dynamic factors and their impact on tactical selection in the cases examined can be found in Table C.2.

Previous Actions

Nonstate actors mobilized by a set of grievances make decisions and take actions in their efforts to have them redressed. Their government responds. These tactical decisions are a function of the conflict environment and its context, as well as the changing nature of the relationships between conflict actors. Of course, it should be clear that the actions and reactions that make up a conflict trajectory are not simply between the nonstate actor and its government. Instead, there is a complex set of interactions across conflicts within the state, as well as interactions involving outside actors. This web of interactions determines the patterns and types of violence in a conflict, the tactics conflict actors employ in order to achieve their goals, and ultimately whether the conflict will terminate or endure.

These dynamics were illustrated in the presentation of the cases. The relative capacity of actors and the nature of the conflict influenced their tactical choices,

TABLE C.2 Comparison of Key Dynamic Factors and Tactical Choices across the Cases

Country	Group	Key dynamic factors and tactical choice
Sierra Leone	RUF AFRC Kamajors	Relative capacity, including the number of actors and their ability to secure financing, was vitally important in these conflicts. The government in this case took the unique step of seeking to build its capacity by hiring private military contractors. The government's capacity was also supplemented by answered calls for intervention by the UN, ECOWAS, and African countries that contributed forces to the fight against the RUF. Group capacity was augmented by Charles Taylor's support through most of the conflict. It was also increased when the RUF and AFRC joined forces to govern. In contrast, it was decreased by the blood diamonds campaign, which significantly impacted its funding stream. The RUF and AFRC engaged in violence against civilians to increase their capacity by forcing people into their ranks, increasing their ability to fund themselves with diamonds, and instilling fear among citizens. Where other groups might court popular support, the RUF chose to use fear to deter public opposition.
Republic of the Congo	Cobras Ninjas Cocoyes Ninjas	Tactical decisions to employ ethnic cleansing kept these elite-led militias relatively small in number. Further, the political nature of the disputes allowed for successful negotiations at times when elites were offered positions in the government. Ultimately, however, decisive intervention by Angola bolstered rebel Sassou N'Guesso over the Lissouba government, resulting in victory and subsequent negotiations to bring the remaining rebels into the fold, with the exception of the Pool region splinter.
Sri Lanka	JVP	The JVP group goal shifted from secession to representation and policy change at specific times, largely based on its relative losses to government or extremist Tamil groups.
	LTTE	The LTTE's capacity was increased by tapping into the Tamil diaspora. At one point, its strength was diminished by the Indian government's intervention in the conflict; however, those forces left the country after suffering significant losses. The LTTE's capacity was sometimes decreased by having to fight both government and other Tamil groups. The group's decision to employ a chemical agent in one case was influenced by its perception of an imminent shift in its relative capacity. This action resulted in a decrease of the group's capacity in terms of popular support, as it resulted in the injury of Tamil civilians. Prabhakaran's charismatic leadership largely increased its capacity. However, his actions reduced capacity at times: when he had a falling out with other Tamil leaders that resulted in group splintering, and when they turned public opinion against him. All of these factors led to the LTTE's shifting tactics between conventional warfare, guerrilla warfare, and terrorism tactics. The group's perception of its relative capacity was a determining factor of this decision.
	TELO EPRLF	TELO and EPRLF lacked the capacity to compete with the LTTE or government forces, which led to the use of terrorism as a tactic.

Myanmar	Arakan Kachin Karen Mon Shan Communists	Ethnic and Communist insurgencies benefited heavily from intergroup collaboration and outside assistance. Resources were bolstered as a result. The shift by both China and Thailand to work with the SLORC rather than against it, coupled with the government's increasingly brutal tactics against civilians, led to a series of negotiated ceasefires that did not address underlying grievances. These frequently tenuous agreements also led to intergroup fighting, which has only diminished the capacity of the remaining rebellions. Some splinter factions have also chosen economic enterprise (i.e., illicit drug trade) over autonomy or secessionist goals.
Indonesia	DI	DI was a nationwide group that occasionally built its capacity by joining forces with regional secessionist groups. It lost public support, however, at times when citizens became upset over the group's attacks on noncombatants. The political party Masyumi increased the group's capacity by backing it. Terrorism was frequently employed by the group, due to its identification of non-Muslims as legitimate targets for violence.
	Permestas	Little detail was found about the capacity of the Permestas, aside from during the periods that it joined forces with the DI under the auspices of the PRRI.
	PRRI	The PRRI combined the DI, Permestas, and other groups to fight the government and, at one point, to create an alternate rebel government consisting of both regionalist separatists and supporters of Islam. Key leaders also had personal attributes that undermined unity. The PRRI's abilities were increased when it was supported by the DI. However, U.S. government support and the Indonesian government's fighting on multiple fronts at the time built the group's relative capacity to a point that it could achieve victory. This divide in the goals of the group's members reduced its ability to build a coordinated action. Eventually, the increase in the DI's popularity pulled support from the PRRI, further undermining its capacity. As with the DI, the identification of non-Muslim citizens as legitimate targets for violence resulted in the frequent use of terrorism as a tactic, particularly when the group's capacity decreased.
	South Moluccas	The rebellion was carried out by roughly 1,000 ex-Dutch military forces who engaged mainly in guerrilla warfare tactics. Citizens in the region largely supported the movement, which built its capacity, minimizing the impetus to engage in terrorism. However, the government engaged in a concerted and escalatory campaign against the rebels that not even international negotiation could counter. In the end, there were more than 15,000 government forces mobilized to the island, which eventually overcame the rebels.
	OPM	The group was not a well-organized or trained force, largely due to the diversity in the region, which complicated efforts to create a united front. The government's actions against the OPM were specifically designed to reduce its capacity by undermining public support (by using indiscriminate violence against them), diminishing its ability to fundraise and recruit, and reducing the number of rebels. Over time, the group's goals shifted from independence to special autonomy and a greater share of locally generated wealth, as its capacity versus the government diminished. The group engaged in guerrilla warfare and frequently appealed for international assistance.

(continued)

TABLE C.2 Continued

Country	Group	Key dynamic factors and tactical choice
	FRETILIN	FRETILIN suffered from significant lack of capacity early in its fight, which was exacerbated by the U.S. and Australian support for the government, which could not be overcome by the Portuguese support for Timor. Its capacity was limited by the fact that the people of East Timor could not agree on the desirability of independence. FRETILIN's capacity was so limited that it needed to disengage from fighting to fundraise and build support. The government's capacity was also diminished by the fact that it was fighting multiple groups in different parts of the country at the same time. Given this, neither side had the capacity necessary to achieve military victory, resulting in peace talks and East Timorese independence in 2002. FRETILIN employed terrorism against those Timorese citizens who opposed terrorism. It appealed for international assistance when the government became particularly brutal.
	GAM	After the loss of East Timor, the government's resolve (an important part of capacity) to not lose Aceh was hardened, as was international pressure to maintain the territorial integrity of the country. Again, however, the government's brutal repression of the rebellion led to increased support for GAM (which employed largely guerrilla warfare as a tactic) among the people of Aceh and the international community. The reaction led to both a new generation of rebels for the cause and an increase in the amount of territory controlled by GAM. However, the group's main leadership lived in exile, which resulted in disagreements in strategy between the leaders abroad and those on the battlefield and an eventual splintering of the group. The only time either side was willing to negotiate (calls for international assistance) was when it was clear it could not win, but even then it did not engage in good faith. The 2004 Asian tsunami had a profound impact on the group's capacity, leading to its capitulation to government.
Peru	ELN MIR	Both of these insurrections were episodic in nature, lacking significant dynamic aspects.
	MRTA Sendero Luminoso	Sendero's targeting of civilians meant collaboration with MRTA, which would have increased its capacity vis-à-vis the government, was unlikely. As both groups were labeled terrorist organizations, negotiations never occurred. Further, the centralized leadership style of Sendero and its isolated nature did not encourage outside appeals for assistance.

which influenced future phases of the conflict and the subsequent actions of each of the actors. In Sierra Leone, repeated successes by the rebels led the government to seek to increase its capacity by calling in external actors, including the private security firms. Those participants then influenced the RUF and became a factor that pushed the RUF to peace talks at one point and were part of the content of the mediation itself. Once those external actors were removed, the RUF responded to that change in the dynamic and capacity of the government by attacking more fiercely.

In the case of Sri Lanka, relatively peaceful student protests either failed to get a reaction from the government or, quite to the contrary, were met with violent repression. In response, the dissatisfied Tamil groups formed the LTTE. It began building its capacity in India, purchasing weapons and training in Tamil Nadu. As the LTTE's capacity increased, Sri Lanka struggled to gain the advantage, escalating the conflict and gaining Indian support in suppressing the rebels. Both the Tamil and Sinhala extremists responded by turning their aggression against the Indian peacekeeping forces.

In Indonesia, the case of Aceh is a good example. The Free Aceh Movement (GAM) formed in 1976 when Acehnese citizens became frustrated with government repression and revocation of autonomy from the region in 1950. When the civil conflict began in 1990 government reaction was repressive, which resulted in the cessation of hostilities. After the 1997 Asian economic crisis and Suharto's removal from power, however, GAM perceived weakness in the government and responded with increased hostilities. By 2001, there was a stalemate in the conflict, which brought both parties into mediation. One of the major provisions in that agreement was the return of special autonomy status to Aceh. When GAM continued fighting because some members felt nothing short of independence would be acceptable, the government's response was to increase its capacity in the region and establish a special military base. This round of fighting was sustained until the 2004 Asian tsunami, which completely devastated GAM's capacity.

No one decision or action, then, should be seen as determining a conflict's trajectory. It is, instead, the reciprocal actions taken by the participants over time and their dynamic interaction that have a determinant effect on decision making from the point of initiating armed struggle to termination. Understanding intrastate conflicts and increasing the ability to bring them to an end, then, requires a deeper understanding of the factors that influenced each decision.

Leadership and Cohesion

Cohesion also appears to be a determinant of conflict trajectory. Governments that are facing multiple, simultaneous conflicts are compelled to divide their resources. This likely detracts from their ability to achieve victory, as it diminishes the capacity that can be devoted to any one dispute. This was the case in Myanmar, Peru, Indonesia, and Sri Lanka. In Myanmar, when rebels worked together, they increased their capacity relative to the government and were more effective. However, the junta adopted a strategy of turning any group it defeated against the others and managed to weaken the rebels. As a result, rebel factions began to fold, choosing to accept ceasefire terms without political concessions. In Peru, MRTA and Sendero Luminoso did not work together and potentially missed taking advantage of the fact that one of those groups was dominant in the high Sierras while the other was doing quite well in the coastal cities. As a result, they were not able to maintain their resistance as effectively following the anti-insurgency policies of Fujimori. Of course, it is difficult to know if either group would have been able to maintain its capacity with the capture of their respective leaders. Sendero Luminoso, in particular, was incredibly centralized. As a result, the capacity of that group was in a significant way tied to Guzman and his ability to indoctrinate members and supporters. The government of Indonesia benefited from the lack of cohesion among the many groups that supported change to an Islamic government in the country. Had the Darul Islam Movement been better able to coordinate action among its troops or its sympathizers in the various regions of the country, it may have fared better against the government, which would have had to divide its forces across many different fronts. A similar situation existed in Sri Lanka. Had the LTTE approach been to mobilize and coordinate the actions of the many Tamil factions in the country, it would have increased its capacity versus the government. Instead, the group either defeated other Tamil entities or compelled them to come into line before the LTTE leadership, minimizing their collective impact.

Centralized leadership and charismatic leaders appear to be both positive and negative factors in group capacity. Strong leaders with dedicated followings increase group capacity by creating cohesion and decrease the chance of splintering. Such leaders can also improve the group's ability to recruit and raise funds. If the personalization of leadership power becomes too extreme, however, it may become problematic when those leaders are eliminated, as has been demonstrated. Group splintering occurred in Myanmar when the leader of Burmese independence, Aung San, was assassinated. His charismatic leadership may have been able to avoid the disintegration of Burma and work to create a unified government. With his death, this fragile set of ethnic alliances crumbled, and the enduring conflicts that were examined in this book began. Similarly, while the charismatic leadership of Prabhakaran in Sri Lanka served to consolidate support behind the LTTE, his death may have doomed the group to failure. Given the massive, coordinated attacks of the government in 2009, however, it may have been that the group's capacity was diminished to a point that even Prabhakaran could not have continued the effort.

Furthermore, conflicts that are defined in large part by their leadership may make working together more difficult. It is unlikely that Polay of MRTA and Guzman of Sendero Luminoso could have ever found common ground to work collectively against the Peruvian government. Similarly, had Prabhakaran not created a schism when he alienated Karuna and his eastern Tamils, the group's extra capacity may have allowed it to fare better against government forces.

Relative Capacity

Economic issues appeared crucial to several of the conflict trajectories. Clearly, unequal access to resources has been known to motivate groups to rebel in the first place (see the work of Gurr 1993, 1971). This was certainly the case in Indonesia, Peru, Sierra Leone, and Sri Lanka. In the cases of Indonesia and Sierra Leone, a significant motivation for their respective rebellions was the desire to control natural resource wealth. Indonesian regions that were resource rich sought to either secede or gain beneficial policies in order to assure that more of the funds generated by local wealth benefited their citizens. In Sierra Leone, the two sides were motivated by greed and sought to control the country's diamond wealth for profit.

The importance of economic issues does not stop there, however. The mismanagement of the national economy in Peru can partly be blamed for the resurgence in leftist activity in the early 1980s, but it also contributed to conflict escalation in the late 1980s. In addition to the arrest of the Sendero and MRTA leadership, the de-escalation of the conflict in both situations coincided with an economic recovery. It would seem that Kaufmann (1996) was correct in his assessment that it is difficult to mobilize the economically satisfied. In Indonesia, the 1997 Asian economic crisis led to the country's poor financial performance and subsequent ouster of Suharto, which caused escalation in the violence in West Papua, East Timor, and Aceh.

Sendero Luminoso may also have been able to endure despite the lack of external support because of its ability to capture resources within the state. By providing protection to the coca producers in the Huallaga Valley, Sendero generated the revenue it needed to sustain its campaign. The rebel-drug connection occurred in other cases as well. Several of the groups in Myanmar provided security for drug routes in the Golden Triangle. The nature of group goals changed in some of these cases, which made it easier for the government to come to terms with them. Once a rebel group goal shifts from representation or secession to protecting their economic livelihood, the government may be more willing and able to negotiate for conflict termination. The military junta in Myanmar offered such groups the right to maintain control over the drug trade routes if they agreed to stop their armed struggle against the government and join it instead, which subsequently pitted them against other groups.

In contrast, in Sierra Leone and Sri Lanka drugs played roles in the conflict that contributed to the strife. In the Sri Lankan case the LTTE engaged in the drug trade in its effort to fund the cause. It is likely that the LTTE would have lost some power versus the government if this revenue stream were not available to it, which essentially means that the drug trade may have extended the duration of the conflict. An even more detrimental impact from drugs was present in the case of Sierra Leone, where the RUF used drugs to control and stimulate violence among its young rebels.

Government policies for land redistribution or transmigration have an unsettling effect, both before and during conflicts. Indonesia transmigration policies that moved Javanese citizens into outlying regions influenced unrest in West Papua, East Timor, and Aceh in Indonesia. During a conflict, such efforts can be undertaken with the goal of changing the nature of the battlefield. In Sri Lanka, the government instituted policies to provide incentives to Sinhala citizens to migrate into areas traditionally dominated by the Tamils. The government's goal was to dilute the concentration of Tamils in these areas, both to reduce their impact on elections and to undermine Tamil claims that the territories were their traditional homelands that continued to be dominated by Tamil citizens. Similar efforts to change a disputed territory's demographics have occurred in the Philippines (most notably in Mindanao) and in Kosovo, two cases not examined here. Doing so changed the nature of resolution efforts by undermining, or attempting to undermine, previously defendable secessionist or right-to-self-determination claims.

A review of all six countries and their intrastate conflicts illustrates a major benefit a government typically has over groups in terms of capacity. Groups require a window of opportunity during which time there is hope they can achieve at least a portion of their goals through the use of armed conflict. This is more likely to occur during a time when such rivals perceive some weakness or vulnerability in the government. However, the cases demonstrate that states have a greater reserve of potential capacity than do groups. In the case of Sierra Leone, for instance, the government started the conflict with its forces in a shambles. They had been disempowered by Stevens, leaving the government with a military of only about two thousand troops who were untrained, poorly armed, and underfed. It is not surprising that the RUF thought it could achieve victory. While governments may start out with such weaknesses, they have the ability to increase their capacity by moving troops from one area to another to concentrate forces (Indonesia, Peru), conscripting additional military personnel (Congo, Myanmar, Sierra Leone, Sri Lanka, Indonesia), reallocating budgets

to focus on defeating the rebels (Sri Lanka), hiring private contractors to augment their capacity (Sierra Leone, Congo), appealing to international actors for
funds and arms (Congo, Myanmar, Indonesia, Sierra Leone), and controlling
media access and the flow of information to keep news of the group's plight
secret (Myanmar, Sri Lanka). In addition, in the post–9/11 world, governments
have gained a powerful tool against rebels. As was seen in Sri Lanka and the
Aceh region in Indonesia, governments that can successfully identify their competitors as terrorists within the international community can potentially interfere with the group's ability to raise and move funds, acquire arms, and recruit
and secure international support. In this sense, Islamic fundamentalist terrorist
groups have replaced the Communist "menace" of the Cold War era.

TACTICAL OPTIONS

The comparative framework applied to the cases examined in this book illustrates that civil war actors evaluate and reevaluate their tactical decisions
throughout the conflict. Their decisions are based on static factors, dynamic
factors relating to their relative capacity, and actors' goals. How those actors
view their position in the dispute relative to their opponent(s) will determine if
they choose to employ traditional or guerrilla warfare, terrorist tactics, appeal
for outside assistance or intervention, or engage in negotiations. What follows
is a discussion of tactical decisions made by the conflict actors examined in this
book and what helped to inform those decisions.

Terrorism

The cases also provide insight into the factors that appear to influence whether
groups or governments will terrorize their populations with indiscriminate approaches to killing. It has been argued that terrorism is a tactic employed by the
weak (Bueno de Mesquita 2008) and, therefore, would seem to be influenced
heavily by group capacity. The conflict histories examined in this book, however,
demonstrate that the decision to employ terrorist tactics is more complex. Indiscriminate killing of civilians was identified in every case: Sierra Leone (RUF
against civilians); the Congo (through ethnic cleansing in Brazzaville); Sri Lanka
(reciprocal LTTE/Tamil/Sinhala); Myanmar (by the government against those
populations unwilling to accept the government's ceasefire terms); Indonesia
(groups against complicit civilians or Javanese); and Peru (involving Sendero
and the Peruvian government).

The use of indiscriminate violence in Sierra Leone was relatively unusual. In
this case, while the government largely avoided violence against civilians, the
nonstate actor (RUF) engaged in terrorism throughout the conflict. The only

time that the government attacked civilians was during the brief time when the RUF joined in a junta to rule the country. The government did, however, engage in violence against members of the RUF. This is likely attributable to the fact that the key goal of the RUF was to control the diamonds rather than some sort of ideological or identity-based aspiration. Anyone who was perceived to pose a threat to the RUF's control of diamonds could be targeted. Meanwhile, citizens and the government sought to protect themselves from the violence that was being wrought, while at the same time attempting to find some way to provide for themselves.

In the Congo, the targeting of civilians can be viewed as a tool by political rivals who employed instrumentalist tactics (see the work of Saideman 1997). The conflicts in the Congo never did seem to be about identity-based representation but rather about the leadership and their position in government. By fanning the flames of identity-based politics, Lissouba, Kolelas, and Sassou were able to rally their militias to the point of ethnic cleansing.

Sri Lanka's experience also included significant terrorism. In part, this was due to the LTTE's (Prabhakaran's) indiscriminate use of violence against the Sinhala population, international tourists, and Tamils who aligned themselves with other Tamil groups. Anyone who could be deemed as being complicit with the Sri Lankan government's occupation of the island was a potential target. The government targeted civilians as well. At key points in time, it intentionally put civilians in harm's way rather than protecting them, especially if they were Tamils. During the 2009 conquest of the LTTE, the government killed Tamils without regard to their affiliation.

Myanmar rebels, for the most part, as well as Peruvian MRTA, the ELN, and the MIR, embraced the populations they sought to save and did not target civilians. MRTA, however, was identified internationally as a terrorist group because of the tactics it employed. Yet, MRTA was careful not to indiscriminately target civilians in these attacks and risk alienating its support base.

Violence was directed against civilians in many of Indonesia's conflicts and was carried out by both the government and associated groups. The government's population redistribution practices (*transmigrasi*) resulted in Javanese civilians being targeted in the regions to which they were sent. They were different from the local populations in almost every way and were seen as being representatives of the government's domination. The conflict in West Papua was a particularly violent case, where citizens turned against one another based on different opinions about whether the region should be independent.

In Peru, the "us versus them" mentality that was indoctrinated through ideological training led by Guzman made the targeting of uncooperative civilians possible. For its part, the Peruvian government also targeted civilians thought to be sympathizing with rebels. Both viewed members of the indigenous population as easily expendable if they did not cooperate. A similar situation ensued in Myanmar when the SLORC decidedly targeted civilian populations as it sought to punish rebel factions that would not accept their terms.

Intervention

The role of external actors was quite evident in the most enduring conflicts that were studied. China's decision to support the Communist Party of Burma, as well as any ethnic groups that were willing to accept the CPB's primary role in any alliance, altered the trajectory of those conflicts. The Communists and their allies were able to take over a large swath of land and hold that territory for some time. When that assistance was revoked, the groups were severely weakened, particularly because China not only withdrew aid but also began working more directly with the Myanmar government. External intervention in Sierra Leone was crucial to the enduring nature of its conflict as well. In that case, Charles Taylor of Liberia supported the RUF from the early phases of the conflict through its termination. His intervention was initially in response to his anger at Sierra Leone's support of ECOWAS activities to terminate the civil conflict in Liberia. Later in the war, Taylor continued support in order to maintain the income stream associated with the Sierra Leone diamonds that were being smuggled through his state. At the same time as Taylor was a force for continuing the conflict, ECOWAS and individual African states were intervening in an effort to bring the brutal war to an end. In addition, a major factor in the termination of the war in Sierra Leone was an economic intervention. When the United Nations banned the trade in uncut diamonds from Sierra Leone until they could be certified as not conflict diamonds, it posed a significant threat to the RUF's funding as well as Taylor's profits.

External intervention in the case of Sri Lanka was varied and complex. Early in the conflict India provided support for the LTTE in the form of weapons and training in Tamil Nadu. As the fighting wore on, however, India became concerned that the support that was being provided to the LTTE would create unrest in Tamil Nadu. India then engaged in a peace agreement with the Sri Lankan government and sent in peacekeeping troops to aid with the fight against the LTTE. After those Indian troops were compelled to withdraw in the face of extensive opposition in Sri Lanka, the interventions in the conflict were relatively limited. The LTTE continued to be able to acquire arms and funds internationally throughout the conflict. In part this took the form of coerced payments from the Tamil diaspora community abroad. This was seriously curtailed by new counterterrorism laws after 9/11, which limited the group's ability to move funds and acquire weapons. The group effectively lost its ability to maintain or build capacity.

In Indonesia external intervention took many forms depending on the location and nature of the dispute. With the Republic of South Moluccas, the United Nations Commission for Indonesia put international pressure on the Indonesian government but was unsuccessful in creating a mediated end to the conflict. In the case of West Papua, both Papua New Guinea and Australia were active in using diplomatic intervention to try to bring about an end to the conflict. In East Timor, U.S. and Australian diplomatic support was initially behind the government as there were fears that the region would become Communist if independent. The United Nations played a strong role in this case and deployed a peacekeeping mission to East Timor for six years. This was necessary because, even when the government and FRETILIN could come to a negotiated agreement, neither side could pacify the domestic population, which was split over the question of independence. Intervention in Aceh was influenced by the case of East Timor in two ways. First, concerns about further erosion of the integrity of the Indonesian state arose, creating international pressure on the rebels to support a negotiated settlement. The second impact was on the government, as international backlash against its brutal repression in East Timor caused diplomatic pressure on it to achieve peace in Aceh.

There was not, however, international intervention in all of the enduring conflicts. Peru's Sendero Luminoso and MRTA were able to survive without third-party support. Their tactical decisions were important in this regard. MRTA never engaged in guerrilla warfare, choosing instead to remain (mostly) in Lima and in the coastal cities and targeting foreign and government assets. Its approach was one that was aimed at gaining support among Peruvians and, therefore, was careful to avoid civilian casualties. Sendero, on the other hand, had the numbers and the ideology to use guerrilla warfare effectively. It was also operating in mountainous terrain among a population of sympathizers that had experienced severe inequality and deprivation at the hands of multiple Peruvian regimes. It also employed force or coercion in order to gain support. This may have ultimately undercut sympathies, both domestically and internationally, and their potential base, but its campaign endured for over a decade.

As demonstrated previously, most of the enduring conflicts in Indonesia were terminated under pressures from the international system. These were brought to bear on both government and groups. The government's goal to become more integrated into the international system facilitated these terminations as Indonesia attempted to show that it could resolve internal conflict and avoid human rights violations. In the case of Aceh, however, it is unclear if the negotiated settlement would have held if not for the 2004 Asian tsunami. Another complex case in Indonesia is the continued dissatisfaction with the secular nature of the regime. This cause was championed by the DI Movement from 1952 to 1961, at which time the violence stopped, but the desire for an Islamic state continued for many. This has manifested itself in the formation of Jemaah Islamiyah, a terrorist organization that operates in Indonesia as an umbrella for various Islamist groups. In some cases, while the conflict may have terminated, the sentiment lives. The conflict in Sierra Leone was terminated through a combination of increased government capacity and international pressures on the RUF. The government was relatively constrained in its use of force, particularly against civilians. In order to achieve termination, international actors had to convince the RUF to give up the fight. Finally, in Sri Lanka the government seems to have achieved a decisive victory over the LTTE in 2009, which is discussed further below.

Termination

One of the goals of this book was to gain a better understanding of the types of factors that effectively bring about conflict termination. A comparison of the conflict outcomes for the cases examined in the book is presented on Table C.3. The shorter, episodic conflicts seem to be clearly impacted by relative group and government capacities, as one actor was able to achieve victory somewhat easily. This was true in the case of the Congo, as the military strength of the Mbochi coupled with the Angolan troops triumphed. The cases of lasting conflict, not surprisingly, are more complicated. Group goals do seem to complicate resolution efforts in the long term. Resource goals are clearly easier to negotiate than issues involving representation and certainly secession. This is not that surprising (see, e.g., Rothman 1997). What was more interesting was the changing nature of goals in light of the availability of resources. Groups such as the Shan and Wa armies in Myanmar or the RUF in Sierra Leone, which became more interested in controlling wealth than obtaining political goals, were more amenable negotiating partners. Of course, the civilian population in such situations often bears the brunt of the decisions. This was the case in Peru as well.

The enduring conflicts that appear to have been terminated include several in Myanmar and all of those in Indonesia, Sierra Leone, and Sri Lanka. Of course, few of these (with East Timor being a possible exception) addressed the underlying grievances that brought about conflict in the first place. As a result, there is simmering popular discontent that may not reach the minimum battle death threshold to be considered an armed conflict, at least at this time. The conflicts in Myanmar were "ended" essentially through coercion. Groups were given the option to give up their campaign, keep their armies intact, and join forces with the government in exchange for the right to control trade routes through their territory, or they would face an onslaught of destruction in which civilians would be treated the same as combatants. Most groups gave in under such an arrangement. Issues of autonomy or representation were never addressed. It was not surprising, then, that the pro-democracy movement, which emerged in 1989, found common ground with many of the ethnicities that sympathized with or fought alongside the ethnic groups.

TABLE C.3   Comparison of Means of Termination across the Cases

Country	Group	Means of termination
Sierra Leone	RUF	Lomé Peace Agreement mediated by ECOWAS, the UN, and others. Required the creation of the UNMOSIL to serve as a peacekeeping force.
	AFRC	Group seized government in 1997 and joined with the RUF. It lost government power in early 1998 and was routed in combat in January 1999.
	Kamajors	Worked against the RUF alongside the government, except for the period when the RUF and AFRC formed a junta to govern, at which time it fought them. Worked with Liberian and ECOMOG forces against them, which brought about negotiations and the end of hostilities.
Republic of the Congo	Cobras Ninjas Cocoyes	Government military victory in the face of Angolan intervention.
	Ninjas	This splinter conflict has been inactive since 2002, following successful negotiations
Sri Lanka	JVP	Pursued political means to have its dispute addressed and continued to hold power in the Sri Lankan government at the time of writing
	LTTE	In 2009 the government abrogated the 2002 ceasefire and escalated conflict with a major offensive against the LTTE in the north. Both sides engaged in extensive violence against civilians. The LTTE called for a ceasefire in February 2009, but the government was close to victory, so it refused. Government forces killed Prabhakaran in May 2009. Given his intense charismatic leadership style (which supported the group's capacity), this helped assure the government's victory
	TELO EPRLF	Defeated by LTTE in intergroup violence
Myanmar	Arakan Kachin Karen Mon Shan	All these insurrections have had factions sign ceasefire agreements with the Myanmar government. The lack of substance to the agreements and continued civilian abuse have made these agreements tenuous at best. Some groups, such as the Kachin, Karen, and at least one faction of the Shan, have continued their rebellion.
	Communists	The aging Communist leadership accepted retirement in China at the time the Chinese decided to stop funding their cause and begin to work with the Myanmar government. The Communist insurrection was defeated as a result.
Indonesia	DI Permestas PRRI	The group experienced low supply levels, low morale, and defection of members when the government offered amnesty, decreasing the capacity of the groups and leading many to surrender and to the eventual negotiation of peace with the groups. However, Islamist tendencies continue to exist in the country.

TABLE C.3   Continued

Country	Group	Means of termination
	South Moluccas	Government military victory
	OPM	Government defeat by killing or capturing the group's leaders, leading to a lack of will to fight among its members
	FRETILIN	When East Timor gained independence, FRETILIN entered the political realm as a party in the new state's government. At the time of publication, the group still was a major political force in the country.
	GAM	Mediated end to the conflict was facilitated by the 2004 Asian tsunami, which devastated the region and allowed the government to leverage its plight to gain a peace agreement
Peru	ELN MIR	Swift government military victory
	MRTA	MRTA has moved into the political realm and given up armed struggle
	Sendero Luminoso	Sendero appeared defeated in the face of Guzman's arrest. A splinter faction did emerge, however, and seems to have moved more directly into the drug trade.

It has been well noted that negotiated outcomes are challenging to first achieve, then to maintain, in civil disputes (Licklider 1995; Gurr 1990; Smith 1986). After an in-depth look at the cases in this book, it becomes even more clear as to why that might be the case. External actors often pressure civil war governments and nonstate actors to come to terms. However, unless both entities act in good faith and there is either a certain amount of trust in the process or a guarantor of the peace, these negotiated agreements are unlikely to be fulfilled (see Johnston 2007). In the case of Sri Lanka, for instance, when the government reached a negotiated settlement for the Tamil issue with India in 1985, Prabhakaran reluctantly agreed to a ceasefire as he believed the arrangement would go forward regardless of his objection. His continued devotion to victory through violence demonstrated his lack of commitment to the ceasefire agreement. In Sierra Leone, the Abidjan Accord in 1996 and then the Lomé Agreement in 1999 both failed to bring about lasting peace. It was only when the RUF's income stream was threatened and the United Nations increased the size of its peacekeeping force that the conflict was terminated.

Conversely, military victories, such as those in Sri Lanka and the Congo, do appear to terminate conflicts. However, again, if underlying issues are not addressed, it is unclear whether even those can stand the test of time. This is certainly the case with Sri Lanka, where the government's victory in 2009 is too recent to know if there will be a return to violence. Peru's MRTA appears to have been terminated with the arrest of Polay, although even that group made one last effort to garner support for its cause with the 1996 embassy takeover. The decision to shift toward the political arena seems to have signaled an end to the conflict more definitively. The JVP in Sri Lanka made a similar decision in 1990.

VALUE OF THE COMPARATIVE FRAMEWORK

The cases examined have demonstrated how incredibly complex civil conflicts can be. While cases like the South Moluccas were short lived, others persisted. Not surprisingly, cases thought to be episodic in nature tended to reemerge when their underlying issues were not addressed during or after previous bouts of violence. This was the case in Peru, Myanmar, and Sri Lanka, among others. While there are differences between the cases examined here, there are also similarities in terms of what drives actors to behave in particular ways. Tactical decisions made by actors are a function of the conflict context, group or government capacity, and group goals. The comparative framework put forth and used to compare the cases presented in this book allows one to flesh out the complexity of civil conflicts and even embrace it. Both static and dynamic factors interact and sometimes result in civil war actors choosing terrorism over more traditional forms of civil warfare, for example. While some factors appear more relevant than others, depending on the dispute examined, all are captured in the framework presented. As a result, a better understanding of the direction that any particular group may take, or the tactics it might employ, can be achieved by applying the comparative framework presented in this volume.

As international norms have shifted, particularly in the post–Cold War era, the international community appears determined to address more effectively the types of disputes examined here. Minimizing the amount of violence against civilians has become a primary goal in dealing with intrastate conflict. The framework utilized here helps illustrate the conditions under which groups make such tactical decisions and identify the factors that move groups toward negotiated outcomes. Without outside intervention, relative group capacity can be influenced in ways that could potentially minimize the level of civilian violence experienced in the midst of war rather than exacerbate it. While previous research on civil wars tended to focus on causes and outcomes, what is suggested here is that in order to understand civil war behavior, a more comprehensive approach has to be taken. The shifting nature of relative group capacity (measured in many different ways), coupled with dynamic group goals, determines the tactical decisions and path that civil war actors will take. The case studies illustrate the relevance of third parties to this process and how tactical decisions can be influenced by their interventions. Application of the framework to conflicts in the system provides an improved understanding of the path of rebellion and the influence various factors may have on the decisions made by the actors involved.

NOTES

Introduction

1. This is the same distinction that Correlates of War researchers make, in that in order for a civil conflict or war to occur, both sides must be engaged in the armed conflict demonstrating effective resistance (Small and Singer 1982). This allows armed conflict to be differentiated from one-sided violence or a massacre.

Chapter 1. Conflict Dynamics

1. An enduring rivalry is defined as a dyadic conflictual relationship between two opponents that is long lasting and that involves repeated militarized engagement (DeRouen and Bercovitch 2008; Kriesberg 1998; Goertz and Diehl 1993). Rivalry involves multiple engagements between elites, creating an enduring history of conflict. All rivalries are conflicts, then, but not all conflicts are rivalries.

2. There is a difference between strategy and tactic. The use of tactic here is with intent. A strategy of terrorism, for instance, would likely take the form of a campaign of attacks designed to achieve some overarching goal. Terrorism as a tactic might be limited to one attack against civilians. The focus here is on tactics because it is fairly rare to find reliable strategy documents for nonstate actors. In contrast, tactics are more easily observed.

3. See also the work of Rauchhaus (2009), Kuperman (2008), and Crawford and Kuperman (2006) on the moral hazard of intervention into civil wars.

4. Coalition forming has been studied quite extensively through research on the American Congress or parliamentary systems. What motivates various forms of coalitions, however, is likely to be quite different depending on the context (Reisinger 1986).

5. It is not the intention of this work to provide a comprehensive listing or analysis of definitions. Rather, its intent is to focus on the common aspect of targeting civilians or innocents that is present in the literature. Che Guevara's classic work on guerilla warfare specified that guerilas target "the oppressor and his agents," which is read by many to mean government and its bureaucratic implements.

6. *Keesing's World News Archive* (formerly *Keesing's Record of World Events* and *Keesing's Contemporary News Archive* in electronic and print versions) is a fee-based online collection of news. The source began collecting materials in 1931 and currently includes in excess of 114,000 entries.

Chapter 2. Resources and Conflict

1. The Uppsala Conflict Data Program (UCDP) has collected information and data on armed conflict since 1946 and has built the reputation of being one of the most reliable sources

for both statistical data and up-to-date summaries of conflict dynamics in the field. One of its products that was used extensively for this book is the UCDP *Conflict Encyclopedia*, which is an online resource (http://ucdp.uu.se/?id=1). The authors accessed the source throughout this multiyear project. Because the source is regularly updated, material used here may no longer be available.

2. Taylor's support for the RUF was described by the SCSL (2004) as follows: "[Prosecution] submits that [Taylor] was the "father" or "godfather" of the RUF in the sense that he created the RUF as a viable organized armed force; nurtured and sustained it by providing a secure training environment, supplies, instructors, and new recruits; ensured its continued survival; taught it how to terrorize civilians; directed it in its first endeavours, protected it from outside threats to its existence, and strengthened the basic unity of the group" (14–15).

Chapter 3. Elite-Led Episodic Rivalry

1. Brazzaville is the capital of the Republic of the Congo. As a result, references to the Republic of the Congo are frequently made as Congo-Brazzaville allowing readers to easily distinguish the Republic of the Congo from the Democratic Republic of the Congo.

2. Clark (1998) actually suggests two cleavages existed. The first involved the international Cold War divisions.

3. Instrumentalist tactics are employed by politicians to rally support. They typically involve ethnocentric pleas to their ethnic kin at the expense of other identity groups in society. See the work of Saideman (1997) or Olson Lounsbery and Pearson (2009) for more on this topic.

Chapter 4. Ethnic Conflict over Time

1. According to Hassan (2009), the Tamil diaspora numbers about seventy million and served as the main source of funding for the Tamils. The Tamil approach to fundraising within the diaspora communities is unique in that it includes the use of threats and violence to ensure that the Tamils abroad continue to pay. After the end of hostilities, in fact, a French court convicted twenty-one LTTE members of extorting millions from the expatriate Tamils in France (Falksohn and Rao 2008). It is likely that this can be attributed to the group's committed drive to increase its capacity, resulting in the identifying of those Tamils who were not actively supporting the cause as being complicit with government.

2. One of the unique strategies adopted by the LTTE through the years was the systematic use of suicide bombers. The Black Tigers were an elite suicide attack group within the LTTE. The group was so influential that the government demanded its disbandment as a condition of a ceasefire in 2002 (Hopgood 2005). "Black Tigers serve two main strategic purposes for the LTTE: first, to compensate for a lack of heavier weaponry; and second, to engage in commando-like actions to secure inaccessible or difficult targets, including assassinations. They are best understood, in other words, as elite soldiers selected for the most dangerous missions—ones with very little chance of survival, and none at all in many cases" (Hopgood 2005, 46). The Black Tigers are therefore fairly unusual in the world of suicide attacks. They go into the attack, at least in some cases, with the possibility of survival if their actions are sufficiently skillful. Furthermore, whereas other suicide bombing tactics focus on killing as

many in one attack as possible, the use of the Black Tigers was more to take out the government's strategically important assets (individuals, materiel or economic assets). In some ways it is a tactic of warfare rather than terrorism, as the goal is the military advantage rather than instilling fear or inflicting casualties. The Black Tigers are important in the context of this study in that they represent a method that the LTTE employed in an attempt to overcome the government's superior capacity.

Chapter 5. A Case of Enduring Rivalries

1. The State Law and Order Restoration Council (SLORC), a military junta that seized power in 1988, renamed the country of Burma to Myanmar. Much of the international community resisted this change and continued to refer to the country as Burma in protest to the SLORC's decision to retain control over the country after the National League for Democracy (NLD) won a landslide election in 1990. Recently, the U.S. government has moved to refer to the country as Myanmar in response to political developments that seem to indicate the government moving in the direction of openness. For the purposes of the chapter, *Burma* is used when referencing the country prior to 1988. The country is referred to as *Myanmar* in post-1988 discussions and more generally.

2. The pro-democracy movement, led by the National League for Democracy (NLD) and popularized by Aung San Suu Kyi, daughter of revolutionary leader Aung San, is not examined in this chapter as an armed conflict. The ABSDF emerged from this movement, and several ethnic rebel groups gained membership and support from participating students (particularly those forced to flee Rangoon). The movement itself, however, is a nonviolent struggle and, as such, does not constitute a rivalry, which by definition requires the militarization of conflict (see Goertz and Diehl 1992; Olson Lounsbery 2005).

3. Silverstein (1997) estimates that approximately one million Burmese citizens were missing from the census counts, most of whom resided in border or frontier areas where the central government has little control. As a result, the minority groups, such as the Karen, are more likely to be undercounted.

4. In 1988, the Burmese government appeared to be democratizing by holding national elections. The National League for Democracy and Suu Kyi won many seats but were not permitted to take them, resulting in massive protests ultimately leading to the arrest of Suu Kyi, among others, and more government repression. The debacle led to a large-scale Western boycott and sanctions of Burmese goods.

Chapter 6. Challenges of a Heterogeneous Population

1. One outcome of this was that soldiers (South Moluccas citizens both from there and those who had been in the military and stationed in Java) who had yet to be demobilized and had fought against Sukarno for the independence of South Moluccas (numbering about five thousand including their families) were subsequently sent to the Netherlands with the promise that they could return, but they were never allowed to do so. This resulted in agitation and demonstrations in the Netherlands as the deportees attempted to get the Dutch government to intervene on their behalf and on that of the Republic of South Moluccas.

Chapter 7. Rivals, Conflict, and Ideology

1. For an explanation of determining poverty and extreme poverty rates, see World Bank (1993, 13).

2. Peru is separated into twenty-four administrative departments.

REFERENCES

Abdullah, Ibrahim. 1998. "Bush Path to Destruction: The Origin and Character of the Revolutionary United Front / Sierra Leone." *Journal of Modern African Studies* 36(2): 203–235.

Agence France-Presse. 2015a. "Congo since the Return to Power of Sassou Nguesso." October 25. http://reliefweb.int/report/congo/republic-congo-return-power-sassou-nguesso, accessed August 10, 2016.

Agence France-Presse. 2015b. "Former Separatist Fighters Surrender in Indonesia's Aceh Province." *NDTV.com*. http://www.ndtv.com/world-news/former-separatist-fighters -surrender-in-indonesias-aceh-1260232, accessed January 27, 2016.

Agence France-Presse. 2015c. "Sierra Leone Loses Track of Millions in Ebola Funds." *New York Times*, February 14. http://www.nytimes.com/2015/02/15/world/africa/sierra-leone -loses-track-of-millions-in-ebola-funds.html?ref=topics&_r=1, accessed January 27, 2016.

Alifandi, Anton. 2015. "Indonesia's Islamic State–Affiliated Militant Group More Likely to Attack Security Forces and Entertainment Targets Outside Jakarta." *Jane's Intelligence Review*, November 30. http://www.janes.com/article/56393/indonesia-s-islamic-state-affiliated -militant-group-more-likely-to-attack-security-forces-and-entertainment-targets-outside -jakarta, accessed January 29, 2016.

Amnesty International. 1999. "Republic of Congo: An Old generation of Leaders in New Carnage." March 25. Index no. AFR 22/001/1999.

Amnesty International. 2015. "A 'Lost Decade' for Victims of Indonesia's Aceh Conflict." Gale Group Targeted News Service, August 14. http://go.galegroup.com/ps/i.do?p=STND&u =ncliveecu&id=GALE|A425375542&v=2.1&it=r&sid=summon&userGroup=ncliveecu &authCount=1, accessed January 27, 2016.

"Amnesty Request for Din Minimi to Be Processed." *Jakarta Post*, January 1, 2016. http://www .thejakartapost.com/news/2016/01/01/amnesty-request-din-minimi-be-processed.html, accessed January 27, 2016.

Ananta, Aris. 2006. "Changing Ethnic Composition and Potential Violent Conflict in Riau Archipelago, Indonesia: An Early Warning Signal." *Population Review* 45(1): n.p.

Archibald, Steven, and Paul Richards. 2002. "Converts to Human Rights? Popular Debate about War and Justice in Rural Central Sierra Leone." *Africa: Journal of the International African Institute* 72(3): 339–367.

Arifianto, Alexander. 2009. "Explaining the Cause of Muslim-Christian Conflicts in Indonesia: Tracing the Origins of *Kristenisasi* and *Islamisasi*." *Islam and Christian-Muslim Relations* 20(1): 73–89.

Asplund, Knut. 2009. "Resistance to Human Rights in Indonesia: Asian Values and Beyond." *Asia-Pacific Journal on Human Rights and the Law* 10(1): 27–47.

Atlantic. 2015. "Burma Doesn't Want the Rohingya Muslims but Insists on Keeping Them." June 12.

Australia West Papua Association, Sydney. 1995. *West Papua Information Kit*. http://www.cs .utexas.edu/users/cline/papua/core.htm#top, accessed August 26, 2014.

Azca, Muhammad Najib. 2006. "In between Military and Militia: The Dynamics of the Security Forces in the Communal Conflict in Ambon." *Asian Journal of Social Science* 34(3): 431–455.

Badcock, James. 2015. "U.S.-Belgian Businessman Arrested on Sierra Leone 'Blood Diamonds' Charge in Spain." *Telegraph*, August 31.

Baer, Suzie. 2003. *Peru's MRTA: Tupac Amaru Revolutionary Movement*. New York: Rosen.

Balch-Lindsay, Dylan, Andrew J. Enterline, and Kyle A. Joyce. 2008. "Third-Party Intervention and the Civil War Process." *Journal of Peace Research* 45(3): 345–363.

Ballentine, Karen, and Heiko Nitzschke. 2003. "Beyond Greed and Grievance: Policy Lessons from Studies in the Political Economy of Armed Conflict." IPA Policy Report, October.

Bandarage, Asoka. 2009. *The Separatist Conflict in Sri Lanka: Terrorism, Ethnicity, Political Economy* New York: Routledge.

Bapat, Navin. 2005. "Insurgency and the Opening of Peace Processes." *Journal of Peace Research* 42(6): 699–717.

BBC News. 2003. "Foday Sankoh: The Cruel Rebel." July 30. http://news.bbc.co.uk/go/pr/fr/-/2 /hi/africa/3110629.stm.

BBC News. 2015a. "Sri Lanka Profile–Timeline." January 9. http://www.bbc.com/news/world -south-asia-12004081, accessed January 26, 2016.

BBC News. 2015b. "What's Happening in Syria?" February 20. http://www.bbc.co.uk/news round/16979186.

Beeson, Mark. 2008. "Civil-Military Relations in Indonesia and the Philippines: Will the Thai Coup Prove Contagious?" *Armed Forces & Society* 34(3): 474–490.

Béjar, Hector. 1969. *Peru 1965: Notes on a Guerrilla Experience*. New York: Monthly Review Press.

Berg, Ronald H. 1994. "Peasant Responses to Shining Path in Andahuaylas." In Palmer, *Shining Path of Peru*, 101-122.

Bertrand, Jacques. 2008. "Ethnic Conflicts in Indonesia: National Models, Critical Junctures, and the Timing of Violence." *Journal of East Asian Studies* 8(3): 425–449.

Bhattacharji, Preeti. 2009. "Backgrounder: Liberation Tigers of Tamil Eelam (aka Tamil Tigers) (Sri Lanka, Separatists)." *Council on Foreign Relations*, May 20, 2009. http://www.cfr .org/publication/9242/, accessed October 14, 2009.

Bilveer, Singh. 2000. "Civil-Military Relations in Democratizing Indonesia: Change amidst Continuity." *Armed Forces & Society* 26(4): 607–633.

Biswas, Bidisha. 2009. "Can't We Just Talk? Reputational Concerns and International Intervention in Sri Lanka and Indonesia (Aceh)." *International Negotiation* 14(1): 121–147.

Blair, David. 2012. "Liberian Warlord Charles Taylor Is Jailed for 50 Years." *Telegraph*, June 5.

Blenkinsop, Philip. 1998. "Behind the Lines . . . with Timor's Forgotten Guerrillas." *Far Eastern Economic Review*, September 3, 25–27.

Bottom, William P., James Holloway, Scott McClurg, and Gary J. Miller. 2000. "Negotiating a Coalition: Risk, Quota Shaving, and Learning to Bargain." *Journal of Conflict Resolution* 44(2): 147–169.

Boulding, Kenneth. 1989. *The Three Faces of Power*. Newbury Park, CA: Sage Publications.

Boulding, Kenneth. 2009. "A Proposal for a Research Program in the History of Peace." *Peace & Change* 14(4): 461–469.

Brecher, Michael, and Jonathan Wilkenfeld. 1997. *A Study of Crisis*. Ann Arbor: University of Michigan Press.

Brown, Catherine. 1999. "Burma: The Political Economy of Violence." *Disasters* 23(3): 234–256.

Brown, Derek. 2000. "Who is Foday Sankoh?" *Guardian*, May 17. http://www.theguardian .com/world/2000/may/17/sierraleone/print.

Brown, Graham. 2005. *Horizontal Inequalities, Ethnic Separatism, and Violent Conflict: The Case of Aceh, Indonesia.* UNDP Human Development Report. New York: United Nations, 2005.

Brundige, Elizabeth, Winter King, Priyneha Vahali, Stephen Vladeck, and Xiang Yuan. 2004. "Indonesian Human Rights Abuses in West Papua: Application of the Law of Genocide to the History of Indonesian Control." Paper prepared for the Indonesia Human Rights Network. April.

Bueno de Mesquita, Ethan. 2005. "The Quality of Terror." *American Journal of Political Science* 49(3): 515–530.

Bueno de Mesquita, Ethan. 2008. "Conciliation, Counterterrorism, and Patterns of Terrorist Violence." *International Organization* 59 (Winter): 145–176.

Bueno de Mesquita, Ethan, and Eric Dickson. 2007. "The Propaganda of the Deed: Terrorism, Counterterrorism, and Mobilization." *American Journal of Political Science* 51(2): 364–381.

Bullion, Alan. 1995. "War Eclipses Peace in Sri Lanka." *World Today* 51(12): 227-229.

Burgoyne, Major Michael L. 2010. "The Allure of Quick Victory: Lessons from Peru's Fight against Sendero Luminoso." *Military Review,* September-October, 68–73.

Capizzi, Elaine, Helen Hill, and Dave Macey. 1976. "FRETILIN and the Struggle for Independence in East Timor." *Race & Class* 17(4): 381–395.

Carment, David, and Patrick James. 1996. "Two-Level Games and Third-Party Intervention: Evidence from Ethnic Conflict in the Balkans and South Asia." *Canadian Journal of Political Science* 29(3): 521–554.

Carment, David, and Patrick James. 1998. *Peace in the Midst of Wars: Preventing and Managing International Ethnic Conflicts.* Columbia, S.C.: University of South Carolina Press.

Cederman, Lars-Erik, and Kristian Skrede Gleditsch. 2009. "Introduction to Special Issue 'Disaggregating Civil War.'" Special issue, *Journal of Conflict Resolution* 53(4): 487–495.

Center for Defense Information. 2003. "In the Spotlight: Sendero Luminoso." Terrorism Project. http://www.cdi.org/terrorism/sendero.cfm, accessed October 8, 2016.

CEPAL (Comision Economica Para America Latino y el Caribe). 1990. *Magnitud de la Probreza en America Latina en los Anos Ochenta.* May. Reported in World Bank (1993).

Champion, Margaret Y. 2001. "Nationalization and Privatization in Peru: Socio-Economic Images in Perpetual Conflict?" *Journal of Socio-Economics* 30(6): 517–532.

Charlé, Suzanne. 2003. "Losing Friends in Indonesia." *Nation,* December 29, 19–22.

Chen, Matthew E. 2007. "Chinese National Oil Companies and Human Rights." *Orbis* 51(1): 41–54.

Chopra, Anuj. 2006. "Sri Lankan Talks a Welcome Step for Weary Observers." *Christian Science Monitor,* October 30. http://www.csmonitor.com/2006/1030/p04s02-wosc.html, accessed October 8, 2016.

Christia, Fotini. 2012. *Alliance Formation in Civil Wars.* New York: Cambridge University Press.

Clark, John. 1997. "Petro-Politics in Congo." *Journal of Democracy* 8(3): 62–76.

Clark, John. 1998. "Foreign Intervention in the Civil War of the Congo Republic." *Issue: A Journal of Opinion* 26(1): 31–36.

Clark, John. 2002a. "The Neo-Colonial Context of the Democratic Experiment of Congo-Brazzaville." *African Affairs* 101(403): 171–192.

Clark, John. 2002b. "Resource Revenues and Political Development in Sub-Saharan Africa Congo Republic in Comparative Perspective." *Africa Spectrum* 37(1): 25–41.

Clark, John. 2008. *The Failure of Democracy in the Republic of Congo.* Boulder, Colo.: Lynne Rienner.

Cochrane, Joe. 2012. "Aceh Peace Process at Risk in Indonesia?" *Wall Street Journal*, January 31. http://blogs.wsj.com/indonesiarealtime/2012/01/31/aceh-peace-process-at-risk-in-indonesia/, accessed September 28, 2016.

Coker, Christopher. 2002. "Globalization and Insecurity in the Twenty-First Century: NATO and the Management of Risk." Special issue, *Adelphi Papers* 42 (345).

Collier, Paul, and Anke Hoeffler. 1998. "On Economic Causes of Civil War." *Review of Economic Studies* 50(4): 563–573.

Collins, Elizabeth Fuller. 2002. "Indonesia: A Violent Culture." *Asian Survey* 42(4): 582–604.

Colombijn, Freek. 2002. "Explaining the Violent Solution in Indonesia." *Brown Journal of World Affairs* 9(1): 49–56.

Cook, Alethia, and Marie Olson Lounsbery. 2010. "Choose Your Weapon (or Strategy)! An Analysis of the Factors Influencing Strategy in Civil Wars." *Democracy and Security* 6(3): 256–277.

Coppel, C. A. 2006. "Violence: Analysis, Representation and Resolution." In *Violent Conflicts in Indonesia: Analysis, Representation, Resolution*, edited by C. A. Coppel, 3–18. London: Routledge, 2006.

Cormick, Craig. 1994. "Xanana Gusmao: Fighting for Freedom with Words." *Green Left Weekly*, May 25, n.p. http://www.greenleft.org.au/node/6530, accessed September 17, 2014.

Cornwell, Svante E. 2005. "The Interactions of Narcotics and Conflict." *Journal of Peace Research* 42(6): 751–760.

CQ Press. 2003. "Sri Lankan Government and Rebels on Cease-Fire." In *Historic Documents of 2002*, 92. Washington, D.C.: CQ Press. http://dx.doi.org/10.4135/9781483302591.n2, accessed September 24, 2016.

CQ Press. 2007a. "International Diplomats on the Peace Process in Sri Lanka." In *Historic Documents of 2006*, 249–56. Washington, D.C.: CQ Press, 2007. http://dx.doi.org/10.4135/9781483302638 accessed September 24, 2016.

CQ Press. 2007b. "Sri Lanka." In *Political Handbook of the World 2007*, edited by Arthur S. Banks, Thomas C. Muller, and William R. Overstreet, 1155–67. Washington, D.C.: CQ Press. http://library.cqpress.com/phw/phw2007_srilanka, accessed September 24, 2016.

CQ Press. 2009a. "Peru." In *Political Handbook of the World*. CQ Press Online Editions. http://library.cqpress.com/phw/document.php?id=phw2009_Peru&type=toc&num=144, accessed September 24, 2016.

CQ Press. 2009b. "Sri Lanka." In *Political Handbook of the World*. http://library.cqpress.com/phw/document.php?id=phw2009_SriLanka&type=toc&num=171, accessed October 20, 2009.

CQ Press. 2011a. "Republic of the Congo." In *Political Handbook of the World*. CQ Press Online Editions. http://library.cqpress.com/phw/document.php?id=phw2011_Republicofthe Congo&type=toc&num=43, accessed September 24, 2016.

CQ Press. 2011b. "Sierra Leone." In *Political Handbook of the World: Online Edition*. http://library .cqpress.com/phw/document.php?id=phw2011_SierraLeone&type=toc&num=164, accessed September 24, 2016.

Crabtree, John. 2002. "The Impact of Neo-Liberal Economics on Peruvian Peasant Agriculture in the 1990s." *Journal of Peasant Studies* 29(3–4): 131–161.

Crawford, Timothy, and Alan Kuperman, eds. 2006. *Gambling on Humanitarian Intervention: Moral Hazard, Rebellion, and Internal War*. New York: Routledge.

Cronin, Audrey K. 2002/2003. "Behind the Curve: Globalization and International Terrorism." *International Security* 27(3): 30–58.

Cronin, Audrey K. 2006. "How al-Qaida Ends." *International Security* 31(1): 7–48.

Cronin, Audrey K. 2010. "When Should We Talk to Terrorists?" United States Institute of Peace Special Report. https://www.usip.org/sites/default/files/SE240Cronin.pdf, accessed June 29, 2015.

Cunningham, David E. 2006. "Veto Players and Civil War Duration." *American Journal of Political Science* 50 (4): 875–92.

Cunningham, David E., Kristian Skrede Gleditsch, and Idean Salehyan. 2009. "It Takes Two: A Dyadic Analysis of Civil War Duration and Outcome." *Journal of Conflict Resolution* 53(4): 570–597.

Dalpino, Catharin E. 2002. "Indonesia's Democratic Difficulty: The Center Will Not Hold." *Brown Journal of World Affairs* 9(1): 85–94.

De Angelis, Martin. 2015. "Peru's Shining Path Insurgency Reemerges as a Security Threat." *Global Risk Insights*, August 17. http://globalriskinsights.com/2015/08/perus-shining-path -insurgency-reemerges-as-security-threat/.

deBeer, Hanlie, and Richard Cornwell. 1999. "Congo-Brazzaville: The Deep End of the Pool." Occasional Paper no. 41. Pretoria: Africa Early Warning Programme, Institute for Security Studies.

de Jonge, Huub, and Gerben Nooteboom. 2006. "Why the Madurese? Ethnic Conflicts in West and East Kalimantan Compared." *Asian Journal of Social Science* 34(3): 456–474.

De Rosayro, Gaston. 1997. "Explosion Betrays Tigers' Desperation." *South China Morning Post*, October 16.

DeRouen, Karl R., Jr., and Jacob Bercovitch. 2008. "Enduring Internal Rivalries: A New Framework for the Study of Civil War." *Journal of Peace Research* 45(1): 55–74.

DeRouen, Karl R., Jr., Jacob Bercovitch, and Jun Wei. 2009. "Duration of Peace and Recurring Civil Wars in Southeast Asia and the Pacific." *Civil Wars* 11(2): 103–120.

De Silva, K. M. 1981. *A History of Sri Lanka*. Berkeley: University of California Press.

DeVotta, Neil. 2000. "Control Democracy, Institutional Decay, and the Quest for *Eelam*: Explaining Ethnic Conflict in Sri Lanka." *Pacific Affairs* 73(1): 55–76.

DeVotta, Neil. 2009. "The Liberation Tigers of Tamil Eelam and the Lost Quest for Separatism in Sri Lanka." *Asian Survey* 49(6): 1021–1051.

de Witt, Ton, and Vera Gianotten. 1994. "The Center's Multiple Failures." In Palmer, *Shining Path of Peru*, 63–75.

"Discourse: Threat Looms from IS Returnees, 600 Freed Former Terrorists." 2015. *Jakarta Post*, December 11. http://www.thejakartapost.com/news/2015/12/11/discourse-threat-looms-is -returnees-600-freed-former-terrorists.html.

Djuli, M. N., and Robert Jereski. 2002. "Prospects for Peace and Indonesia's Survival." *Brown Journal of World Affairs* 9(1): 35–48.

Driscoll, Jesse. 2012. "Commitment Problems or Bidding Wars? Rebel Fragmentation as Peace Building." *Journal of Conflict Resolution* 56(1): 118–149.

Dugger, Celia W. 2000. "The Blood All Over." *New York Times*, October 8.

"East Timor President Accepts New Cabinet Roster." 2015. Kyodo News Service, February 11.

Eaton, David. 2006. "Diagnosing the Crisis in the Republic of Congo." *Africa* 76(1): 44–69.

Economist. 1992. "Myanmar's Monsters." February 29. http://www.economist.com/node /1974062/print.

Economist. 1998. "A Tooth for a Tooth." January 29. http://www.economist.com/node/111669.

Economist. 2003. "Obituary: Foday Sankoh: Foday Saybana Sankoh, an African Revolutionary, Died on July 29th, Aged 65." August 7. http://www.economist.com/node/1974062.

Economist. 2004. "Asia: Deep Freeze; Myanmar." November 27. http://www.economist.com /node/3429072.

Economist. 2005. "The Mess That the Army has Made." July 23. http://www.economist.com /node/4197705.

Economist. 2007. "Oil, Votes and Ninjas: The Smaller Congo Goes to the Polls." August 9. http://www.economist.com/node/9621999.

Elson, R. E., and Chiara Formichi. 2011. "Why Did Kartosuwiryo Start Shooting? An Account of Dutch-Republican-Islamic Forces Interaction in West Java, 1945–49." *Journal of Southeast Asian Studies* 42(3): 458–486.

Ethnic Nationalities Council (Union of Burma). 2007. 60th Anniversary of the Panglong Agreement. Chang Mai, Thailand: Chang Mai University.

Falksohn, Rüdiger, and Padma Rao. 2008. "Extorting the Diaspora: Tamil Tigers Exploit Exiles Abroad to Fund Insurgency." *Spiegel Online*, February 14. http://www.spiegel.de /international/world/extorting-the-diaspora-tamil-tigers-exploit-exiles-abroad-to-fund -insurgency-a-535316.html, accessed October 8, 2016.

Fearon, James, and David Laitin. 2003. "Ethnicity, Insurgency, and Civil War." *American Political Science Review* 97(1): 75–90.

Feith, Herbert, and Daniel Lev. 1963. "The End of the Indonesian Rebellion." *Pacific Affairs* 36(1): 32–46.

Feldman, Andreas, and Maiju Perala. 2004. "Reassessing the Causes of Nongovernmental Terrorism in Latin America." *Latin American Politics and Society* 46(2): 101–132.

Findley, Michael. 2012. "Bargaining and the Interdependent Stages of Civil War Resolution," *Journal of Conflict Resolution* 57(5): 905–932.

Fison, Darren, and Suzanne Werner. 2002. "A Bargaining Model of War and Peace." *American Journal of Political Science* 46(4): 819–838.

Formichi, Chiara. 2012. *Islam and the Making of the Nation.* Leiden: KITLV Press.

Forsberg, Erika. 2009. "Neighbors at Risk: A Quantitative Study of Civil War Contagion." PhD dissertation, Uppsala University.

Francis, David. 1999. "Mercenary Intervention in Sierra Leone: Providing National Security or International Exploitation." *Third World Quarterly* 20(2): 319–338.

Franck, Raphael, and Ilia Rainer. 2012. "Does the Leader's Ethnicity Matter? Ethnic Favoritism, Education, and Health in Sub-Saharan Africa." *American Political Science Review* 106(2): 294–319.

Freeman, Colin. 2015. "Guinea and Sierra Leone Tried to Cover Up Ebola Crisis, Says Medecins Sans Frontieres." *Telegraph.* http://www.telegraph.co.uk/news/worldnews/ebola /11488726/Guinea-and-Sierra-Leone-tried-to-cover-up-Ebola-crisis-says-Medecins-Sans -Frontieres.html, accessed January 27, 2016.

Fritz, Mark. 1994. "Africa's Youngest Dictator Keeps Tight Rein." *Los Angeles Times*, March 20.

Fuller, Thomas. 2009. "Sri Lanka Rejects Tamil Call for Cease-Fire." *New York Times*, April 26. http://www.nytimes.com/2009/04/27/world/asia/27lanka.html, accessed October 8, 2016.

Galloy, Martine-Renée, and Marc-Éric Gruénais. 1997. "Fighting for Power in the Congo." *LaMonde*, November.

Ganguly, Rajat. 2004. "Sri Lanka's Ethnic Conflict: At a Crossroad between Peace and War." *Third World Quarterly* 25(5): 903–917.

Gargan, Edward. 1993. "Suicide Bomber Kills President of Sri Lanka." *New York Times*, May 2.

Gberie, Lansana. 2003. "West Africa: Rocks in a Hard Place: The Political Economy of Diamonds and Regional Destabilization." In *The Diamonds and Human Security Project*, edited by Ian Smillie. Ottawa: Partnership Africa Canada.

Gberie, Lansana. 2005. *Dirty War in West Africa: The RUF and the Destruction of Sierra Leone.* Bloomington: Indiana University Press.

Gberie, Lansana. 2007. "Liberia and Sierra Leone: Civil Wars, 1989–2004." In *Daily Lives of Civilians in Wartime Africa: From Slavery Days to Rwanda*, edited by John Laband, 195–226. Westport, Conn.: Greenwood.

Gberie, Lansana. 2011. "How Sierra Leone Fell into the Hands of Young Soldiers." *New African*, April, 48–53.

Ghosh, P. A. 1999. *Ethnic Conflict in Sri Lanka and Role of Indian Peace Keeping Force (IPKF)*. New Delhi: A.P.H.

Giblin, Susan. 2007. "Violent Conflicts in Indonesia." *International Journal of Human Rights* 11(4): 517–527.

Gleditsch, Nils Peter, Peter Wallensteen, Mikael Eriksson, Margareta Sollenberg, and Havard Strand. 2002. "Armed Conflict, 1946–2001: A New Dataset." *Journal of Peace Research* 39(5): 615–637.

Globalsecurity.org. N.d. "Mong Tai Army (MTA), United Wa State Army (UWSA)." http://www.globalsecurity.org/military/world/para/wa.htm.

Goertz, Gary, and Paul F. Diehl. 1992. "The Empirical Importance of Enduring Rivalries." *International Interactions* 18(2): 151–183.

Goertz, Gary, and Paul F. Diehl. 1993. "Enduring Rivalry: Theoretical Constructs and Empirical Patterns." *International Studies Quarterly* 37(2): 147–171.

Gonzales, José E. 1994. "Guerrillas and Coca in the Upper Huallaga Valley." In Palmer, *Shining Path of Peru*, 123–143.

Gorriti, Ellenbogen Gustavo. 1999. *The Shining Path: A History of the Millenarian War in Peru*. Chapel Hill: University of North Carolina Press.

Gregory, Kathryn. 2009. "Backgrounder: Shining Path, Tupac Amaru (Peru, Leftists)." Council on Foreign Relations, August 27.

Greig, J. Michael. 2001. "Moments of Opportunity: Recognizing Conditions of Ripeness for International Mediation between Enduring Rivals." *Journal of Conflict Resolution* 45(6): 691–718.

Grundy-Warr, Carl. 1993. "Coexistent Borderlands and Intra-State Conflicts in Mainland Southeast Asia." *Singapore Journal of Tropical Geography* 14(1): 42–57.

Guardian. 2015. "Burma's Birth Control Law Exposes Buddhist Fear of Muslim Minority." May 25.

Gurr, Ted Robert. 1971. *Why Men Rebel*. Princeton, N.J.: Princeton University Press.

Gurr, Ted Robert. 1990. "Ethnic Warfare and the Changing Priorities of Global Security." *Mediterranean Quarterly* 1(1): 82–98.

Gurr, Ted Robert. 1993. *Minorities at Risk: A Global View of Ethnopolitical Conflicts*. Washington, D.C.: United States Institute of Peace.

Guzman, Abimael. 1993. "Exclusive Comments by Abimael Guzman." *World Affairs* 156(1): 52–57.

Harbom, Lotta, and Peter Wallensteen. 2010. "Armed Conflict, 1946–2009." *Journal of Peace Research* 47(4): 501–509.

Hassan, S. Azmat. 2009. *Countering Violent Extremism: The Fate of the Tamil Tigers*. New York: EastWest Institute.

Havermans, Jos. 1999. "Congo Brazzaville: A Democratization Process Scourged by Violence." In *Searching for Peace in Africa: An Overview of Conflict Prevention and Management Activities*, edited by Monique Mekenkamp, Paul Van Tongeren, and Hans Van der Veen. Utrecht, Netherlands: European Platform for Conflict Prevention and Transformation/European Centre for Conflict Prevention.

Hayami, Yoko. 2011. "Pagodas and Prophets: Contesting Sacred Space and Power among Buddhist Karen in Karen State." *Journal of Asian Studies* 70(4): 1083–1105.

Hefner, Robert. 2003. "Roots of Violence in Indonesia: Contemporary Violence in Historical Perspective." *Journal of Asian Studies* 62(2): 1005–1007.

Henderson, Errol, and J. Singer. 2002. "'New Wars' and Rumors of 'New Wars.'" *International Interactions* 28(2): 165–190.

Herriman, Nicholas. 2006. "Fear and Uncertainty: Local Perceptions of the Sorcerer and the State in an Indonesian Witch-hunt." *Asian Journal of Social Science* 34(3): 360–387.

Hindu. 1986. "The View from the Tigers: Part 1 and 2." September. (two-part interview with Velupillai Prabhakaran).

Hirsch, John. 2001. *Sierra Leone: Diamonds and the Struggle for Democracy*. Boulder, Colo.: Lynne Rienner.

Hoffman, Bruce. 1998. *Inside Terrorism*. New York: Columbia University Press.

Hoffman, Bruce. 2009. "The First Non-State Use of a Chemical Weapon in Warfare: The Tamil Tigers' Assault on East Kiran." *Small Wars & Insurgencies* 20(3): 463–477.

Hoffman, Danny. 2002. "The Meaning of a Militia: Understanding the Civil Defence Forces of Sierra Leone." *African Affairs* 106(425): 639–662.

Holliday, Ian. 2005. "Doing Business with Rights and Violating Regimes Corporate Social Responsibility and Myanmar's Military Junta." *Journal of Business Ethics* 61(4): 329–342.

Holliday, Ian. 2008. "Voting and Violence in Myanmar: Nation Building for a Transition to Democracy." *Asian Survey* 48(6): 1038–1058.

Homer-Dixon, Thomas. 1999. *Environment, Scarcity, and Violence*. Princeton, N.J.: Princeton University Press.

Hopgood, Stephen. 2005. "Tamil Tigers, 1987–2002." *Making Sense of Suicide Missions*, edited by Diego Gambetta, 43–76. Oxford: Oxford University Press..

Horikoshi, Hiroko. 1975. "The Dar ul-Islam Movement in West Java (1948–62): An Experience in the Historical Process." *Indonesia*, no. 20, 58–86.

Hulst, Wiecher. 1991. "From Now On, It is Not Just Free Acheh but Free Sumatra." http://Aceh net.tripod.com/sumatra.htm, accessed September 9, 2014.

Human Rights Watch. 1995a. *Peru: The Two Faces of Justice*. Human Rights Watch report 7(9), July. New York: Human Rights Watch. https://www.hrw.org/sites/default/files/reports /PERU957.pdf, accessed September 24, 2016.

Human Rights Watch. 1995b. *Playing the "Communal Card": Communal Violence and Human Rights*. New York: Human Rights Watch. https://www.hrw.org/legacy/reports/1995 /communal/, accessed September 24, 2016.

Human Rights Watch. 1996. "Sri Lanka." *Human Rights Watch World Report 1996*. https:// www.hrw.org/reports/1996/WR96/Asia-08.htm#P735_195262, accessed October 8, 2016.

Human Rights Watch. 1997. "Sri Lanka." *Human Rights Watch World Report 1997*. New York: Human Rights Watch. https://www.hrw.org/reports/1997/WR97/ASIA-06.htm#P487 _223952, accessed October 8, 2016.

Human Rights Watch. 1998. *Burma/Thailand: Unwanted and Unprotected: Burmese Refugees in Thailand*. Human Rights Watch report 10(6), September. New York: Human Rights Watch. https://www.hrw.org/legacy/reports98/thai/Thai989-03.htm, accessed September 24, 2016.

Human Rights Watch. 1999a. "Sierra Leone: Getting Away with Murder, Mutilation, and Rape." Human Rights Watch report 11(3A), July. New York: Human Rights Watch. https:// www.hrw.org/legacy/reports/1999/sierra/, accessed September 24, 2016.

Human Rights Watch. 1999b. "Sri Lanka." *Human Rights Watch World Report 1999*. New York: Human Rights Watch. https://www.hrw.org/legacy/worldreport99/asia/srilanka.html, accessed October 8, 2016.

Human Rights Watch. 2002. *Indonesia: Accountability for Human Rights Violations in Aceh.* Human Rights Watch report 14(1), March. New York: Human Rights Watch. https://www .hrw.org/reports/2002/aceh/, accessed September 24, 2016.

Human Rights Watch. 2005. *"They Came and Destroyed Our Village Again": The Plight of Internally Displaced People in the Karen State.* Human Rights Watch report 17(4C), June. New York: Human Rights Watch. https://www.hrw.org/report/2005/06/09/they-came-and -destroyed-our-village-again/plight-internally-displaced-persons accessed October 8, 2016.

Human Rights Watch. 2006. "Sri Lanka." *Human Rights Watch World Report 2006.* New York: Human Rights Watch. https://www.hrw.org/legacy/english/docs/2006/01/18/slanka12252 .htm accessed October 8, 2016.

Human Rights Watch. 2012. *"The Government Could Have Stopped This": Sectarian Violence and Ensuring Abuses in Burma's Arakan State.* New York: Human Rights Watch. https:// www.hrw.org/sites/default/files/reports/burma0812webwcover_0.pdf, accessed September 24, 2016.

Hunter, Helen-Louise. *Sukarno and the Indonesian Coup: The Untold Story.* Westport, Conn.: Praeger Security International, 2007.

IRIN News. 2000. "Sierra Leone: IRIN Interview with Johnny Paul Koroma." IRIN News, a service of the UN Office for the Coordination of Humanitarian Affairs. June 6.

IRIN News. 2003. "West Africa: Bockarie's Death Boost Chances for Peace." IRIN News, a service of the UN Office for the Coordination of Humanitarian Affairs. May 9.

Isbell, Billie Jean. 1994. "Shining Path and Peasant Responses in Rural Hyacucho." In Palmer, *Shining Path of Peru*, 77–99.

Jagan, Larry. 2009. "Junta Has 'Stolen Billions' in Gas Revenue." *National*, September 13.

Jane's. 2012. "Procurement (Myanmar), Procurement." *Sentinel Security Assessment—Southeast Asia.* Coulsdon, Surrey UK: Jane's Information Group.

Jane's Intelligence Weekly. 2015. "Resignation of East Timor PM Will Be Managed Transition, but Protest and Riot Risks Increase." February 11.

Johnston, Patrick. 2007. "Negotiated Settlements and Government Strategy in Civil War: Evidence from Darfur." *Civil Wars* 9(4): 359–377.

Jones, Lucy. 2003. "Bockarie Died a Wanted Man." BBC News, May 8. http://newsvote.bbc.co .uk/mpapps/pagetools/print/news.bbc.co.uk/2/hi/africa/3006851.stm.

Jordan, Jenna. 2009. "When Heads Roll: Assessing the Effectiveness of Leadership Decapitation." *Security Studies* 18(4): 719–755.

Kamaluddin, S. 1992. "Burma-Bangladesh: The Arakan Exodus, Anxious Neighbors." *Far East Economic Review*, March 26.

Kammen, Douglas. 2009. "A Tape Recorder and a Wink? Transcript of the May 29, 1983 Meeting between Governor Carrascalão and Xanana Gusmão." *Indonesia* 87: 73–140.

Kandeh, Jimmy. 2003. "Sierra Leone's Post-Conflict Elections of 2002." *Journal of Modern African Studies* 41(2): 189–216.

Kaufmann, Chaim. 1996. "Possible and Impossible Solutions to Ethnic Civil Wars." *International Security* 20(4): 136–175.

Kay, Cristobal. 1983. "Agrarian Reform in Peru: An Assessment." In *Agrarian Reform in Contemporary Developing Countries*, edited by Ajit Kumar Ghose, 185–239. New York: St. Martin's Press.

Keen, David. 2005. "Liberalization and Conflict." *International Political Science Review* 26(1): 73–89.

Keesing's World News Archive. 1931–2016. Reno, Nev.: Keesings Worldwide LLC. www.keesings .com, accessed May 19, 2010, to May 19, 2011.

Kerry, John. 2015. "In the Matter of the Designation of Mujahidin Indonesia Timur (MIT), aka Mujahideen Indonesia Timor, aka Mujahidin of Eastern Indonesia, aka Mujahidin Indonesia Barat, aka Mujahidin Indonesia Timor, aka Mujahidin of Western Indonesia (MIB), as a Specially Designated Global Terrorist Entity Pursuant to Section 1(b) of Executive Order 13224, as Amended." *Federal Register*. https://www.federalregister.gov/articles/2015 /09/30/2015-24898/in-the-matter-of-the-designation-of-mujahidin-indonesia-timur-mit -aka-mujahideen-indonesia-timor-aka, accessed January 29, 2016.

Kingsbury, Damien. 2007. "Indonesia in 2006: Cautious Reform." *Asian Survey* 47(1): 155–161.

Kipp, Rita Smith. 2004. "Indonesia in 2003: Terror's Aftermath." *Asian Survey* 44(1): 62.

Kriesberg, Louis. 1998. *Constructive Conflicts: From Escalation to Resolution*. Lanham, Md.: Rowman and Littlefield.

Kuperman, Alan. 2008. "The Moral Hazard of Humanitarian Intervention: Lessons from the Balkans." *International Studies Quarterly* 52(1): 49–80.

Kurlantzick, Joshua. 2001. "Indonesia's Splintering." *World & I* 16(7): n.p.

Lacina, Bethany, and Nils Petter Gleditsch. 2005. "Monitoring Trends in Global Combat: A New Dataset of Battle Deaths." *European Journal of Population* 21(2–3): 145–166.

Lanka Newspapers. 2007. "President Orders Recruitment of 50,000 More Youths to Forces." *Sri Lankan News & Discussions*, June 19. http://www.lankanewspapers.com/news/2007/6 /16057.html, accessed October 8, 2016.

Lavalie, A. M. 1985. "Government and Opposition in Sierra Leone, 1968–78." In *Sierra Leone Studies at Birmingham 1983: Symposium Proceedings*, edited by A. Jones and P. K. Mitchell, 77–106. Birmingham: University of Birmingham, Centre of West African Studies.

Le Billon, Phillipe. 2005. *Fueling War: Natural Resources and Armed Conflict*. London: Routledge, for the Institute for Strategic Studies.

Le Billon, Phillipe, and Estelle Levin. 2009. "Building Peace with Conflict Diamonds? Merging Security and Development in Sierra Leone." *Development and Change* 40(4): 693–715.

Lee, Thomas J., Luke C. Mullany, Adam K. Richards, Heather K. Kulper, Cynthia Maung, and Chris Beyrer. 2006. "Mortality Rates in Conflict Zones in Karen, Karenni, and Mon States in Eastern Burma." *Tropical Medicine and International Health* 11(7): 1119–1127.

Licklider, Roy. 1995. "The Consequences of Negotiated Settlements in Civil Wars, 1945–1993." *American Political Science Review* 89(3): 681–690.

Lilja, Jannie. 2010. *Disaggregating Dissent: The Challenges of Intra-Party Consolidation in Civil War and Peace Negotiations*. Uppsala: Uppsala Universitet.

Lintner, Bertil. 1990. *Outrage: Burma's Struggle for Democracy*. Ann Arbor, Mich.: White Lotus.

Lintner, Bertil. 1991. "Unexpected Karen Rebel Push Worries Ruling Junta." *Far Eastern Economic Review*, November 14.

Lintner, Bertil. 1992. "The Arakan Exodus." *Far Eastern Economic Review*, March 26.

Lintner, Bertil. 1993. "One More to Go." *Far Eastern Economic Review*, October 21.

Lintner, Bertil. 1994. *Burma in Revolt: Opium and Insurgency since 1948*. Boulder, Colo.: Westview Press.

Liong, Liem Soei. 1988. "Indonesian Muslims and the State: Accommodation or Revolt?" *Third World Quarterly* 10(2): 869–896.

Litse, Janvier. 2015. Foreword to *Development Effectiveness Review 2015: Sierra Leone*, by African Development Bank Group, 1. Country Report. Abidjan, Côte d'Ivoire: African Development Bank Group.

Little, David. 1994. *Sri Lanka: The Invention of Enmity*. Washington, D.C.: United States Institute of Peace Press.

Los Angeles Times. 1989. "The World—February 05, 1989." February 5. http://articles.latimes .com/1989-02-05/news/mn-2347_1_victor-polay-campos.

Magnusson, Bruce A., and John F. Clark. 2005. "Understanding Democratic Survival and Democratic Failure in Africa: Insights from Divergent Democratic Experiments in Benin and Congo (Brazzaville)." *Comparative Study of Society and History* 47(3): 552–582.

Manwaring, Max G. 1995. "Peru's Sendero Luminoso: The Shining Path Beckons." *The Annals of the American Academy of Political and Social Science* 541(1): 157–166.

Marshall, C. Andrew. 2000. "The Republic of Congo on the Brink: Mission of the Henry Dunant Centre for Humanitarian Dialogue to the Republic of Congo on behalf of the Inter-Agency Standing Committee Working-Group, 5–15 April 2000." Geneva: Henry Dunant Center for Humanitarian Dialogue. http://www.hdcentre.org/uploads/tx_news /224-The-Republic-of-Congo-on-the-Brink.pdf.

Marshall, Monty, and Ted Robert Gurr. 2003. *Peace and Conflict, 2003: A Global Survey of Armed Conflicts, Self-Determination Movements, and Democracy*. College Park, Md.: Center for International Development and Conflict Management.

Martel, Frances. 2015. "Peru: Long-Diminished Shining Path Terror Group May Now Have Up to 350 Members." August 6. http://www.breitbart.com/national-security/2015/08/06 /peru-long-diminished-shining-path-terror-group-may-now-have-up-to-350-members/.

Maung, Mya. 1990. "The Road from the Union of Burma to Myanmar." *Asian Survey* 30: 602–624.

Mayilvaganan, M. 2009. "Is It Endgame for LTTE?" *Strategic Analysis* 33(1): 25–39.

McClintock, Cynthia. 1989. "The Prospects for Democratic Consolidation in a 'Least Likely' Case: Peru." *Comparative Politics* 21(2): 127–148.

McDonnell, Ted. 2015. "Timor President Urged to Resign over Role in Party." *Australian*, November 18, 10.

Mercury. 1950. "Ambon Rebellion Expected to Spread to Celebes." April 28. http://trove. nla.gov.au/newspaper/article/26692821?searchTerm=Ambon+Bay, accessed October 8, 2016.

Miall, Hugh. 1992. *The Peacemakers: Peaceful Settlement of Disputes since 1945*. London: Macmillan.

Mietzner, Marcus. 2002. "Politics of Engagement: The Indonesian Armed Forces, Islamic Extremism, and the 'War on Terror.'" *Brown Journal of World Affairs* 9(1): 71–84.

"Military Reform from Above." 1992. In *Peru: A Country Study*, edited by Rex A. Hudson. 4th ed. Washington, D.C.: Government Printing Office for the Library of Congress. http:// countrystudies.us/peru/21.htm.

Minorities at Risk Project. 2009. "Minorities at Risk Dataset." College Park, Md.: Center for International Development and Conflict Management. http://www.cidcm.umd.edu/mar/, July 30, 2015.

Muggah, Robert, Philippe Maughan, and Christian Bugnion. 2003. "The Long Shadow of War: Prospects for Disarmament Demobilisation and Reintegration in the Republic of Congo: A Joint Independent Evaluation for the European Commission, UNDP and the MDRP Secretariat." February 13–March 6.

Mullany, L. C., C. I. Lee, L. Yone, P. Paw, E. K. S. Oo, C. Maung, et al. 2008. "Access to Essential Maternal Health Interventions and Human Rights Violations among Vulnerable Communities in Eastern Burma." *PLoS Med* 5(12): e242. doi:10.1371/journal.pmed.0050242.

Nadarajah, Suthaharan, and Dhananjayan Sriskandarajah. 2005. "Liberation Struggle or Terrorism: The Politics of Naming the LTTE." *Third World Quarterly* 26(1): 87–100.

Nawawi, Mohammed. 1969. "Stagnation as a Basis of Regionalism: A Lesson from Indonesia." *Asian Survey* 9(12): 934–945.

Ndumbe, J. Anyu, and Babalola Cole. 2005. "The Illicit Diamond Trade, Civil Conflicts, and Terrorism in Africa." *Mediterranean Quarterly* 16(2): 52–65.

New York Times. 1948. "Burmese Rebels Hurt by Sea-Air Assault." August 20.

New York Times. 1958. "Indonesia Split Traced Far Back." February 16.

New York Times. 1961. "Surrender of Arms Ordered." April 25.

New York Times. 2009. "Tamil Tigers." May 18.

Nieto, W. Alejandro Sanchez. 2008. "A War of Attrition: Sri Lanka and the Tamil Tigers." *Small Wars & Insurgencies* 19(4): 573–587.

Norwegian Refugee Council/Global IDP Project. 2005. "Profile of Internal Displacement: Republic of Congo (Brazzaville)." Compilation of the information available in the Global IDP Database of the Norwegian Refugee Council, Geneva, Switzerland.

O'Flaherty, Michael. 2004. "Sierra Leone's Peace Process: The Role of the Human Rights Community." *Human Rights Quarterly*, 26(1): 29–62.

Olson Lounsbery, Marie. 2005. "Enduring Intrastate Rivalries in Southeast Asia: A New Direction in Intrastate Conflict Exploration." Paper presented at the Annual Meeting of the American Political Science Association, Washington D.C., September.

Olson Lounsbery, Marie. 2015. "Foreign Military Intervention and Rebel Group Cohesion." Unpublished manuscript.

Olson Lounsbery, Marie, and Alethia Cook. 2010. "Rebellion, Mediation, and Group Change: An Empirical Investigation of Competing Hypotheses." *Journal of Peace Research* 48(1): 73–84.

Olson Lounsbery, Marie, and Karl DeRouen Jr. 2015. "Foreign Intervention and Civil War Peace Agreement Provisions." Unpublished manuscript.

Olson Lounsbery, Marie, and Frederic Pearson. 2009. *Civil Wars: Internal Struggles, Global Consequences.* Toronto: University of Toronto Press.

Onís, Paco, Peter Kinoy, Pamela Yates, and Karen Duffy. *State of Fear.* New York: Skylight Pictures, 2005.

Palmer, David Scott, ed. 1994. *Shining Path of Peru.* New York: St. Martin's Press.

"Papuan Leader Says Netherlands Created OPM to Oppose Indonesia." 2014. AntaraNews.com, May 12. http://www.antaranews.com/en/news/94013/papuan-leader-says-netherlands-created-opm-to-oppose-indonesia, accessed November 12, 2014.

Parlina, Ina. 2016. "Govt to Take 'Soft Approach' in Papua." *Jakarta Post*, January 5. http://www.thejakartapost.com/news/2016/01/05/govt-take-soft-approach-papua.html, accessed January 27, 2016.

Parnini, Syeda Naushin. 2013. "The Crisis of the Rohingya as a Muslim Minority in Myanmar and Bilateral Relations with Bangladesh." *Journal of Muslim Minority Affairs* 33(2): 281–297.

PBS. 1999. "War in Europe." *Frontline.* http.://www.pbs.org/wgbh/pages/frontline/shows/kosovo, accessed July 30, 2015.

Pearson, Frederic S., and Robert Baumann. 1993. *International Military Intervention, 1946–1988.* Inter-University Consortium for Political and Social Research (ICPSR), Data Collection 6035. Ann Arbor: Institute for Social Research, University of Michigan.

Pearson, Frederic S., Marie Olson Lounsbery, Scott Walker, and Sonja Mann. 2006. "Replicating and Extending Theories of Civil War Settlement." *International Interactions* 32(2): 109–128.

Pearson, Frederic S., John Sislin, and Marie Olson. 1998. "Arms Trade, Economics of." In *The Encyclopedia of Violence, Peace and Conflict*, edited by Lester Kurtz. San Diego: Academic Press.

Pemberton, John. 1999. "Open Secrets: Excerpts from Conversations with a Javanese Lawyer, and a Comment." In *Figures of Criminality in Indonesia, the Philippines, and Colonial Viet-*

nam, edited by Vicente L. Rafeal, 193–209. Ithaca, N.Y.: Southeast Asia Program, Cornell University.

Peruvian Times. 1990. "Peru Journalists Remember Fallen Colleagues on 26th Anniversary of Uchuraccay Massacre." January 28.

Peruvian Times. 2012. "Peru's Poverty Rate Falls 3 Percent in 2011." May 31.

Pfaffenberger, Bryan. 1987. "Sri Lanka in 1986: A Nation at the Crossroads." *Asian Survey* 27(2): 155–162.

Powell, Robert. 2004. "Bargaining and Learning While Fighting Over the Distribution of Power." *American Journal of Political Science* 48(2): 344–361.

Prabhakaran, V. 1994. "Heroes Day Speech 1994." *Eelam View*, November 27. As translated by eelamaran and posted November 7, 2012. http://www.eelamview.com/2012/11/07/leader-v -prabakarans-heros-day-speech-1994/.

Prabhakaran, V. 1995. "Heroes Day Speech 1995." *Eelam View*, November 27. As translated by eelamaran and posted November 7, 2012. http://www.eelamview.com/2012/11/07/leader-v -prabakarans-heros-day-speech-1995/.

Prabhakaran, V. 1999. "Heroes Day Speech 1999." *Eelam View*, November 27. As translated by eelamaran and posted November 7, 2012. http://www.eelamview.com/2012/11/07/leader-v -prabakarans-heros-day-speech-1999-2/.

Pratap, Anita. 1984. "Velupillai Pirabaharan: Interview with Anita Pratap." *Sunday Magazine, India*, March 11–17. http://tamilnation.co/ltte/vp/interviews/8403%20anita%20pratap.htm.

Radio Free Asia. 2015. "Armed Ethnic Groups Call for an End to Myanmar Military Offen- sives." November 3. http://www.rfa.org/english/news/myanmar/armed-ethnic-groups -call-for-an-end-to-myanmar-military-offenses-11032015150042.html.

Radio Free Asia. 2016. "Myanmar Army Vows to Eliminate Armed Ethnic Rebels in Rah- kine State." January 8. http://www.rfa.org/english/news/myanmar/myanmar-army-vows -to-eliminate-armed-ethnic-rebels-in-rakhine-state-01082016153351.html?searchterm :utf8:ustring=KIA+Myanmar.

Rajah, Ananda. 2002. "A 'Nation of Intent' in Burma: Karen Ethno-Nationalism, Nationalism and Narrations of Nation." *Pacific Review* 15(4): 517–537.

Rajasingham-Senanayake, Darini. 2009. "Transnational Peace Building and Conflict Lessons from Aceh, Indonesia and Sri Lanka." *Sojourn: Journal of Social Issues in Southeast Asia* 24(2): 211–234.

Raman, Nachammai. 2009. "A History of Violence." *Alternatives International*, July 21. http:// www.alterinter.org/article3330.html?lang=fr, accessed October 16, 2009.

Ramesh, Randeep. 2007. "Tamil Tigers Used Truce to Rearm, Says Former Commander." *Guardian*, April 4. https://www.theguardian.com/world/2007/apr/04/srilanka, accessed October 8, 2017.

Rashid, Ismail. 2016. "Sierra Leone: The Revolutionary United Front." In *Criminalized Power Structures: The Overlooked Enemies of Peace*, edited by Michael Dziedzic, 81–110. Lanham, Md.: Rowman & Littlefield.

Ratnayake, K. 2004. "A Split in the LTTE Heightens Danger of War in Sri Lanka." *World Social- ist Web Site*, March 18. https://www.wsws.org/en/articles/2004/03/ltte-m18.html.

Rauchhaus, Robert. 2009. "Principal-Agent Problems in Humanitarian Intervention: Moral Hazards, Adverse Selection, and the Commitment Dilemma." *International Studies Quar- terly* 53(4): 871–884.

Regan, Patrick M. 2000a. *Civil Wars and Foreign Powers*. Ann Arbor: University of Michigan Press.

Regan, Patrick M. 2000b. "The Substitutability of U.S. Policy Options in Internal Conflicts." *Journal of Conflict Resolution* 44(1): 90–106.

Reisinger, William M. 1986. "Situational and Motivational Assumptions in Theories of Coalition Formation." *Legislative Studies Quarterly* 11(4): 551–563.

Reno, William. 1996. *Corruption and State Politics in Sierra Leone.* Cambridge, Mass.: Cambridge University Press.

Reno, William. 1998. *Warlord Politics and African States.* Boulder, Colo.: Lynne Rienner.

Report of the Secretary-General's Panel of Experts on Accountability in Sri Lanka. 2011. United Nations, March 31. http://www.un.org/News/dh/infocus/Sri_Lanka/POE_Report_Full .pdf, accessed July 10, 2012.

Richards, Joanne. 2014. *An Institutional History of the Liberation Tigers of Tamil Eelam (LTTE).* Geneva: Centre on Conflict, Development and Peacebuilding.

Richards, Paul. 2005. "West-African Warscapes: War as Smokes and Mirrors." *Anthropological Quarterly* 78(2): 377–402.

Ricklefs, Merle. 2003. "The Future of Indonesia." *History Today* 53(12): 46–53.

Riker, William H. 1962. *The Theory of Political Coalitions.* New Haven, Conn.: Yale University Press.

Rotberg, Robert I. 1999. *Creating Peace in Sri Lanka: Civil War and Reconciliation.* Washington, D.C.: Brookings Institution Press.

Rothman, Jay. 1997. *Resolving Identity-Based Conflict in Nations, Organizations, and Communities.* San Francisco: Jossey-Bass.

Rothman, Jay, and Marie Olson. 2001. "From Interests to Identities: Toward a New Emphasis in International Conflict Resolution." *Journal of Peace Research* 38(3): 289–305.

Rupesinghe, Kumar. 1988. "Ethnic Conflicts in South Asia: The Case of Sri Lanka and the Indian Peace-Keeping Force." *Journal of Peace Research* 25(4): 337–350.

Rupesinghe, Kumar. 1998. *Civil Wars, Civil Peace: An Introduction to Conflict Resolution.* London: Pluto Press.

Saddique, Haroon. 2007. "Tamil Tigers Attack Airforce Base." *Guardian,* October 22. https:// www.theguardian.com/world/2007/oct/22/srilanka, accessed October 8, 2016.

Saideman, Stephen. 1997. "Explaining the International Relations of Secessionist Conflicts: Vulnerability versus Ethnic Ties." *International Organization* 51(4): 721–753.

Sandy, Denis. 2016. "The Dark Side of Sierra Leone's Development—Part One." *Sierra Leone Telegraph.* http://www.thesierraleonetelegraph.com/?p=11446#more-11446, accessed January 27, 2016.

Saravanamuttu, Paikiasothy. 2000. "Sri Lanka: The Intractability of Ethnic Conflict." In *The Management of Peace Processes,* edited by John Darby and Roger MacGinty, 195–227. New York: St. Martin's Press.

Schock, Kurt. 1999. "People Power and Political Opportunities: Social Movement Mobilization and Outcomes in the Philippines and Burma." *Social Problems* 46(3): 355–375.

Schulze, Kirsten. 2002. "Laskar Jihad and the Conflict in Ambon." *Brown Journal of World Affairs* 9(1): 57–69.

Schulze, Kirsten. 2004. *The Free Aceh Movement (GAM): Anatomy of a Separatist Organization.* Policy Studies no. 2. Washington, D.C.: East-West Center.

SCSL (Special Court for Sierra Leone). 2003. *The Prosecutor against Charles Ghankay Taylor, Also Known as Charles Ghankay Macarthur Dapkpana Taylor: Indictment.* March 7. Case no. SCSL-03-01-I.

SCSL (Special Court for Sierra Leone). 2004. *Trial Chamber II: Judgment: Prosecutor v. Alex Tamba Brima, Brima Bazzy Tamara, and Santigie Borbor Kanu.* May 18. Case no. SCSL-04-16-T.

SCSL (Special Court for Sierra Leone). 2009. *Trial Chamber II: Judgment: Prosecutor v. Issa Hassan Sesay, Morris Kallon, and Augustine Gbao.* March 2. Case no. SCSL-04-T-2234 D.

SCSL (Special Court for Sierra Leone). 2012. *Trial Chamber II: Judgment: Prosecutor v. Charles Ghankay Taylor*. May 18. Case no. SCSL-03-01-T.

Sengupta, Somini. 2015. "U.N. Delays Release of Report on Possible War Crimes in Sri Lanka." *New York Times*, February 16. http://www.nytimes.com/2015/02/17/world/asia/united -nations-postpones-report-possible-war-crimes-sri-lanka.html?ref=topics&_r=0, ac- cessed January 26, 2016.

Silverstein, Josef. 1997. "Fifty Years of Failure in Burma." In *Government Policies and Ethnic Relations in Asia and the Pacific*, edited by Michael Brown and Sumit Ganguily, 167–196. Cambridge, Mass.: MIT Press.

Singer, Marshall. 1992. "Sri Lanka's Tamil-Sinhalese Ethnic Conflict: Alternative Solutions." *Asian Survey* 32(8): 712–722.

Singh, Bilveer. 2004. "The Challenge of Militant Islam and Terrorism in Indonesia." *Australian Journal of International Affairs* 58(1): 47–68.

Sisk, Timothy. 2009. *International Mediation in Civil Wars: Bargaining with Bullets*. New York: Routledge.

Sislin, John, and Frederic Pearson. 2001. *Arms and Ethnic Conflict*. Lanham, Md.: Roman & Littlefield.

Sislin, John, and Frederic Pearson. 2006. "Arms and Escalation in Ethnic Conflicts: The Case of Sri Lanka." *International Studies Perspectives* 7(2): 137–158.

Skeen, Lisa. N.d. "A Shining Path Resurgence?" *NACLA: Reporting on the Americas since 1967*. https://nacla.org/news/shining-path-resurgence.

Slantchev, Branislav. 2003. "The Principle of Convergence in Wartime Negotiations." *American Political Science Review* 97(4): 621–632.

Small, Melvin, and J. David Singer. 1982. *Resort to Arms: International and Civil Wars, 1816– 1980*. Beverly Hills, Calif.: Sage.

Smillie, Ian, Lansana Gberie, and Ralph Hazleton. 2000. *The Heart of the Matter: Sierra Leone, Diamonds and Human Security*. Ottawa: Partnership Africa Canada.

Smith, Anthony D. 1986. "Conflict and Collective Identity: Class, Ethnie, and Nation." In *International Conflict Resolution*, edited by Edward D. Azar and John W. Burton, 64–73. Boulder, Colo.: Lynne Rienner.

Snyder, Richard, and Ravi Bhavnani. 2005. "Diamonds, Blood, and Taxes: A Revenue- Centered Framework for Explaining Political Order." *Journal of Conflict Resolution* 49(4): 563–597.

Soebardi, S. 1983. "Kartosuwiryo and the Darul Islam Rebellion in Indonesia." *Journal of Southeast Asian Studies* 14(1): 109–133.

Somba, Nethy Dharma. 2016. "Hundreds of Papuans Hide in the Woods after the Death of TNI Officer." *Jakarta Post*, January 7. http://www.thejakartapost.com/news/2016/01 /07/hundreds-papuans-hide-woods-after-death-tni-officer.html, accessed January 27, 2016.

Spencer, Jonathan. 1990. "Collective Violence and Everyday Practice in Sri Lanka." *Modern Asian Studies* 24(3): 603–623.

Sri Lanka Project. 2004. "Sri Lanka Project Briefing." Sri Lanka Project, International Section, Refugee Council. London: Refugee Council.

Stedman, Stephen J. 1997. "Spoiler Problems in Peace Processes," *International Security* 22(2): 5–53.

Strong, Simon. 1992. *Shining Path: Terror and Revolution in Peru*. New York: Times Books.

Subramanian, Nirupama. 1995. "Fight to the Finish." *India Today*, November 30.

Sullivan, Mark P. 2010. "Latin America: Terrorism Issues." *Congressional Research Service Re- port*, October 26.

Svensson, Isak. 2009. "Who Brings Which Peace? Neutral versus Biased Mediation in Institutional Peace Arrangements in Civil Wars." *Journal of Conflict Resolution* 53(3): 446–469.

Synge, Richard. 2002. "Sierra Leone: Recent History." In *Africa South of the Sahara, 2003*, edited by Katharine Murison, 916–922. London: Europa.

Tadjoeddin, Mohammad Zulfan, and Anis Chowdhury. 2009. "Socioeconomic Perspectives on Violent Conflict in Indonesia." *Economics of Peace and Security Journal* 4(1) 39–46.

Tajima, Yuhki. 2008. "Explaining Ethnic Violence in Indonesia: Demilitarizing Domestic Security." *Journal of East Asian Studies* 8(2008): 451–472.

Tambiah, S. J. 1986. *Sri Lanka: Ethnic Fratricide and the Dismantling of Democracy*. Chicago: University of Chicago Press.

Tanter, Richard, Desmond Ball, and Gerry Van Klinken, eds. 2006. *Masters of Terror: Indonesia's Military and Violence in East Timor*. Lanham, Md.: Roman & Littlefield.

Taylor, Robert H. 2008. "Finding the Political in Myanmar, a.k.a. Burma." *Journal of Southeast Asian Studies* 39(2): 219–237.

Thompson, Virginia. 1948. "Burma's Communists." *Far Eastern Survey* 17(9): 103–105.

UCDP (Uppsala Conflict Data Program). 1975-2016. *UCDP Conflict Encyclopedia*. Uppsala, Sweden: Uppsala University. http://www.ucdp.uu.se, accessed September 5, 2008, to October 8, 2016.

UCDP/PRIO (Uppsala Conflict Data Program / Peace Research Institute Oslo). 2014. *UCDP/PRIO Armed Conflict Dataset—2014*. Vol. 4-2014, 1946–2013. http://www.pcr.uu.se/research/ucdp/datasets/ucdp_prio_armed_conflict_dataset/, accessed August 12, 2014.

UN News Centre. 2007. "China and Russia Veto U.S./UK-Backed Security Council Draft Resolution on Myanmar." January 12.

U.S. CIA (Central Intelligence Agency). 2012, 2016. *World Factbook*. https://www.cia.gov/library/publications/the-world-factbook/geos/sl.html, accessed August 29, 2012, and January 27, 2016.

U.S. Department of State. 2009a. "Background Note: Peru." Country Reports on Human Rights Practices. http://www.state.gov/outofdate/bgn/peru/123821.htm, accessed September 24, 2016.

U.S. Department of State. 2009b. "Background Note: Republic of the Congo." Country Reports on Human Rights Practices. Bureau of African Affairs. August. http://www.state.gov/outof date/bgn/congobrazzaville/127941.htm, accessed September 24, 2016.

U.S. Department of State. 2009c. *Report to Congress on Incidents during the Recent Conflict in Sri Lanka*. Washington, D.C.: U.S. Government Printing Office. http://reliefweb.int/sites/reliefweb.int/files/resources/4792D63B35FAD909492576580005B2E2-Full_Report.pdf, accessed on September 24, 2016.

U.S. Department of State. 2015. "Designations of Foreign Terrorist Fighters." September 29. http://www.state.gov/r/pa/prs/ps/2015/09/247433.htm, accessed January 29, 2016.

U.S. Department of the Treasury. 2009. "Treasury Targets U.S. Front for Sri Lankan Terrorist Organization." *Press Center*, February 11. https://www.treasury.gov/press-center/press-releases/Pages/tg22.aspx, accessed October 14, 2009.

U.S. Energy Information Administration. 2014. "Congo (Brazzaville)." January 29. http://www.eia.gov/beta/international/analysis_includes/countries_long/Congo_Brazzaville/congo.pdf.

Van Bruinessen, Martin. N.d. "Islamic State or State Islam? Fifty Years of State-Islam Relations in Indonesia." In *Indonesien am Ende des 20. Jahrhunderts*, edited by Ingrid Wessel, 19–34. Hamburg: Abera-Verlag.

Vandenbosch, Amry. 1952. "Nationalism and Religion in Indonesia." *Far Eastern Survey* 21(18): 181–185.

van der Kroef, Justus. 1958a. "Disunited Indonesia." *Far Eastern Survey* 27(4): 49–63.

van der Kroef, Justus. 1958b. "Disunited Indonesia II." *Far Eastern Survey* 27(5): 73–80.

Varagur, Krithika. 2015. "World's Largest Islamic Organization Tells ISIS to Get Lost." *Huffington Post*, December 3. http://www.huffingtonpost.com/entry/indonesian-muslims -counter-isis_us_565c737ae4b072e9d1c26bda, accessed January 28, 2016.

Varshney, Ashutosh. 2008. "Analyzing Collective Violence in Indonesia: An Overview." In "Collective Violence in Indonesia," special issue, *Journal of East Asian Studies* 8(3): 341–359.

Varshney, Ashutosh, Mohammad Zulfan Tadjoeddin, and Rizal Panggabean. 2008. "Creating Datasets in Information-Poor Envioronments: Patterns of Collective Violence in Indonesia, 1990–2003." In "Collective Violence in Indonesia," special issue, *Journal of East Asian Studies* 8(3): 361–394.

Vines, Alex. 2005. "Combating Light Weapons Proliferation in West Africa." *International Affairs* 81(2): 341–360.

Wall Street Journal. 2010. "World News: Myanmar Moves Troops to Borders." March 12.

Washington Post. 1988. "Peruvian Rebel Offers Grim Prophecy." August 19.

Wax, Emily. 2009. "Without Me, They Couldn't Win the War." *Washington Post*, February 11.

Weatherbee, Donald. 2002. "Indonesia: Political Drift and State Decay." *Brown Journal of World Affairs* 9(1): 23–33.

Weber, Max. 1964. *The Theory of Economic and Social Organization.* New York: Free Press.

Weiner, Myron. 1996. "Bad Neighbors, Bad Neighborhoods: An Inquiry into the Causes of Refugee Flows." *International Security* 21(1): 5–42.

Wirajuda, N. Hassan. 2002. "The Democratic Response." *Brown Journal of World Affairs* 9(1): 15–21.

Woods, Larry J., and Timothy R. Reese. 2008. "Military Interventions in Sierra Leone: Lessons from a Failed State." Long War series, occasional paper 28. Ft. Leavenworth, Kan.: Combat Studies Institute Press.

World Bank. 1993. "Peru Poverty Assessment and Social Policies and Programs for the Poor." Report no. 11191-PE. May 5.

"World Development Indicators." 1960–2014. Poverty rates. World Bank. http://data.world bank.org/data-catalog/world-development-indicators.

Yaeger, Carl. 2008. "Menia Muria: The South Moluccans Fight in Holland." *Terrorism* 13(3): 215–226.

Yin Hlaing, Kyaw. 2004. "Myanmar in 2003: Frustration and Despair?" *Asian Survey* 44(1): 87.

Zack-Williams, Alfred. 1999. "Sierra Leone: The Political Economy of Civil War, 1991–98." *Third World Quarterly* 20(1): 143–162.

Zack-Williams, Alfred, and Stephen Riley. 1993. "Sierra Leone: The Coup and Its Consequences." *Review of African Political Economy* (56): 91–98.

Zartman, I. William. 1989. *Ripe for Resolution: Conflict and Intervention in Africa.* 2nd ed. New York: Oxford University Press.

Zartman, I. William. 1993. "The Unfinished Agenda: Negotiating Internal Conflicts." In *Stopping the Killing: How Civil Wars End*, edited by Roy Licklider, 20–34. New York: New York University Press.

Zartman, I. William. 2000. "Ripeness: The Hurting Stalemate and Beyond." In *International Conflict Resolution after the Cold War*, edited by Paul Stern and Daniel Druckman, 225–250. Washington, D.C.: National Academies Press.

Zartman, I. William, and Saadia Touval. 1985. "International Mediation: Conflict Resolution and Power Politics." *Journal of Social Issues* 41(2): 27–45.

Zartman, I. William, and Katharina R. Vogeli. 2000. "Prevention Gained and Prevention Lost: Collapse, Competition, and Coup in Congo." In *Opportunities Missed, Opportunities Seized: Preventative Diplomacy in the Post-Cold War Era*, edited by Bruce W. Jentleson, 265–292. Lanham, Md.: Rowman & Littlefield.

Zenn, Jacob. 2013. "East Indonesian Islamist Militants Expand Focus and Area of Operations." *Terrorism Monitor* 11(11). A report by the Jamestown Foundation. http://www.jamestown .org/single/?tx_ttnews[tt_news]=40960&no_cache=1#.Vqu_SU9bjsA, accessed January 29, 2016.

INDEX

Aceh, 9, 113, 115–116, 120–125, 127–129, 131, 136; conclusions about, 172–173, 175–177, 180; conflict progression, 139–145

African Development Bank (AfDB), 47

All Burma Student's Democratic Front (ABSDF), 104, 187n2 (chap. 5)

All People's Congress (Sierra Leone; APC), 31, 34, 36–37, 40, 47

alluvial, 7, 31, 40

Al Qaeda, 1, 132–133

American Popular Revolutionary Alliance (APRA), 148, 151–154, 161

Anti-Corruption Revolutionary Movement (ACRM), 34, 36

Anti-Fascist People's Freedom League (AFPFL), 96

Arakan Parties, 98, 108; conflict progression, 107–109

Arbulu Galliani, Guillermo, 151

Armed Forces Revolutionary Council (AFRC), 33, 35, 37, 48, 50, 166, 170, 182; conclusions about, 166, 170, 182; conflict progression, 43–46

Association of Southeast Asian Nations (ASEAN), 107, 143

Aung San, 93, 96, 174

autonomy: Aceh, 139–140, 142; conclusions about, 171, 173, 181; Congo, 64; Indonesia, 116, 122, 125–126, 131; Myanmar, 93–94, 109–110; Sri Lanka, 69, 75, 78, 80, 82–85, 90; theoretical importance, 5, 15, 21, 27; West Papua, 134–136

Ayacucho, 149, 151, 153–154, 156

Bakongo, 52, 57

Bangladesh, 91, 94; influence on Arakan rivalry, 98, 107–109

Bejar, Hector, 156–157

Belaunde Terry, Fernando, 149–151, 158

Bio, Julius Maada, 35, 42–43

Bitsangou, Frederic (Ntoumi), 57–59, 65

Black Tigers, 186–187

Bloku Unidade Popular (BUP), 138

Bockarie, Sam, 35, 45

Bongo, Omar, 54, 60–61, 66

Bustamante, Jose Luis, 151

capacity, government, 4–5, 7, 187n2 (chap. 5); conclusions about, 166–184; Congo, 54; Indonesia, 117, 120, 130, 135, 142, 144–145; Myanmar, 102, 107, 111; Peru, 159; Sierra Leone, 32, 38–39, 41–44, 46, 50; Sri Lanka, 78, 82–83, 87–90; theoretical importance, 14–15, 17–20, 22, 27–28

capacity, rebel, 2–5, 8, 186n1 (chap. 4); conclusions about, 166–184; Congo, 54, 62; Indonesia, 123, 130–135, 139–145; Myanmar, 91, 93, 96, 102–104, 109–111; Peru, 154–157, 161–163; Sierra Leone, 38–39, 41, 43–46, 48–50; Sri Lanka, 74, 77, 80–81, 83–86, 88–90; theoretical importance, 14–15, 17–20, 22–23, 27–28

Chin, 93, 95

China, influence on conflicts: conclusions about, 166, 171, 179, 182; Indonesia, 121; Myanmar, 93–95, 99–100, 102–104, 107, 110; Peru, 155

Chinese Kuomintang (KMT), 94, 99, 103, 109

Coalition, 2, 37, 42; Congo, 55–56, 61, 65; Indonesia, 129, 138; Myanmar, 97, 99, 110–112; Sierra Leone, 37, 42, 46, 49–50; theoretical importance, 19–20, 185n4 (chap. 1)

Cobras, 9, 55, 57–58, 166, 170, 182; conflict progression, 59–65

Coca, 159–160, 175

Cocoyes, 9, 54, 57–58, 166, 170, 182; conflict progression, 59–65

Printed in the USA
CPSIA information can be obtained
at www.ICGtesting.com
LVHW091130240923
759127LV00003B/206

9 780820 358833